Classwide Positive Behavioral Interventions and Supports

The Guilford Practical Intervention in the Schools Series

Kenneth W. Merrell, Founding Editor
Sandra M. Chafouleas, Series Editor

www.guilford.com/practical

This series presents the most reader-friendly resources available in key areas of evidence-based practice in school settings. Practitioners will find trustworthy guides on effective behavioral, mental health, and academic interventions, and assessment and measurement approaches. Covering all aspects of planning, implementing, and evaluating high-quality services for students, books in the series are carefully crafted for everyday utility. Features include ready-to-use reproducibles, appealing visual elements, and an oversized format. Recent titles have Web pages where purchasers can download and print the reproducible materials.

Recent Volumes

Executive Function Skills in the Classroom:
Overcoming Barriers, Building Strategies
Laurie Faith, Carol-Anne Bush, and Peg Dawson

The RTI Approach to Evaluating Learning Disabilities,
Second Edition
Joseph F. Kovaleski, Amanda M. VanDerHeyden,
Timothy J. Runge, Perry A. Zirkel, and Edward S. Shapiro

Effective Bullying Prevention:
A Comprehensive Schoolwide Approach
Adam Collins and Jason Harlacher

Social Justice in Schools:
A Framework for Equity in Education
Charles A. Barrett

Coaching Students with Executive Skills Challenges,
Second Edition
Peg Dawson and Richard Guare

Social, Emotional, and Behavioral Supports in Schools:
Linking Assessment to Tier 2 Intervention
Sara C. McDaniel, Allison L. Bruhn, and Sara Estrapala

Family–School Success for Children with ADHD:
A Guide for Intervention
Thomas J. Power, Jennifer A. Mautone, and Stephen L. Soffer

School Crisis Intervention: An Essential Guide for Practitioners
Scott Poland and Sara Ferguson

Classwide Positive Behavioral Interventions and Supports,
Second Edition: A Guide to Proactive Classroom Management
Brandi Simonsen and Diane Myers

Family–School Collaboration in Multi-Tiered Systems of Support
S. Andrew Garbacz, Devon R. Minch, and Mark D. Weist

Overcoming Test Anxiety:
Tools to Support Students from Early Adolescence to Adulthood
Alex Jordan and Benjamin J. Lovett

Classwide Positive Behavioral Interventions and Supports

A Guide to Proactive Classroom Management

SECOND EDITION

BRANDI SIMONSEN
DIANE MYERS

gp

THE GUILFORD PRESS
New York   London

For product and safety concerns within the EU, please contact *GPSR@taylorandfrancis.com*,
Taylor & Francis Verlag GmbH, Kaufingerstraße 24, 80331 München, Germany.

Last digit is print number: 9   8   7   6   5   4   3   2

Library of Congress Cataloging-in-Publication Data

Names: Simonsen, Brandi, author. | Myers, Diane, author.
Title: Classwide positive behavioral interventions and supports : a guide
    to proactive classroom management / Brandi Simonsen, Diane Myers.
Description: Second edition. | New York : The Guilford Press, [2025] |
    Series: The Guilford practical intervention in the schools series |
Includes bibliographical references and index.
Identifiers: LCCN 2024046145 | ISBN 9781462556656 (paperback) |
    ISBN 9781462556663 (hardcover)
Subjects: LCSH: Classroom management. | Problem children—Behavior
    modification. | School psychology. | Behavior disorders in children. |
    Behavior modification,
Classification: LCC LB3013 .S576 2025 | DDC 371.102/4—dc23/eng/20241018
LC record available at *https://lccn.loc.gov/2024046145*

About the Authors

Brandi Simonsen, PhD, is Professor in the Department of Educational Psychology and Co-Director of the Center for Behavioral Education and Research at the University of Connecticut. She is Co-Director of the National Technical Assistance Center on Positive Behavioral Interventions and Supports, Co-Principal Investigator of the Integrated Multi-Tiered Systems of Supports Research Network, and Senior Advisor to the National Center on Intensive Intervention. Dr. Simonsen's primary interests include Tier 1 schoolwide positive behavioral interventions and supports (PBIS) in alternative settings, classwide PBIS, and more intensive supports for students with challenging behavior. Her publications include numerous journal articles and book chapters and the coauthored book *Implementing Classwide PBIS: A Guide to Supporting Teachers.*

Diane Myers, PhD, is Senior Vice President of Special Education for Specialized Education Services, Inc. Her prior academic appointments include serving as Professor of Special Education and Chair of the Department of Teacher Education at Texas Woman's University. Dr. Myers's research interests include implementing PBIS at the school, classroom, and individual student levels; teacher training and professional development; classroom management; and supporting students with challenging behavior. Her publications include numerous journal articles and book chapters and the coauthored book *Implementing Classwide PBIS: A Guide to Supporting Teachers.*

Preface

Welcome to the second edition of *Classwide Positive Behavioral Interventions and Supports*. A decade ago, when we wrote the first edition, we strongly believed in the importance of writing a book that (1) presented empirically supported classroom management and behavioral support practices in a user-friendly way, (2) provided follow-up activities to move teachers toward more systematic implementation, and (3) discussed classwide practices in the context of schoolwide positive behavioral interventions and supports (PBIS). A decade later, we continue to believe these areas are critical to the field. The second edition is still organized in three main sections: Part I: PBIS Foundations and Basic Principles, Part II: Classwide PBIS Practices, and Part III: Additional Tiers of Support for Students.

Although we maintained many of the organizational structures that worked well in the first edition, we made significant updates to the text.

- Within each section, we updated resources and tools, incorporated new research, and expanded our examples.
- Throughout the second edition, we expanded our focus on culturally responsive and inclusive practice to promote equitable access to, engagement in, and benefit from classroom instruction for each and every student. Although we included this focus in our first edition, we enhanced our guidance, examples, and tools to help educators prioritize equity in their classroom PBIS implementation.
- In Part II, we increased our focus on establishing and maintaining positive connections with students and families, creating positive and inclusive classroom environments, and actively engaging students and families in designing, implementing, and monitoring practices.
- We substantially revised Part III: Additional Tiers of Support for Students. In the first

edition, we focused on implementation of specific, additional Tier 2 (Chapter 9) and Tier 3 (Chapter 10) practices and systems. In this edition, we focused instead on how to differentiate and integrate more intensive, targeted (i.e., Tier 2) supports within a universal classwide PBIS model and how those supports could be further individualized (i.e., Tier 3) for students with the most intensive needs. The revisions more accurately reflect a continuum of supports and capitalize on opportunities to enhance and advance the evidence-based, culturally relevant practices explored in previous chapters.

We hope you enjoy the second edition. More importantly, we hope it enables you to (1) collaborate with your students to design a classroom where everyone is included; (2) support and respond to each of your students' social, emotional, and behavioral needs; and (3) implement advanced tiers of support to further enhance your students' experiences and outcomes.

ACKNOWLEDGMENTS

Thank you to the students, educators, researchers, and mentors who have provided the foundational content for this book. We are honored to share your experiences and work in a way that we hope will promote positive classrooms for many students in years to come.

Contents

PART III. ADDITIONAL TIERS OF SUPPORT FOR STUDENTS

CHAPTER 1

Foundations of Classwide Positive Behavioral Interventions and Supports

---

CHAPTER OBJECTIVES

By the end of this chapter, you should be able to . . .

1. Describe positive behavioral interventions and supports (PBIS).
2. Summarize the supporting evidence for organizing empirically supported practices within a PBIS framework.
3. Identify the theoretical foundations of PBIS.

Imagine This: *It is your first day of teaching. You have spent days creating the perfect visual displays in your classroom to enhance learning, you've arranged desks so that there are perfect 90-degree angles everywhere you turn, and your well-planned lesson is ready to go. As the bell rings, your students arrive for first period, wearing shirts that advertise bands you have never heard of (even though you don't think of yourself as that much older than these students) and looking at the latest video circulating social media on their phones. The first few students enter the room and walk through (rather than around) the groups of neatly arranged desks and destroy your perfect right angles. You hear a pair of students making fun of your colorful visual displays, and you look out on a group of students who are giving you suspicious looks. All of a sudden, you are not sure where to begin.*

OVERVIEW OF POSITIVE BEHAVIORAL INTERVENTIONS AND SUPPORTS

Teaching is an exciting and sometimes overwhelming profession. You are asked to identify evidence-based practices; differentiate your instruction to meet the needs of each of your students, who enter your classroom with a variety of academic and behavioral strengths and challenges; deliver high-quality instruction in an engaging manner; assess students' learning relative to established standards; and complete a myriad of other tasks (that were likely left out of your job description). To meet any of these demands, you must also support and respond to students' social, emotional, and behavioral needs. Unfortunately, many teachers—especially those early in their career—feel unprepared to support students' social, emotional, and behavioral needs (Gable et al., 2012; Reinke, Stormont, et al., 2011) and express concerns about student behavior (Bushaw & Lopez, 2010; Harrison et al., 2012).

Luckily, researchers have spent decades identifying specific practices that will allow you to create and maintain a welcoming, positive, organized, and effective classroom environment, and we have distilled that research into a user-friendly text that will set you up for success in creating a classroom environment that supports your students' educational, social, emotional, and behavioral needs. We have also organized these strategies within a **positive behavioral interventions and supports (PBIS)** framework, which provides the theoretical and empirical foundations for the classroom management strategies we discuss. In this chapter, we provide an overview of PBIS, describe the empirical support for PBIS, discuss the theoretical foundations for PBIS, and introduce the phases of learning, which we use throughout this book to organize follow-up activities for each chapter. We conclude this chapter with an overview of the remaining chapters in the book.

PBIS Is a Prevention Framework

PBIS is a prevention **framework** for organizing evidence-based practices within your school and classroom to meet the needs of individual students (Center on PBIS, 2023b). In other words, PBIS is *not* a curriculum or a "packaged" approach. PBIS *is* a problem-solving approach (e.g., Lewis et al., 2010) that emphasizes (1) providing a continuum of support for all students; (2) evaluating the implementation and outcomes of those supports; and (3) using data to guide decision making about how to improve or sustain implementation, when to identify additional interventions for students (or staff) who require more support to be successful, and how to provide and monitor those supports to promote success. Thus, PBIS counteracts the traditional "wait-to-fail" models that characterized the old way of doing business and moves us toward a prevention-based approach.

PBIS is based on decades of work in public health and prevention science (e.g., Caplan, 1964; Walker et al., 1996), which has taught us to invest in universal prevention (Tier 1) for all, identify and provide secondary prevention (Tier 2, or targeted supports) for individuals who have elevated needs, and provide tertiary prevention (Tier 3, or individualized and intensive supports) for individuals with chronic or significant needs (e.g., Sugai & Horner, 2006; Walker et al., 1996). This continuum of support, often depicted as a triangle (see Figure 1.1), is also known in schools as a multi-tiered system of support (MTSS) framework (e.g., Sugai & Horner, 2009) or a similar name (see I-MTSS Research Network, 2023). This approach may (and should!) be applied to supporting students across both academic and behavioral support (see *www.mtss.org*). PBIS refers to the "triangle" as it applies to supporting students' social, emotional, and behavioral needs, and the next paragraphs describe what PBIS looks like across each tier.

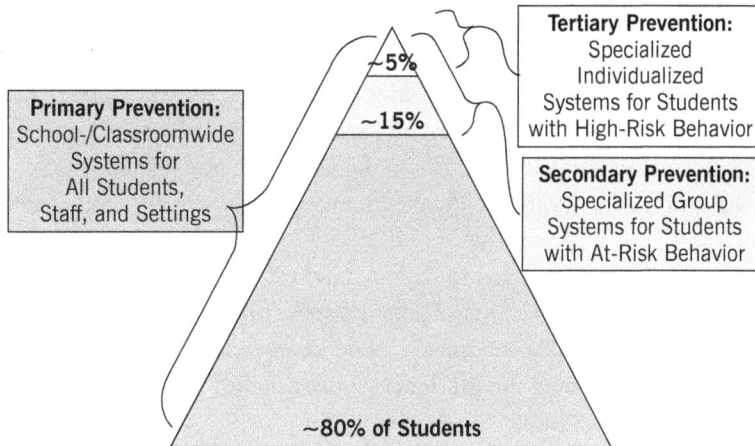

FIGURE 1.1. Continuum of academic and behavioral support. Adapted from *www.pbis.org*. Used with permission from the National Technical Assistance Center on Positive Behavioral Interventions and Supports.

Tier 1 Support

All staff members provide Tier 1 support for *all* students across *all* settings. In other words, Tier 1 supports should be universal and inclusive—ensuring that all students, including students with disabilities, are able to access, engage in, and benefit from Tier 1 support (Meyer et al., 2021; Simonsen et al., 2020). Although members of each school community should collaboratively identify culturally and contextually relevant practices for their setting (e.g., Leverson et al., 2021; Sugai et al., 2012), there are common practices that occur within Tier 1. Specifically, members of the school community:

- Identify a few (three to five) positively stated expectations or norms for their school (e.g., safety, kindness, and responsibility).
- Define and explicitly teach these expectations or norms across school and classroom settings and routines (e.g., "What does it look like to be safe in the cafeteria?" "How do you show kindness when entering the classroom?").
- Arrange the school and classroom environment to promote contextually appropriate behavior (i.e., those behaviors that are consistent with classroom community norms) and prevent contextually inappropriate behavior (i.e., behaviors that are not consistent with norms). That is, increase visual prompts, modify the physical environment, and increase active supervision across all settings.
- Implement a continuum of strategies to recognize students for contextually appropriate behavior (i.e., focus on "catching" and increasing contextually appropriate behavior).
- Implement a continuum of strategies to supportively respond to students following contextually inappropriate behavior or mistakes (i.e., respond predictably to contextually inappropriate behavior with an instructional focus to help prevent similar mistakes in the future).
- Use data to guide and evaluate implementation of supports for all students.

To implement Tier 1 support, a representative team of school staff, family members, students, and community members with diverse areas of expertise and backgrounds (e.g., administrator, teachers who are representative of grades or content areas, specialized or support staff, noncertified staff, students, families, community mental health providers) participate in training activities, develop an action plan to guide implementation, and provide ongoing professional development to all staff in the building. This team meets regularly to plan, monitor, and evaluate implementation of Tier 1 support across all school environments (classroom and nonclassroom). This team also develops systems to support and recognize staff implementation efforts. We describe schoolwide implementation of Tier 1 support in Chapter 3. When Tier 1 support is implemented with fidelity (i.e., as intended), schools can expect most students (approximately 80%) to be successful; however, some students (approximately 20%) will continue to require additional layers of support.

Tier 2 Support

Students who continue to demonstrate elevated social, emotional, and behavioral needs across settings (e.g., repeated low-level disruptions, frequent requests to visit the nurse for reasons that are not known to be medically necessary) may benefit from Tier 2, or targeted, support. Generally, you can think of Tier 2 as intensifying each of the practices included in Tier 1 (listed in the dot points in the previous section). For example, if you are prompting, teaching, and reinforcing expectation-following behaviors in Tier 1, you would want to (1) *increase* the number and salience of prompts, (2) *intensify* instruction (i.e., increase explicitness, decrease group size, target specific skills), and (3) *enhance* the schedule and intensity of available reinforcement in Tier 2. Because one size does not fit all, schools typically offer a "menu" of empirically supported Tier 2 interventions including, for example, Check-In/Check-Out (CICO), or the Behavior Education Program (Fairbanks et al., 2007; Hawken et al., 2021); small-group social skills training (Cho Blair et al., 2020; Kern et al., 2020; Lane et al., 2003); self-management approaches (Briesch & Chafouleas, 2009); First Step to Success (Walker et al., 1997) for younger (PreK–3) learners; Check & Connect (Anderson et al., 2004; Sinclair et al., 1998, 2005); Check, Connect, and Expect (CCE; Cheney et al., 2009); or some combination of these approaches. We explore these intervention approaches further in Chapter 9.

To implement Tier 2 supports, each school identifies a team of staff members with educational and behavioral expertise (e.g., administrator, special educator, counselor, social worker, school psychologist, general educator) who (1) review existing student data and nominations (e.g., teacher, student, or family requests for support) to identify students in need of Tier 2 support, (2) use data to identify an appropriate Tier 2 intervention "match" for each identified student, (3) plan for and ensure implementation of the selected intervention, (4) review data regularly (weekly or biweekly) to monitor each student's response to Tier 2 intervention, and (5) make decisions about each student's ongoing intervention (i.e., fade support and return to Tier 1, maintain or adjust support in Tier 2, increase support to Tier 3). Although most students who require additional support will respond to Tier 2, some students will need even more intensive and individualized Tier 3 support.

Tier 3 Support

Students who have significant or consistently unmet social, emotional, and behavioral needs (e.g., students who engage in highly disruptive or dangerous behavior, students who experience anxiety that interferes with their day) are candidates for the intensive and individualized support provided in Tier 3. To implement Tier 3 support, an individualized team is formed, including members with social, emotional, and behavioral expertise (e.g., school psychologist, school counselor, special educator, community mental health provider), student expertise (family and student), and educational expertise (e.g., special educator, general educator), to guide the assessment and intervention process. First, the team members plan, conduct, and review results of a **functional behavioral assessment (FBA)**. An FBA is a systematic process for studying a student's behavior using multiple sources of information generated by multiple informants and documenting patterns of behavior over time (e.g., student records, interviews with team members, and direct observations). The FBA should identify the ABCs: antecedents (A) that predict when contextually inappropriate behaviors are likely to occur, describe the specific nature of the contextually inappropriate behaviors (B), and document the consequences (C) that typically follow (and likely reinforce) the contextually inappropriate behaviors (Crone et al., 2015). In other words, the FBA should articulate the "function," or purpose, the contextually inappropriate behaviors serve for the learner. All behaviors function to either get/obtain access to or escape/avoid various stimuli (e.g., attention, items, activities, stimulation). We explore the ABCs of behavior and function in Chapter 2, and we take a closer look at (1) ways to intensify your classroom practice to meet the needs of students with individualized social, emotional, and behavioral needs and (2) how to participate in FBA and individualized intervention planning in Chapter 10.

Once an FBA has identified the function of a student's contextually inappropriate behavior, the team should work to develop an individualized and positive **behavior support plan (BSP)**. A comprehensive BSP should include (1) antecedent strategies that modify the environment to prompt or occasion contextually appropriate behavior and remove triggers for contextually inappropriate behavior, (2) instructional strategies to explicitly teach contextually appropriate behaviors that "replace" the contextually inappropriate behavior and shape toward long-term desired behaviors (e.g., instead of ripping up work, please ask for a break), and (3) consequence strategies that ensure that contextually appropriate behaviors "work" for the student (i.e., result in reinforcement) and contextually inappropriate behaviors do not. The individualized team should ensure that all staff members who support the student are trained to implement the BSP, monitor implementation and outcomes, and adjust the plan, if necessary, based on data (Crone et al., 2015).

In addition to school-based interventions documented in a BSP, some students will need supports that extend beyond the walls of the school building. For example, students involved with multiple agencies (e.g., child protective services, external mental health agencies, juvenile justice) may benefit from student- and family-centered supports that are identified, planned, implemented, and monitored via a person-centered planning (e.g., Artesani & Mallar, 1998) or wraparound process (e.g., Scott & Eber, 2003). If you have a student who requires this level of support, contact your school- or district-based social worker, administrator, school counselor, or other local expert to request assistance.

Essential Elements of PBIS

Across each of the tiers, PBIS emphasizes five essential elements: equity, outcomes, data, practices, and systems (Center on PBIS, 2023b), which are illustrated in Figure 1.2. As depicted in that graphic, teams center **equity** to ensure they are making decisions that reflect their students', families', and educators' unique and collective cultural backgrounds and learning histories (i.e., the experiences they bring with them that affect how they experience school). Equity is a throughline that connects all other essential elements.

Outcomes are locally determined, contextually and culturally relevant, observable, and measurable goal statements that describe indicators of successful implementation of PBIS for students and staff. For example, a school may want to decrease the number (or percentage) of students suspended or expelled by the end of the year. A possible outcome statement for that school may be "Given schoolwide implementation of PBIS with fidelity, we will decrease the number of students suspended or expelled by 25% by the end of the school year." As another example, a teacher may notice issues with homework completion during the first quarter and may want to increase her students' homework completion during the second quarter. An appropriate outcome for this situation may be "As a result of teaching and rewarding homework completion, students in my classroom will submit homework on 80% of opportunities across the second quarter."

To know which outcomes are relevant and to set realistic criteria for success, schools and teachers must collect and use data (Simonsen & Sugai, 2007; Simonsen et al., 2019). In this context, the word **data** refers to quantitative indicators of implementation fidelity and effectiveness. Schools and teachers routinely collect data on students' social, emotional, and behavioral strengths and needs (e.g., brief rating scales or screeners, observations of students' skills), academic performance (e.g., curriculum-based assessments, teacher-created measures, district- or statewide test scores), requests for support (e.g., mental health requests, visits to nurse), attendance (e.g., tardiness and truancy), discipline (e.g., office referrals, suspensions, expulsions), and other key indicators of strengths and needs. In addition, schools and teachers should collect data on fidelity of implementation to ensure that interventions are being implemented as intended.

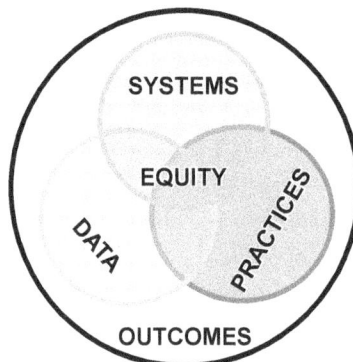

FIGURE 1.2. Essential elements of PBIS: equity, outcomes, data, practices, and systems. Adapted from *www.pbis.org*. Used with permission from the National Technical Assistance Center on Positive Behavioral Interventions and Supports.

By reviewing data regularly, school teams can make decisions to select, adjust, or discontinue practices within or across each of the tiers.

Practices are the interventions and supports for students. As you recall (or you may flip back to review), we described examples of practices within each tier in the previous section. Given the diversity of students, staff, and school settings, all practices should be selected and adjusted to ensure they are culturally and contextually relevant (Leverson et al., 2021). For example, teaching, prompting, and reinforcing agreed upon norms or expectations should be taught across all grade levels, but it "looks" different in kindergarten than it does in 12th grade. Similarly, involving family members in developing a Tier 3 BSP may look different depending on whether it will be implemented in a suburban elementary school, a middle school on a reservation, an urban high school, or a rural K–12 school. Therefore, it is critical that staff and teachers involve partners across their school community (staff, students, and families) to identify, implement, and evaluate evidence-based practices to ensure that both the practices and the implementation are culturally and contextually relevant (Leverson et al., 2021).

To promote the sustained implementation of practices with fidelity (i.e., consistently implementing practices as they are designed), schools invest in **systems** to support staff. Systems include supportive administrator participation; teaming structures (i.e., schoolwide team to support Tier 1, advanced tiers system team(s) to support Tier 2 and/or Tier 3, and individual student-centered teams to support each student receiving supports in Tier 3); professional development (ongoing training and coaching); staff recognition; data structures that facilitate easy input and flexible output; and other organizational supports for staff. Of all the essential elements, systems to support staff are perhaps the most critical for you: without a positive work environment and engaged, positive, and dedicated staff members, none of the other elements are possible!

In summary, PBIS schools center *equity* and select locally meaningful, measurable *outcomes* to evaluate their *data-driven* implementation of student-focused *practices* and staff-focused *systems*. In Chapters 3 and 4, we describe these five essential elements of implementing PBIS within your school (schoolwide PBIS) and your classroom (classwide PBIS) in much greater detail. For now, we turn to the empirical support for PBIS.

EMPIRICAL SUPPORT FOR PBIS

Before we continue to discuss PBIS, we thought you might appreciate a quick overview of the research that supports PBIS. That way, you don't have to take our word for it; you can decide for yourself if this is an approach that you think will work in your classroom, school, or both. We briefly describe the evidence supporting implementation of each tier of support, and interested readers are encouraged to view a more complete description presented by Santiago-Rosario et al. (2023).

Support for Tier 1

There are numerous randomized control trials (considered a "gold standard" in research) that support positive outcomes for schools implementing Tier 1 of schoolwide PBIS (e.g., Bradshaw et al., 2008, 2009, 2010, 2012, 2015; Horner et al., 2009; Waasdorp et al., 2012). In particular, research has demonstrated that schools that implement PBIS experience increases in students' prosocial behavior (Bradshaw et al., 2012); decreases in exclusionary discipline (documented by office referrals, suspensions, and expulsions; Bradshaw et al., 2010, 2012; Horner et al., 2009); increases in organizational health (Bradshaw et al., 2008, 2009); decreases in reported instances of bullying (Waasdorp et al., 2012); and tentative (i.e., promising but not statistically significant) improvements in academic outcomes (Bradshaw et al., 2010; Horner et al., 2009) relative to control schools. Among student groups, some studies have shown the greatest effects for students with the greatest needs (e.g., Bradshaw et al., 2015; Condliffe et al., 2022); and other research has demonstrated promising effects for students with disabilities (e.g., Center on PBIS, 2022d). Further, evidence suggests that schools that implement with high fidelity outperform schools that implement with lower fidelity (e.g., Simonsen, Eber, et al., 2012), and schools that center equity begin to close discipline gaps between students of color and white peers (e.g., Santiago-Rosario et al., 2022).

Beyond school-level implementation, emerging research supports an important role of districts in promoting fidelity (Kittelman et al., 2023) and sustainability (McIntosh et al., 2018) of schoolwide PBIS implementation. In addition, evaluation studies demonstrate that scaling these supports for districts and states also leads to positive outcomes (e.g., Barrett et al., 2008; McIntosh et al., 2011; Muscott et al., 2008). Given this evidence, it is not surprising that so many schools have adopted a schoolwide PBIS framework: there are more than 25,000 schools implementing PBIS in the United States with the support of the National Technical Assistance Center on Positive Behavioral Interventions and Supports (*www.pbis.org*), and additional schools implementing PBIS across the world. (We're going for planet-wide PBIS!)

Support for Tier 2

As described, schools typically offer a menu of Tier 2 supports to meet the diverse needs of students whose behaviors are unresponsive to Tier 1. Fortunately, empirical evidence suggests that the following Tier 2 interventions are associated with positive student outcomes: CICO (Fairbanks et al., 2007; Hawken & Horner, 2003; Hawken et al., 2007; Simonsen et al., 2011); small-group social skills training (Cho Blair et al., 2020; Kern et al., 2020; Lane et al., 2003); self-management (Briesch & Chafouleas, 2009); First Step to Success (Sumi et al., 2013; Walker et al., 2009); Check & Connect (Anderson et al., 2004; Sinclair et al., 1998, 2005); and CCE (Cheney et al., 2009). You should identify the best match between the student and intervention based on data about the type and function of behavioral need. For example, CICO is likely more appropriate for students whose behaviors function to obtain attention than for students whose behaviors function to escape stimuli (March & Horner, 2002; McIntosh et al., 2009), unless adjustments are made to implementation. Therefore, ongoing data collection and monitoring are critical to determine if a student is benefiting from a particular Tier 2 intervention and whether the supports need to be faded (to Tier 1), modified (by selecting a different Tier 2 approach), or intensified (to Tier 3).

Support for Tier 3

Within Tier 3, supports should be individualized, intensified, and function based. Empirical evidence suggests that function-based support (i.e., BSP based on FBA, as previously described) is more effective than similarly intensive supports that are not based on function (e.g., Ingram et al., 2005; Walker et al., 2018). Further, systematic literature reviews and meta-analyses, which summarize numerous individual experimental studies, document the positive effects of function-based support for students (Gage et al., 2012; Goh & Bambara, 2012; Snell et al., 2005). For students with complex needs that extend beyond school-based services, emerging evidence supports the use of person-centered planning (e.g., Artesani & Mallar, 1998; Claes et al., 2010; Kennedy et al., 2001) or wraparound process (e.g., Eber et al., 1996; Olson et al., 2021; Suter & Bruns, 2009) to identify, monitor, and coordinate supports.

In conclusion, empirical evidence upholds providing Tier 1, Tier 2, and Tier 3 supports within a PBIS framework. Perhaps the strongest evidence base exists for schoolwide Tier 1 support, specific Tier 2 interventions, and function-based support at Tier 3. Although the majority of the studies focused on schoolwide implementation, evidence also suggests that it is possible to implement all three Tiers within your classroom (e.g., Fairbanks et al., 2007). Given the quantity and quality of evidence, we hope you are now convinced that organizing empirically supported interventions within a PBIS framework is a good idea for your school and classroom. Now that we have demonstrated that PBIS "works" (i.e., results in positive outcomes), we will turn to *why* it works, or the theoretical foundations of PBIS.

THEORETICAL FOUNDATIONS OF PBIS

PBIS is grounded in behaviorism, a theoretical approach with rich empirical support in psychology, education, and related fields. Behaviorism emerged out of an early scientific emphasis on studying what can be directly observed, which was prevalent in approaches like functionalism and positivism (Alberto et al., 2021). Advances in the natural sciences further influenced behaviorism. For example, Charles Darwin's (1809–1892) observations about natural selection are referenced in both Skinner's description of Thorndike's law of effect (Skinner, 1963) and Skinner's own description of selection by consequences (Skinner, 1953, 1974). Although there are many scientists who have contributed to our understanding of behavioral theory, including Edward Thorndike (1874–1949) and John Watson (1878–1958), perhaps none are better known than Ivan Pavlov (1849–1936) and B. F. Skinner (1904–1990). In the next sections, we explore the major contributions from Pavlov and Skinner: respondent and operant conditioning, respectively. Then we describe a purposeful shift toward an applied science of behavior: applied behavior analysis. Finally, we highlight some of the other influences that continue to shape PBIS.

Early Behavioral Foundations: Respondent and Operant Conditioning

There are two primary methods to explain why behaviors occur within a behavioral approach. **Respondent conditioning** (also known as **classical conditioning**), which was initially documented by Pavlov (1927/1960), focuses on "reflexive," or involuntary, behaviors that are conditioned to occur under different conditions. In contrast, **operant conditioning,** documented by Skinner (e.g., 1953, 1963), focuses on behavior that "acts on the environment to produce consequences" (Skinner, 1969), or voluntary behaviors. We explore each type of conditioning on the following pages.

Respondent Conditioning

Respondent conditioning occurs when an **unconditioned stimulus,** which elicits an **unconditioned response** (i.e., an unlearned behavior or reflex), is consistently paired with a neutral stimulus. As a result of the pairing, the previously neutral stimulus elicits the same response in the absence of the original unconditioned stimulus. Thus, the neutral stimulus becomes a **conditioned stimulus,** and the response is now called a **conditioned response.** In his classic experiment (see Figure 1.3), Pavlov was studying the salivation of dogs (a reflexive response). Specifically, he presented the dogs with food (unconditioned stimulus) and measured their salivation (unconditioned response). However, Pavlov noticed that the dogs also started to salivate when they saw the research assistants in their lab coats, regardless of whether the assistants had food. To understand why that would occur, Pavlov began a series of experiments in which he paired a tone (previously neutral stimulus) with the food and measured salivation. Over time, he found that the tone began to elicit salivation even when food was not present. Thus, the tone had become a conditioned stimulus, which elicited a conditioned response (salivation).

Although examples of this type of conditioning may not be as obvious in your classroom, you may find that some students engage in reflexive behaviors under atypical circumstances as a result of respondent conditioning. For example, a neutral stimulus (e.g., object, person, activity) may have been present when a student initially experienced an unconditioned fight-or-

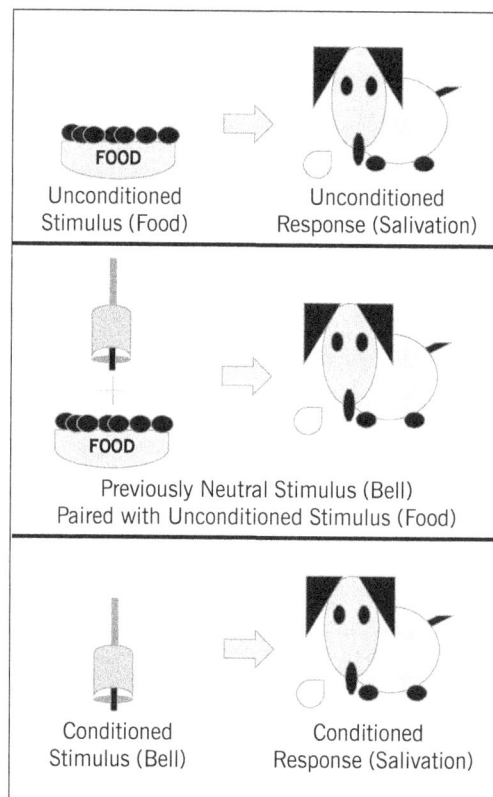

FIGURE 1.3. This simple sequence illustrates respondent, or classical, conditioning.

flight response to an unconditioned stimulus (i.e., pain, imminent threat of harm). This neutral stimulus may have been conditioned to elicit the same fight-or-flight response under seemingly neutral conditions: for example, a student may cower when he smells burnt popcorn if he was hit for burning popcorn in the past. Far more common, however, are behaviors that have been strengthened through operant conditioning.

Operant Conditioning

With operant conditioning, consequences may increase (reinforce) or decrease (punish) a learner's use of a specific behavior. The behaviors are learned and voluntary (i.e., a learner may "choose" to engage in the behavior or not), not reflexive. In Skinner's classic experiments, he worked with hungry rats and pigeons, and he used food to increase a variety of learned behaviors, from pressing or pecking a lever to more elaborate responses. Based on his early work, Skinner documented two key concepts: (1) a **contingency**—or the relation between a behavior and its consequence—affects the future probability of that behavior, and (2) behavior can be **reinforced** (i.e., strengthened or increased) with the use of contingent reinforcers, including those that have biological importance (i.e., food). He also demonstrated that antecedent stimulus conditions affected the probability of behavior occurring if they were consistently associated with the availability of reinforcement (i.e., food). For example, if food was only available when a light was on, then a rat would learn to press the bar only in the presence of the light. In this example, the light was a **discriminative stimulus,** as it signaled the availability of reinforcement (i.e., food). This concept recurs again in Chapter 2, when we discuss the various types of antecedents that affect behavior.

You may see numerous examples of operant conditioning in your classroom. Generally speaking, consider that students continue to engage in behaviors that have resulted in previous reinforcement under similar stimulus conditions (i.e., in a classroom setting). For some students, this means that they are kind, responsible, and safe. For other students, this may mean that they engage in disruptive or withdrawn behavior, especially within specific classroom routines, as those behaviors have provided access to desired stimuli (e.g., getting attention) or allowed the students to escape or avoid undesired stimuli (e.g., difficult tasks). You can use operant conditioning to help your students increase valued and contextually appropriate behaviors and decrease contextually inappropriate behaviors in your classroom, as we discuss in Chapters 7 and 8, respectively.

Applied Behavior Analysis: Bringing the Science from the Lab to the Real World

Although Skinner discussed applications of his theory in "real-world" settings (e.g., Skinner, 1953, 1969), much of the early behavioral research took place in lab settings with animals, rather than humans. Thus, there was a need to bring the science and technology of behaviorism into the real world to solve applied problems (e.g., supporting student behavior in the classroom, enhancing performance of employees in an organization). In the initial volume of the *Journal of Applied Behavior Analysis,* Baer, Wolf, and Risley (1968) described the key dimensions of applied behavior analysis (ABA). ABA is an approach to addressing socially important (*applied*) problems by (1) implementing theoretically sound interventions (grounded in *conceptual sys-*

tems), described in replicable detail (*technological*), to alter observable and measurable actions of individuals (*behavioral*) and (2) demonstrating that the selected intervention is functionally related to the behavior change (*analytic*), producing change that is both meaningful (*effective*) and durable across contexts (*generality*). (The words in italics are the seven dimensions of ABA identified by Baer et al.) In schools, we often think of ABA as services for students with autism spectrum disorders, but ABA is a broad scientific approach that can be applied across a range of individuals and environments.

Other Influences on PBIS

Behaviorism and ABA provide a theoretical and empirical foundation for PBIS. In addition, movements within the disability and special education communities, including person-centered values and the normalization and inclusion movements, have also informed the broader field of positive behavioral support (Carr et al., 2002) and influenced PBIS—the application of positive behavioral support in schools and other organizations that serve students and youth. These influences are reflected in PBIS researchers and practitioners translating technical terminology into more user-friendly language; emphasizing local capacity and expertise, rather than maintaining an expert-driven model; and considering broader outcomes when determining effectiveness (e.g., quality of life across the lifespan, ecological validity; Carr et al., 2002). In a rudimentary way, you may think of PBIS as "ABA for the people." It relies on the same science and theory, but PBIS is presented in a way that may be more accessible to families, educators, and school staff.

PHASES OF LEARNING

When we consider the implications of ABA and PBIS in instructional contexts, one of the key concepts is the phases of learning (Alberto et al., 2021; Cooper et al., 2021). There are four main phases of learning (acquisition, fluency, maintenance, and generalization), and the goal of instruction is to help learners progress through the phases to promote generalization of skills and knowledge (see Figure 1.4). In the next sections, we provide a brief introduction to each phase.

Acquisition

The first phase of learning is focused on the **acquisition** of new skills and concepts. When learners initially acquire a new skill or concept, they often make errors. Therefore, the goal of this phase of learning is *accurate* responding. For example, when students initially learn to read words, they often make errors in pronunciation, misapply phonetic "rules," and make other mistakes related to decoding. Therefore, teachers initially work to assist students in becoming accurate with reading words. Similarly, when students initially learn to ask a peer to play, they may be awkward in their requests, engage in "silly" behavior (e.g., poking a peer) to get peer attention, or otherwise make social mistakes. The teacher's goal should be to facilitate appropriate use of social skills.

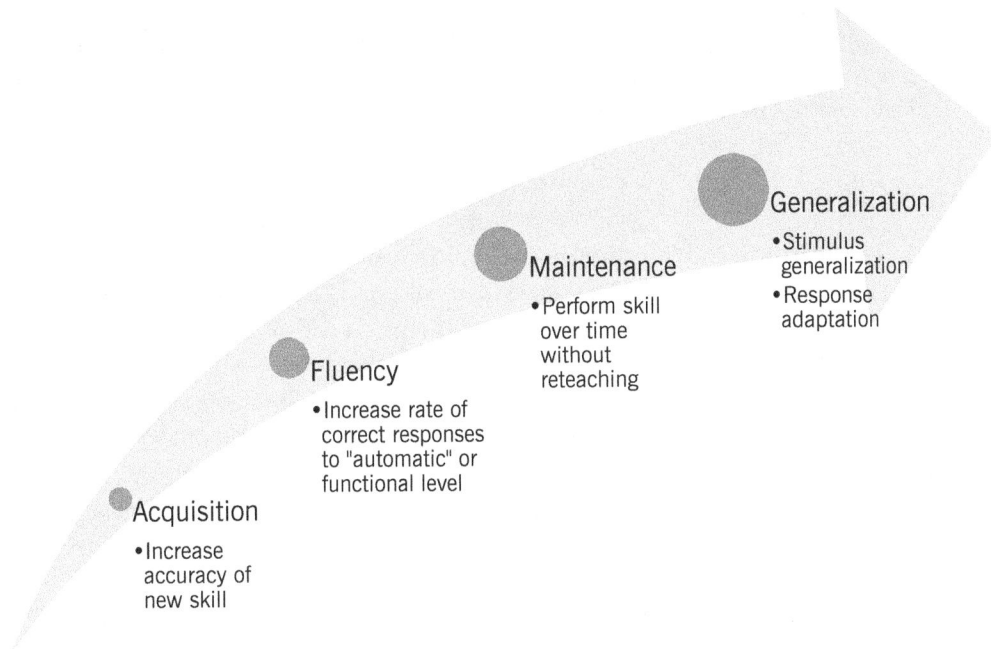

FIGURE 1.4. The goal of instruction is to move learners toward generalization of learned skills and concepts.

Fluency

Once a learner is accurate in responding, the next focus is on the **fluency,** or rate, of responding. Fluency is what makes a skill functional. If it took you 5 minutes to decode each word of this text, you might be an accurate reader, but reading would not be a functional skill. Therefore, the goal of fluency is attaining a rate of accurate responding that is age appropriate or functional. For example, once students have learned to accurately decode words, we shift our focus to the number of words read correctly per minute, or oral reading fluency. Similarly, we want students to demonstrate social skills at a rate that is age appropriate.

Maintenance

Once learners are fluent with a skill or concept, the goal is to have them **maintain** their use of that skill over time and without reteaching. One way to promote maintenance is repeated practice or "overlearning" (Alberto et al., 2021; Cooper et al., 2021). Math fact drills are a good example of this practice; the goal of these drills is **automaticity** (rapid responding that appears "automatic"). Most of us have had sufficient practice with math facts, and we can quickly respond to questions like "What's 2 + 2?" and "What is 4 * 5?" without using our fingers and toes, manipulatives, or other strategies to determine a solution. In contrast, if some of us were asked to integrate a function, we may need to review our calculus text, watch a module on the Kahn Academy website (*www.khanacademy.org*), or call our favorite high school math teacher for a little reteaching. In other words, most of us have maintained our use of basic math, but some of us have not maintained our use of advanced mathematical applications. As you think of other skills that you have not maintained, consider that *all* instruction should promote maintenance of skill and concept use so students can apply that knowledge over time without reteaching.

Generalization

The final phase of learning, and the ultimate goal of instruction, is **generalization.** In this phase, learners are able to both (1) apply the learned skill or concept in a range of appropriate contexts and (2) adjust their application as needed to meet the new context (a process also known as **adaptation**). For example, if we have taught students how to appropriately initiate and conclude a conversation with adults and peers, we would know that they had generalized this skill if they were able to perform the same skill with a range of "untrained" individuals (e.g., principal, future employer, police officer, younger sibling) and adjust their conversational discourse to appropriately interact with each person. There are various strategies to promote generalization (e.g., Stokes & Baer, 1977), including general case programming (Horner & Albin, 1988), which we will discuss in the next chapter.

   As we have stated, the goal of instruction is to ensure that each skill and concept is acquired, performed fluently, maintained across time, and generalized across contexts. For the purposes of this text, we want to increase the likelihood that your learning of key skills and concepts progresses through the relevant phases of learning. To that end, we provide extension activities at the end of each chapter. For some skills and concepts, you may already have progressed through earlier stages of learning (e.g., you may already be fluent in using various consequence strategies to increase contextually appropriate behavior in your classroom), and it may be appropriate to skip those activities to focus on maintenance or generalization. For other skills or concepts, you may need to start at the beginning and work through all four sets of activities. We hope that these activities will help you move past basic acquisition (or comprehension) and toward generalized use of the skills and concepts in this text. In the next section, we provide an overview of the remaining chapters in this book.

OVERVIEW OF THE BOOK

This book provides an introduction to classwide PBIS. We believe this book may be used in a variety of ways, including:

- An applied text for an introductory course in classroom management or PBIS for preservice educators.
- A resource used by inservice teachers to enhance their own classroom practice.
- A guide for school- or district-level PBIS teams to use when providing professional development to staff (who may read a section a month and work on the described skill).
- A resource used by internal or external consultants when they work with an individual teacher who would like to improve their classroom implementation of PBIS.

Given the variety of potential uses, we believe this text will shape the dialogue in the field about how classroom practice can be enhanced with PBIS, what PBIS "looks like" in a classroom, and how teachers can implement these strategies in a variety of school contexts (e.g., those that do and do not implement PBIS).

To that end, we give you a theoretical foundation (Chapter 2) to support the content in the remainder of the book, and we provide an overview of the essential elements of Tier 1 PBIS in your school (Chapter 3) and classroom (Chapter 4) in the remainder of Part I. Then we highlight empirically supported practices for classwide PBIS (Part II) and discuss how to implement them in your classroom (Chapters 5–8). Finally, we introduce strategies to support students who require Tier 2 (Chapter 9) or Tier 3 (Chapter 10) support to be successful in your classroom (Part III). The book ends with a discussion of resources and next steps (Chapter 11).

Part I. PBIS Foundations and Basic Principles

Chapter 2. Behavioral Principles at Work in PBIS

In Chapter 2, we provide a brief primer on the behavioral principles that underlie PBIS. In particular, we discuss the ABCs of behavior, or the three-term contingency. We introduce the concept of setting events and describe how they interact with the other elements of the three-term contingency. We also highlight behavioral approaches to teaching new skills (shaping and chaining) and increasing the likelihood that previously learned behaviors occur in the desired situations (establishing stimulus control).

Chapter 3. Tier 1 Schoolwide PBIS

Chapter 3 is an overview of Tier 1 schoolwide PBIS. We present the defining characteristics of schoolwide PBIS, describe the essential elements (equity, outcomes, data, practices, and systems) in greater depth using schoolwide examples, and highlight how to connect schoolwide PBIS with your own classroom PBIS approach.

Chapter 4. Introduction to Classwide PBIS: Focus on Equity, Outcomes, Data, and Systems

In this chapter, we describe how to apply the essential elements of PBIS in your classroom. Because we discuss classroom practices in Chapters 5–8, Chapter 4 focuses primarily on centering equity, selecting outcomes, collecting and using data to guide your practice, and identifying systems to support your classroom implementation of PBIS.

Part II. Classwide PBIS Practices

Chapter 5. Create an Inclusive, Predictable, Safe, and Engaging Classroom

In Chapter 5, we share strategies for creating an inclusive, predictable, and safe classroom environment by (1) connecting and fostering positive relationships with and among your students, (2) establishing and teaching classroom routines, and (3) arranging your classroom environment in a way that promotes access and contextually appropriate behavior. We also discuss strategies to actively engage your students in relevant instruction, as high-quality instruction is one of the most effective social, emotional, and behavioral support tools!

Chapter 6. Establish and Teach Positively Stated Norms or Expectations

After considering the structure and instruction in your classroom, it is critical to engage your students in selecting, defining, explicitly teaching, monitoring, and reinforcing a small number of positively stated norms or expectations to foster a positive classroom community. This chapter is all about expectations, including a focus on designing and delivering classroom social skills lessons that assist students with acquiring, gaining fluency with, maintaining, and generalizing social, emotional, and behavioral skills (i.e., contextually appropriate behavior) across contexts.

Chapter 7. Implement a Continuum of Strategies to Increase Contextually Appropriate Behavior

In Chapter 7, we teach you to apply the basic principle of reinforcement to increase students' social, emotional, and behavioral skills (i.e., contextually appropriate behaviors) in your classroom. We present a variety of empirically supported reinforcement strategies, describe how to engage your students in designing an appropriate system for your classroom, and discuss how to implement and evaluate your classroom reinforcement system.

Chapter 8. Implement a Continuum of Strategies to Decrease Contextually Inappropriate Behavior

Chapter 8 is the companion to Chapter 7, as we teach you strategies to supportively respond to and decrease social, emotional, and behavioral mistakes, or contextually inappropriate behaviors, in your classroom. Although we discuss strategies that use the behavioral mechanism of punishment (i.e., error correction, overcorrection, response cost, time out from reinforcement), we also (1) highlight strategies designed to strengthen contextually appropriate behaviors to decrease contextually inappropriate behavior (e.g., differential reinforcement), (2) describe a restorative approach, and (3) generally emphasize a supportive and instructional approach that aims to set students up for success and prevent social, emotional, and behavioral mistakes.

Part III. Additional Tiers of Support for Students

Chapter 9. Overview of Tier 2 Support in Your School and Classroom

In Chapter 9, we introduce you to the critical features of Tier 2 support and describe how it can be applied in your school and classroom. We begin by discussing how you can further differentiate your classroom practices (described in Part II) to meet the needs of students who require an additional layer of support. We also review a variety of empirically supported Tier 2 interventions and discuss how they can be used to support a range of student needs in your classroom.

Chapter 10. Overview of Tier 3 Support in Your School and Classroom

We introduce Tier 3 support in Chapter 10, including individualized BSPs based on FBAs and more intensive supports developed through wraparound and person-centered planning processes. We highlight what this may look like within your classroom, and how you may participate in developing and implementing FBAs and BSPs for your students (along with a whole team to support you!).

SUMMARY

Schools and teachers implementing PBIS center equity; identify relevant and meaningful outcomes for implementation; use data to guide decisions and evaluate progress toward outcomes; organize, adopt, and implement evidence-based and culturally responsive practices within a preventive framework; and invest in systems to sustain fidelity of implementation over time. PBIS is grounded in the early science and theory of behaviorism and in more recent applications of ABA. One of the key dimensions of ABA is generality; in an instructional context, this means that our goal is to promote the acquisition, fluency, maintenance, and ultimately generalization of learned skills and concepts. We continue to "unpack" behavioral principles that are foundational to PBIS in Chapter 2.

PHASES OF LEARNING ACTIVITIES: CHAPTER 1

Acquisition

1. Identify examples of respondent and operant conditioning that affect students' behavior in your classroom.
2. Write a definition of PBIS that references the three tiers of support and the five essential elements (equity, outcomes, data, practices, and systems).

Fluency

1. Select a contextually appropriate behavior that you would like to increase for students in your classroom, identify a potentially meaningful reinforcer to provide when the students engage in that behavior, and use operant conditioning to systematically reinforce students' use of that behavior.
2. Briefly describe PBIS to a colleague in your school environment and check for their understanding to evaluate the quality of your description.

Maintenance

1. Once the behavior you targeted in Fluency Activity 1 reaches the desired level, select a new classroom behavior you would like to increase or a new group of students (if you see multiple groups of students throughout the day) and repeat the same process.
2. Review descriptions of PBIS found in resources listed in this book and on the web (e.g., *www.pbis. org*). Determine whether your understanding matches those descriptions, and continue to refine your own descriptions by discussing PBIS with colleagues.

Generalization

1. Use operant conditioning to systematically reinforce one of your own behaviors. That is, identify a behavior you want to increase, identify a reinforcer, and only give yourself access to that reinforcer when you have engaged in the desired behavior.

2. Develop a plan for implementing PBIS within your classroom. (You may need to finish reading this book first!) Consider practices you will implement for all of your students (Tier 1) and supports that you may provide to targeted groups (Tier 2). Consult with a behavioral expert in your school to identify supports for individual students who display chronic or high-risk behavior in your classroom (Tier 3).

PART I

PBIS FOUNDATIONS AND BASIC PRINCIPLES

CHAPTER 2

Behavioral Principles at Work in PBIS

CHAPTER OBJECTIVES

By the end of this chapter, you should be able to . . .

1. Describe the ABCs of behavior and identify common ABCs for students in your classroom.
2. Describe behavioral principles involved in teaching, and select and implement appropriate behavioral teaching strategies within your classroom.

Imagine This: One of your new colleagues is a first-year teacher, and he just purchased a book of 101 classroom management solutions. Exasperated, he comes to you, and states that he has tried every solution in the book and nothing seems to work. He tells you his classroom management skills are great, and his classroom would be perfect if the principal would just move the "problem students" out of his classroom. As he starts to name the offending students, you recognize their names and realize that those students were successful in your classroom the previous year. You also recall that your typical approaches had to be adjusted to meet the needs of a few of these students; just implementing "tricks" from a book is unlikely to work with this group. He needs to understand more about classroom management than his 101 solutions!

OVERVIEW OF BEHAVIORAL PRINCIPLES: WHY SHOULD YOU CARE?

As you learned in Chapter 1, PBIS is based on a long tradition of behavioral theory and science. From this rich theoretical and empirical tradition, we have learned key behavioral principles that are critical to implementing effective schoolwide and classroom behavioral supports for students. At this point, you may be asking, "Why bother to focus on theory? Why not move straight to teaching us the practices or 'tricks'?" The answer is simple: *The tricks will fail you in certain situations, but the theory never will.* By developing an understanding of the theoretical principles that underlie the practices, you will be able to (1) identify which practices are appropriate for whom and under which conditions, (2) assess whether practices are working as intended, and (3) adjust your implementation as necessary. You will develop these more advanced skills as you continue to progress through this text.

In addition, behavioral principles are at work *whether or not* you:

• *Understand them.* Behaviors are constantly being occasioned by antecedent stimuli and reinforced, punished, or extinguished by consequence stimuli. You do not have to understand or even be aware of these contingencies for them to affect behavior (Cooper et al., 2021). Without an understanding of the key behavioral mechanisms (e.g., reinforcement, punishment, stimulus control), you may inadvertently reinforce an undesired behavior or punish a desired behavior.

• *Believe in them.* Skinner (1983) shared a great story about attending a talk by someone who was trying to refute behavioral explanations of human behavior. He passed his colleague a note saying that he would shape the speaker's behavior to make a "chopping motion" with his left hand, and by the end of the talk the speaker was "chopping the air so vigorously that his wristwatch kept slipping over his hand" (Skinner, 1983, p. 151). As this anecdote illustrates, behavioral principles work regardless of your beliefs about them. So, if you work in a building with staff members who believe that behavioral principles don't work, you may think about using the principles to alter their behavior!

• *Implement behavioral interventions,* like practices included in a PBIS framework, in your school or classroom. Thus, the content in this chapter is applicable in any setting with any population at any time. Once you develop a clear understanding of behavioral principles, you will be able to see evidence of them throughout your day and use them to your advantage with your students, colleagues, friends, family, and even yourself!

Therefore, a necessary first step is developing a basic understanding of behavioral principles. In this chapter, we begin with the building blocks, or ABCs, of behavior and progress to examining behavioral principles involved in teaching. To assist you in recognizing and applying these principles, we have also interspersed a series of text boxes illustrating the various behavioral principles "in action." Because this is only one chapter in an applied book, we recommend reading additional texts (e.g., Alberto et al., 2021; Cooper et al., 2021; Vargas, 2020) to develop a more complete understanding of behavioral principles; you will notice we reference these texts throughout this chapter.

ABCs OF BEHAVIOR: THE THREE-TERM (AND FOUR-TERM) CONTINGENCY

There are three basic building blocks for behavior: antecedents, behaviors, and consequences. **Antecedents** are the stimuli (e.g., attention, events, conditions) that occur before a behavior. **Behaviors** are observable and measurable actions (i.e., actions we can directly sense and mea-

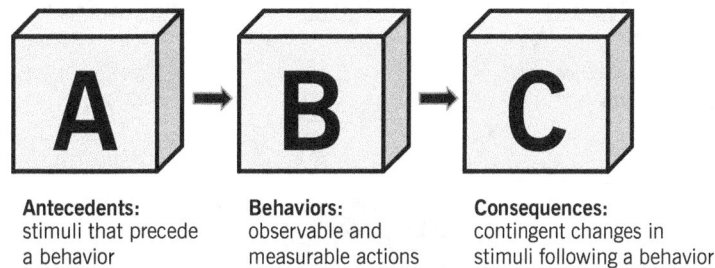

FIGURE 2.1. The building blocks (ABCs) of behavior: The three-term contingency.

sure). **Consequences** are changes in stimuli (i.e., stimuli are added/increased or subtracted/decreased) that occur contingent on a behavior. This "ABC" sequence is often referred to as the three-term contingency (see Figure 2.1). These ABC sequences occur constantly throughout our day. (See if you can identify ABC sequences that typically occur in your classroom, as described in Acquisition Activity 1 at the end of the chapter.) For example, you may ask your students to begin their in-class assignment (antecedent), then they may begin to work quietly (behavior), and you may say, "Thank you for quietly working on your assignment" (consequence). Alternatively, you may deliver the same antecedent, and one student may start to play with materials, talk with peers, and draw on a desk (behaviors). You may provide a different response (consequence) to that student, such as a quick error correction ("Remember, we are supposed to be quietly working on our assignment. If you need help, please raise your hand."). From these examples and from your observations, you may already be anticipating that there are different types of antecedents and consequences that help us explain (1) when behaviors may occur and (2) why some behaviors increase and others decrease (or stop altogether).

Types of Antecedents

There are three main types of antecedent stimuli: discriminative stimulus (S^D), stimulus delta (S^Δ), and discriminative stimulus for punishment (S^{D-} or S^{Dp}).[1] (In behavioral notation, a capital S represents a stimulus, and the superscript indicates the type of stimulus. Because each descriptor of antecedent stimuli is a mouthful, the behavioral shorthand is helpful!) Each type of antecedent is associated with a different type of consequence (reinforcement, neutral, or punishment, respectively) for a particular behavior or response (see Figure 2.2). As a result, a learner who experiences these three types of antecedents responds differentially with their behavior because the same behavior may lead to reinforcement in the presence of one antecedent (S^D) and punishment in the presence of another (S^{D-}). For example, consider a middle school student who engages in teasing behavior. When the student teases in the presence of a peer, the peer laughs and provides desired attention. Thus, the peer is an S^D for teasing, as the student has a history of reinforcement for teasing in the presence of a peer. When the student teases in the presence of a baby sibling, the sibling likely does nothing. The sibling is an S^Δ for teasing,

---

[1]There is not a standard way to note discriminative stimuli associated with punishing consequences (Cooper et al., 2021). In this book we will consistently use S^{D-} to note an S^D associated with a history of punishment for a particular behavior.

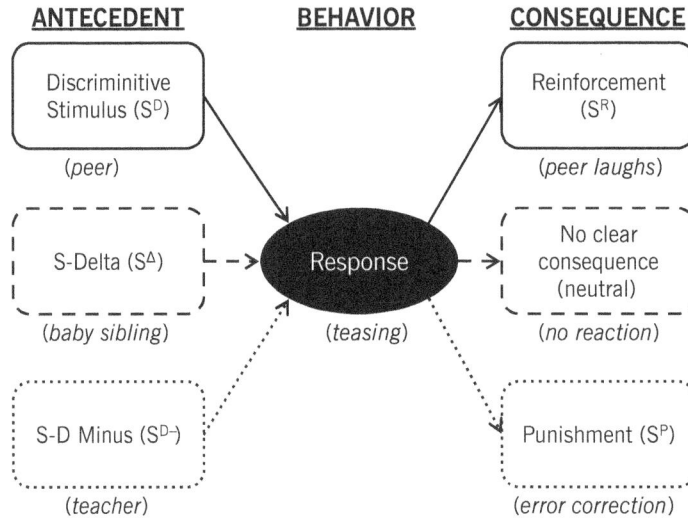

FIGURE 2.2. Relations among each type of antecedent and consequence for the same response (with an illustration of an example related to teasing behavior discussed in text).

as no clear (i.e., neutral) consequences occur. In contrast, if a student teases in the presence of a teacher, the teacher may provide an error correction (e.g., "Teasing is not respectful. What is a better way to get your friend's attention?"). Thus, the teacher is an S^{D-} for teasing, as the student has a history of punishment for teasing in the presence of a teacher. As a result of this learning history, the student's teasing is more likely in the presence of peers, less likely in the presence of a teacher, and not affected by the presence of a baby sibling. In the next paragraphs, we go into a bit more detail about each type of antecedent.

S^D (Discriminative Stimulus)

An antecedent becomes an S^D for a particular behavior by being associated with a history of reinforcement for that behavior. For example, if you teach students a specific problem-solving strategy to use (behavior) every time they encounter a particular type of word problem (antecedent), and they use that strategy successfully to earn full points (reinforcing consequence) on that type of word problem over time, then that type of word problem becomes an S^D for use of that strategy. Similarly, if you show a quiet signal in your classroom (antecedent), students stop what they are doing and quietly listen (behavior), and you praise them for giving you their attention (consequence), then the quiet signal becomes an S^D for quietly paying attention to the teacher. In other words, as a result of a student's learning history (i.e., experiencing reinforcement for a particular behavior consistently in the presence of a particular antecedent), the behavior becomes more likely to occur in the presence of that antecedent, or S^D. In fact, when we say "antecedent" (e.g., "What's the antecedent of that behavior?"), we are typically referring to the S^D, as we are referring to the antecedent that occasions the target behavior due to its association with a history of reinforcement.

S$^\Delta$ (Stimulus Delta)

There are also a variety of other stimuli present in the environment that do not have "discriminative" properties because they are not associated with any particular history of reinforcement or punishment. For example, in the word problem example, there are a variety of other antecedent stimuli in the environment (e.g., color and font on worksheet, teacher's outfit, temperature outside) that are not associated with whether use of a particular problem-solving strategy (behavior) will lead to reinforcement (or punishment). Similarly, there are a variety of other stimuli in the environment (e.g., time of day, teacher's location in the classroom) that are not associated with reinforcement (or punishment) when students stop what they are doing and pay attention to the teacher (behavior). In both examples, these other stimuli are S$^\Delta$s: they are not likely to affect the occurrence of a particular behavior, as they have no association with consequences for that behavior.

S^{D-} (Discriminative Stimulus for Punishment)

Unlike the S$^\Delta$s, an S^{D-} is associated with a history of punishment for a particular response. For example, if a student uses the same problem-solving strategy (behavior) in the presence of a different type of word problem, they may lose points on an assignment or exam (punisher). As a result, the student will be less likely to use that strategy in the presence of the different type of word problem, and that word problem will become an S^{D-} for use of that specific strategy. Likewise, if students stop what they are doing to wait and listen to the teacher (behavior) when they

---

BOX 2.1. ANTECEDENTS IN ACTION: TO ANSWER, OR NOT TO ANSWER

Your phone is ringing, vibrating, lighting up, or doing whatever you've selected as your preferred antecedent stimulus to signal a phone call. This antecedent (S^D) likely occasions a "pick it up and/or look at the phone" response (R) so that you can see who is calling, as at least some of the time you're excited to talk with the caller (i.e., you anticipate reinforcement when you answer the phone; S^{R+}).

However, think about the next step in the sequence. When do you actually answer your phone? Part of your "phone answering" behavior may depend on the name (or face) that appears on your phone indicating who is calling.

- If the name indicates that your best friend or significant other is calling (S^D), you may answer the phone (R$_1$) to receive desired attention or information from a preferred person (S^{R+}).
- If the name indicates that your boss or someone with whom you've recently fought is calling (S^{D-}), you may not answer the phone to avoid hearing about additional work or receiving aversive attention (S^{P+}).
- If you do not recognize the name or number, the likelihood of answering the phone is affected by your history of reinforcement (or punishment) for answering calls from unknown callers. Thus, an unknown caller may be either an S^D or S^{D-}, depending on your personal learning history.

Thus, different antecedent stimuli occasion different responses as a result of their association with reinforcement, punishment, or no clear (neutral) consequences.

were asked to be actively engaged with their peers in cooperative learning groups (antecedent), the teacher may redirect them to work with peers and the students may not earn full points on the group assignment (punisher). Thus, cooperative learning groups will become an S^{D-} for sitting quietly and waiting for a teacher to speak.

To summarize, the three types of antecedents (S^D, S^Δ, S^{D-}) help us explain when behaviors are most (and least) likely to occur due to a history of reinforcing, neutral (or unclear), or punishing consequences for a particular behavior (see Box 2.1). These concepts will come up later in the chapter when we discuss establishing stimulus control. In the next sections we explore the different types of consequences that may occur contingent on a particular behavior.

Types of Consequences

As we stated previously, consequences are changes in stimuli (additions or subtractions) that occur contingent on a particular behavior. We talked about three main categories of consequences in connection with the three types of antecedents: reinforcing, neutral or unclear, and punishing consequences. For our purposes, we are interested in those consequences that have an effect on future behavior; thus, we will explore types of reinforcing and punishing consequences within this section.

Effects on Future Behavior

Consequences may have one of two effects on future behavior: increase or decrease. A consequence (change in stimuli) that results in an *increase* in future behavior is a **reinforcer.** A consequence that results in a *decrease* in future behavior is a **punisher.** Notice that there is no mention of intent or any other value or judgment in those definitions: you only know if something is a reinforcer or punisher by examining the effect (increase or decrease) on future behavior. For example, imagine two students working quietly on an assignment. To each student, you say something like "Wow, I like how you are being responsible by working quietly on your assignment." The first student may be more likely to work quietly in the future as you walk by, and your praise statement may have functioned as a reinforcer for that behavior. However, the second student may not respond to public recognition and may be less likely to work quietly when you are close. For the second student, your statement may have functioned as a punisher for that behavior. For both students, you were trying to provide a nice consequence, but the same consequence functioned as a reinforcer for one and a punisher for the other.

Consider a second example: picture two students engaging in disruptive behavior during your lesson. You send both students to the office with an office referral for classroom disruption. The next time you deliver a lesson with both students in the room, you notice that one is actively listening, but the second student is even more disruptive. If this pattern continues, you may infer that being sent to the office functioned as a punisher for the first student's disruptive behavior, but it functioned as a reinforcer for the second student's disruptive behavior. Again, we only know whether a consequence is reinforcing or punishing by looking at the effect on future behavior. If a behavior continues to occur, you can infer that it is being reinforced. (This concept will come into play when we discuss why students engage in particular behavior—or the *function* of behavior—in Chapter 10.)

Action (Add or Subtract)

We have already noted that consequences are changes in stimuli that occur contingent on a behavior. There are two ways we can change stimuli: we can add ("give") or subtract ("take"). If you focus on the mathematical terms (*add* and *subtract*), you will begin to associate the signs or operations with those words. As a quick refresher, addition is associated with a plus or a *positive* sign, and subtraction is associated with a minus or *negative* sign. Thus, think of the words *positive* and *negative* in terms of mathematical operations (add = *positive* and subtract = *negative*).

A **positive** consequence occurs when stimuli are added contingent on behavior. For example, you may add (give) your attention (e.g., proximity, verbal statement), an item, an activity, or other stimuli contingent on behavior. If these additions have an effect on future behavior, you have provided a positive consequence. In contrast, a **negative** consequence occurs when stimuli are subtracted contingent on behavior. For example, you may subtract (take away) your attention (e.g., walk away, ignore), an item, an activity, or other stimuli contingent on behavior. If these subtractions have an effect on future behavior, you have employed a negative consequence. Again, note that there is no intent and no value statements in those examples—just simple descriptions of addition and subtraction!

Four Types of Consequences

If we put both concepts together (action and effect), we end up with four types of consequences: positive reinforcers, negative reinforcers, positive punishers, and negative punishers (see Figure 2.3). In the next sections, we provide a little more explanation of each type of consequence. It will be helpful to recall our earlier comment about behavioral notation. Remember that a capital *S* refers to a stimulus, and the superscript describes the type of stimulus. A superscript *R* refers

Action

	Give (Add) $+$	Take (Subtract) $-$
EFFECT Increase ↑	S^{R+} Positive Reinforcement	S^{R-} Negative Reinforcement
EFFECT Decrease ↓	S^{P+} Positive Punishment	S^{P-} Negative Punishment

FIGURE 2.3. By examining the action (give or take) and effect (increase or decrease), you can identify four distinct types of consequences. Adapted from Cooper et al. (2021). Copyright © 2021 Pearson Education. Adapted with permission.

to a reinforcing stimulus, a superscript P refers to a punishing stimulus, and the superscript sign (+ or –) indicates whether that stimulus was added (positive) or subtracted (negative).

POSITIVE REINFORCEMENT (S^{R+})

Positive reinforcement occurs when a stimulus is *added* (action) contingent on a particular behavior that *increases* (effect) the future probability of that behavior. Consider the following four examples.

- You give your students a test (antecedent), and a student studies hard and correctly answers questions on the test (behavior). As a result, you "give" a good grade (consequence). If the student is more likely to study and answer correctly in the future, the good grade may have functioned as a positive reinforcer.
- During teacher-directed instruction (antecedent), a student makes an inappropriate comment in class (behavior), and peers laugh and "give" the student attention (consequence). If the student is more likely to make inappropriate comments in the future, peer attention may have functioned as a positive reinforcer.
- During less structured times (antecedent), a student has a "tantrum" (cluster of behaviors including shouting, crying, stomping, and kicking the ground while lying on the floor). The teacher calls members of the crisis team, and they immediately enter the room, ask the student what's wrong, circle around the student, and "calm" them with a gentle hand on their back (consequence). Although this reaction may appear to stop the tantrum in that moment, if tantrums are more likely to occur in the future, then attention from the crisis team may have functioned as a positive reinforcer.
- During quiet classroom routines (antecedent), a student alternates between repeatedly slapping the side of her face, flicking her fingers in front of her eyes or "filtering light," and rocking with her hands tucked tightly in her lap (behavior). As a result of these behaviors, she receives sensory stimulation (tactile sensation from slapping, visual sensation from filtering light, and vestibular sensation from rocking, which are all consequences). If the student continues to engage in these behaviors, the sensory stimulation may have functioned as a positive reinforcer.

In each of these examples, it should be clear that positive reinforcers may be (1) purposefully delivered (e.g., good grade) or not (e.g., peer attention); (2) intended as reinforcers (e.g., good grade) or not (e.g., attention from crisis team); and (3) socially mediated (e.g., first three consequences) or "automatic" (e.g., sensory stimulation resulting from behavior in the fourth example). Thus, the purpose, intention, and mode of delivery may vary; this is also true for all of the consequences described subsequently. The key features of positive reinforcers are the action (add) and effect (increase) on future behavior. We will discuss applications of positive reinforcement in the classroom in Chapter 7.

NEGATIVE REINFORCEMENT (S^{R-})

Negative reinforcement occurs when a stimulus is *subtracted* (action) contingent on a particular behavior that *increases* (effect) the future probability of that behavior. A simple (and often used) example of negative reinforcement occurs each time you get into your car. In most modern cars, there is a noise (and likely other signals on your dashboard or touch screen) that occurs repeatedly (antecedent) until you fasten your seat belt (behavior) and stops once it is fastened (consequence). Assuming you continue to fasten your seat belt in the future (possibly even before turning the car on) to stop (or altogether avoid) that noise, your behavior is likely negatively reinforced.

In a classroom, we also see many examples of negative reinforcement. Consider the following examples:

- A student rips up his paper (behavior) each time a difficult task is presented (antecedent). The teacher may ignore the student or send him to the office, but in either case the work is functionally removed (consequence). If the student continues to rip up his paper each time he is presented with a difficult task, we may infer that his behavior is being negatively reinforced.
- At the start of a group activity (antecedent), a student pulls their hood over their head, puts their head down on their desk, and occasionally looks up to glare at anyone who tries to talk to them (behaviors). Peers move away and stop trying to interact with the student (consequence). If the student is more likely to put their head down during future group activities, peers may be negatively reinforcing their behaviors. (Remember, behavioral principles work whether we realize it or not!)
- Students are working quietly and accurately (behavior) on an assignment (antecedent). The teacher says, "Because you have all worked so hard in class, I'm not going to assign homework on this topic tonight" (consequence). If the students are more likely to work quietly on class assignments in the future, the consequence (removing homework) may have functioned as a negative reinforcer.

Again, the key features of negative reinforcement are action (subtract) and effect (increase), and we will discuss additional applications in Chapter 7.

POSITIVE PUNISHMENT (S^{P+})

Positive punishment occurs when a stimulus is *added* (action) contingent on a particular behavior that *decreases* (effect) the future probability of that behavior. Keep in mind that positive punishers are not inherently "bad." In fact, providing specific feedback (adding a verbal statement) to correct (decrease future) errors is a part of good instruction. For example, if a student responds to the teacher's question "What's 2 plus 2?" (antecedent) with the answer "5" (behavior), the teacher may say, "No, 2 plus 2 is 4" (consequence). If the student stops responding to the question "What's 2 plus 2?" with the answer "5," we can infer that the teachers' correction positively punished the student's incorrect response. (If the student instead provides the correct answer, the teacher may also follow the correct answer with a statement, "You're right; 2 plus 2 is 4"—praise that may function as a positive reinforcer for the correct answer, assuming the student continues to answer the question correctly.) Similarly, if a student engages in unsafe behavior (e.g., throwing materials at peers), the teacher may say, "That is not safe. We use our materials only for the intended purpose." If the student is less likely to throw materials in the future, then the teacher may have positively punished that behavior.

Although positive punishers are part of good instruction and classroom behavioral support, we also want to be clear that some positive punishers should never be used in the classroom (or elsewhere!). It is *never* acceptable (or ethical) to provide a consequence with the intention of humiliating or harming the student. For example, if a student engages in inappropriate behavior, it is *not* acceptable to scream at the student, physically back the student into a corner while berating them, ask the student to wear a different color shirt (or some other identifier) so peers know that they were inappropriate, or make fun of them in front of peers. All of these "added" consequences may sound extreme and farcical, but they are all things we have observed or heard about occurring in our research and practice. Even if these consequences function as positive punishers (i.e., decrease future probability) for contextually inappropriate behavior, they should never be used. In contrast, it would be totally appropriate for a teacher to calmly let a student know that their behavior was not consistent with classroom norms and remind them of the expected behavior. We will continue our discussion of the appropriate (and inappropriate) use of positive punishers in Chapter 8.

NEGATIVE PUNISHMENT (S^{P-})

Negative punishment occurs when a stimulus is *subtracted* (action) contingent on a particular behavior that *decreases* (effect) the future probability of that behavior. For example, a student may lose points (consequence) contingent on providing an incorrect response (behavior) on an exam question (antecedent). If, as a result of points being removed (action), the student is less likely (effect) to make the same error again in the future, then negative punishment has occurred. Negative punishment is often used in classroom consequence systems: teachers may remove items or activities contingent on inappropriate behavior by one or more students, "drop the student's level" in a classroom level system and restrict access to associated privileges contingent on unsafe behavior, or withhold access to particular items or activities contingent on undesired behavior. In each case, if removing or subtracting stimuli results in a decrease in the specified behavior, then the teacher has used negative punishment.

Although these systems may result in decreases in inappropriate behavior, they have not specifically taught or reinforced an appropriate behavior. These systems may also inadvertently cause shame and harm (e.g., clip charts and level systems can have negative side effects; McIntosh et al., 2020). Therefore, we encourage you to transform (or augment) a system that relies on "taking away" to decrease problem behavior (negative punishment) into a system that allows students to earn the same stimuli that you were taking away to increase appropriate behavior (positive reinforcement).

Further, although negative punishment may be used appropriately and effectively, there are some ways in which it should never be used. It is *never* acceptable (or ethical) to remove or restrict a student's access to stimuli that meet basic needs (e.g., withhold food, water, access to a restroom) contingent on problem behavior. Of course, it is acceptable to teach students to take care of basic needs on a regular schedule (we are not suggesting that you let a student visit the restroom or get a drink of water 50 times during a math lesson), but a student should not be prevented from eating, drinking, or using the restroom during a scheduled break contingent on "problem" behavior. We will discuss further applications of negative punishment approaches in Chapter 8.

Extinction

In addition to the four types of consequences, there is a fifth consequence condition that affects the future probability of behavior. When a behavior has a history of reinforcement and when that reinforcement is consistently withheld or removed, the behavior will decrease and eventually stop. This process is called **extinction.** For example, during teacher-directed instruction (antecedent), a student may repeatedly call out (behavior), and the teacher may call on, redirect, or otherwise give attention (positively reinforcing consequence) to the student. Once the teacher realizes that his attention is reinforcing, or increasing, the student's calling-out behavior, the teacher may decide to (1) teach the student to appropriately request attention with a quiet hand raise and (2) ignore (withhold attention from) all future callouts. Initially, the callouts may increase in frequency or intensity; this is called an **extinction burst.** But if the teacher is able to consistently ignore callouts, they will eventually disappear and the teacher will have successfully implemented extinction. We will discuss applications of extinction, like planned ignoring, in Chapter 8.

In summary, the four types of consequences (S^{R+}, S^{R-}, S^{P+}, and S^{P-}) all occur contingent on a particular behavior and are defined by action (add or subtract) and by effect (increase or decrease) on the future probability of that behavior. The fifth consequence procedure (extinction) occurs when reinforcement (S^{R+} or S^{R-}) is withheld from a previously reinforced behavior and results in a decrease in that behavior. Thus, consequences explain why some behaviors continue to occur (history of reinforcement) and some behaviors decrease or stop all together (history of punishment and/or absence of reinforcement). (See additional examples of consequences in action in Box 2.2.) Although knowledge of the different types of antecedents and consequences is critical to explaining when (antecedent conditions) and why behaviors continue (or cease) to occur (consequence conditions), this knowledge does not fully account for the variations in behavior under similar antecedent and consequence conditions. We now turn to a "fourth" term, which we will add to the original three-term contingency.

Adding a Fourth Term: Setting Events

We have all seen that some days are different (i.e., better or worse) than others for each student's behavior, even when the conditions in our classroom appear to be similar. For example, you present an assignment to a student (antecedent), and the student typically completes the assignment (behavior) to receive praise, earn points toward a grade, and access the next activity (consequences). Occasionally, however, you provide a similar assignment, and the student rips it up (or maybe just puts their head down) and refuses to work. Something is different about this ABC sequence, even though the antecedent and available consequences are similar to all of the other times when the student just does the work. Setting events or motivating operations help explain these variations in behavior (Alberto et al., 2021; Cooper et al., 2021). Although there are some slight differences between these two concepts, we will consider them together and use the term *setting event.* **Setting events** are antecedent events or conditions that temporarily alter the value or effectiveness of the consequence(s) for particular behavior (e.g., Horner et al., 1996). In the next sections, we describe three key features of a setting event: (1) antecedent stimuli that (2) alter the value of the consequence(s) for a particular behavior and (3) have a temporary effect.

BOX 2.2. CONSEQUENCES IN ACTION: STUDENT BEHAVIOR DURING TEACHER-DIRECTED INSTRUCTION

Regardless of the age and content you teach (or plan to teach), you probably have an image of what students should be doing when you are delivering instruction. Although the specific topography of the behavior may vary by age, ability, and context, you probably want some demonstration of actively engaged behavior, including active listening, eyes on instruction, feet on the floor, hands and materials used to enhance learning (e.g., taking notes, answering a math problem on a whiteboard), and calm body.

In addition to using antecedent stimuli to occasion and explicit instruction to teach the desired behavior, you may also want to employ consequences to increase the likelihood of actively engaged behavior (and decrease the likelihood of disruptive behavior). To that end, consider how you may use each type of consequence to your advantage.

• **Positive reinforcement (S^{R+}) of actively engaged behavior:** You may provide specific praise and attention contingent on engaged behavior. For young students you may say, "I can tell that you are really listening because your eyes are on me and your body is ready." Or, for older students, you may say, "Thank you for quietly taking notes. This content will be on your quiz, and I'd like to see you all do well." Assuming your specific praise increases actively engaged behavior, you have used positive reinforcement.

• **Negative reinforcement (S^{R-}) of actively engaged behavior:** You may start with a long list of homework tasks related to your instruction. For each 5 minutes that the majority of your students remain actively engaged, you may remove one task. (Of course, you'd only want to do this if the tasks you removed were not critical to students progressing through the phases of learning with those skills.)

• **Positive punishment (S^{P+}) of disruptive behavior:** Each time a student engages in disruptive behavior, you may provide a specific error correction (e.g., "Remember, if you'd like my attention, please raise your hand."). If the student is less likely to engage in disruptive behavior, you have provided positive punishment.

• **Negative punishment (S^{P-}) of disruptive behavior:** If a student is disruptive by talking with peers, you may have that student move to a desk away from peers (i.e., remove access to peers) for 1 minute. If that results in less disruptive behavior in the future, you have employed negative punishment.

As illustrated in these dot points, there are often multiple ways to use consequences to increase desired and decrease undesired behaviors in your classroom. Throughout this text, we encourage you to use consequence strategies as part of an overall positive and preventive classroom management approach. Specifically, consider (1) employing antecedent and instructional strategies to prevent inappropriate behaviors and promote appropriate behaviors; (2) emphasizing consequence strategies that are largely based on positive reinforcement; (3) collecting data to monitor the effects of consequences (or any other behavioral strategy); and (4) adjusting your implementation based on the function of student behavior and data.

Setting Events Are Antecedents Too

One defining feature of setting events is that they are *antecedent* stimuli (i.e., conditions or events); that is, they occur prior to (and occasionally are still present with) the behavior. Setting events can occur in the more remote past (e.g., hours or days before the behavior). For example, you may notice that a student's issues at home, on the bus, or in a nonclassroom setting (e.g., playground, locker room, hallway) affect their behavior in your classroom even though these events occurred hours or days before you observed their effect. But setting events can also occur at the same time as the S^D and may still be present when the behavior occurs. For example, a student may have a cold (or other illness) when you assign independent classwork (S^D), and their illness would still be present when they are expected to complete the work (behavior). The symptoms of the illness may decrease the value of the consequences for completing work (e.g., points) and increase the reinforcing value of putting their head on the desk (e.g., immediate break from work).

Setting Events Alter the Value or Effectiveness of Consequences

Setting events affect the probability of a behavior (i.e., make it more or less likely to occur) because they alter the value or effectiveness of the consequence(s) for that behavior; they make reinforcers or punishers more or less effective. Looking at your own personal life, consider a time when you woke up for work or class after going to bed late and did not get enough sleep. Although you always arrive on time (behavior) to maintain your awesome attendance and time-liness record, which often results in desired attention from your boss or professor (positive rein-forcer), on this morning you hit the snooze button (behavior) for an extra 15 minutes, stopped at your favorite coffee shop to get a large caffeinated beverage (behavior), and arrived at work or class late. In this example, lack of sleep was a setting event, as it (1) decreased the effectiveness (or reinforcing value) of social attention for on-time behavior and (2) increased the effectiveness of sleep and caffeine as reinforcers for hitting the snooze alarm and stopping to get a large caf-feinated beverage, respectively.

The Effects of Setting Events Are Temporary

The definition also states that setting events have a *temporary* effect. As in our example, setting events may include states of deprivation (e.g., tired, hungry, thirsty, cold, long period of time without social interaction) or satiation (e.g., too much sleep, overly full, hot, excessive social interaction), but they can also include other physiological (e.g., sick, experiencing allergy symp-toms), social (e.g., fight with friend, tragedy in family), or environmental (e.g., noise, light) stim-uli. All of these examples are temporary conditions or events. In contrast, disability, cognitive, and/or mental health status is not temporary and cannot function as a setting event; however, a temporary symptom (e.g., active hallucinations) of one of those conditions may function as a setting event if it alters the value of the consequences for specific behaviors. Thus, setting events help us explain variations in behavior because they temporarily alter the value of the consequence(s).

Setting Event (SE)	Discriminative Stimulus (S^D or S^{D-})	Behavior or Response (R)	Consequence (S^R or S^P)
Temporarily alters the value or **effectiveness** *of the consequence*	*Associated with differential* **availability** *of the consequence*	*Observable and measurable* **action** *or response of an individual*	*Contingent change in stimuli (+ or –) that affects the* **future probability** *(↑ or ↓) of a behavior*

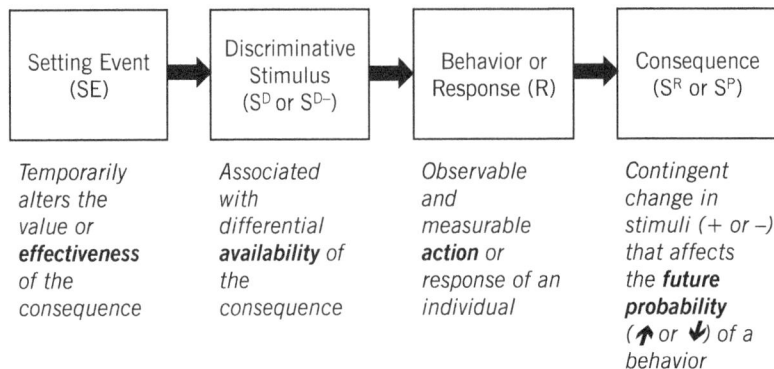

FIGURE 2.4. The expanded, or four-term, contingency considers setting events in addition to the ABCs of behavior.

To summarize, when we examine and explain behavior, we can now consider an expanded and refined four-term contingency (see Figure 2.4). We now know that (1) a behavior is more likely to occur in the presence of an S^D due to its past association with reinforcement (positive or negative) in the presence of that stimulus and (2) the behavior is even more likely to occur if a setting event increases (and less likely to occur if a setting event decreases) the effectiveness or value of the identified reinforcer(s). In contrast, we know that (1) a behavior becomes less likely to occur in the presence of an S^{D-}, as it has been previously associated with punishing consequences (positive or negative) in the presence of that antecedent stimulus and (2) the behavior is even less likely to occur if a setting event increases (and slightly more likely to occur if a setting event decreases) the effectiveness of the punisher. In other words, our ABCs are a little more sophisticated than they were when we started this chapter!

BEHAVIORAL STRATEGIES INVOLVED IN TEACHING

Now that we have a basic understanding of the building blocks of behavior (ABCs), we turn to how we can use this knowledge in teaching. As we learned in Chapter 1, the goal of our instruction is to promote learners' effective and sustained application of skills and knowledge by helping them progress through four phases of learning: *acquisition* of new skills and knowledge, *fluency* (accurately and efficiently using skills and knowledge in the instructional context), *maintenance* of learned skills and knowledge (using skills and knowledge over time without reteaching in the instructional context), and *generalization* (applying and adapting skills and knowledge across a variety of contexts). To facilitate this process, there are four basic teaching principles that we discuss in the next sections: prompting, stimulus control, shaping, and chaining.

Prompting

Prompting is a useful instructional strategy that is often used in combination with other teaching strategies described subsequently. Prompts are antecedent stimuli that are added to the S^D to increase the likelihood of a learner engaging in the desired behavior in response to the S^D

(Alberto et al., 2021). The keys to effective prompting are (1) choosing the "just right" prompt—neither too strong nor too weak—to allow the learner to be successful without distracting from the S^D and (2) fading the prompts as quickly as possible so that the learner responds only to the S^D. For example, when a young child is learning to write, they may trace dotted lines of the letters that the teacher has made based on the child dictating a sentence. This visual prompt is helpful in teaching the child to write with appropriate letter formation and spacing; however, we may be concerned if a college student still required that level of prompting to write legibly on an in-class assignment or quiz. Thus, there should be a plan for fading each prompt before it is even introduced. These two topics (choosing the correct prompt and fading prompts) are discussed in the next sections.

Types of Prompts

There are a variety of types of prompts (cf. Alberto et al., 2021; Cooper et al., 2021; MacDuff et al., 2001), and you should choose the best prompt based on (1) the type of skill (e.g., physical guidance may be needed in teaching a physical activity but should not be needed to teach a student to integrate a function in advanced calculus) and (2) the learner's needs and preferences (e.g., some students will respond to verbal prompts, some may prefer or be more successful with visual prompts, and some may need physical guidance). Within each type of prompt, there are often various "levels" of prompts, and you should select the weakest level possible to still ensure that the learner experiences success. In other words, if a learner can be successful with a hint, providing full step-by-step instructions is not necessary and may actually slow the learner's progress toward independence.

VERBAL PROMPTS

Verbal prompts include any verbal statement added to the S^D to increase the likelihood that a learner responds to the S^D. That is, verbal prompts are reminders about what the learner should do when they encounter a particular situation, activity, instruction, or other type of stimulus. Verbal prompts may include *rules* (e.g., "In our classroom, we are considerate."), *direct verbal* statements or instructions (e.g., "To be considerate during instruction, please raise your hand and wait to be called on before speaking."), *indirect verbal* statements or hints (e.g., "Remember how to get my attention."), and similar verbal reminders of expected behavior in specific situations. Verbal prompts can also be self-operated: a student may be taught to press "Play" on a digital recording of direct verbal prompts or instructions for key situations where the student experiences difficulty. Keep in mind that you eventually want the learner to demonstrate the skill or knowledge without needing a reminder. Therefore, you should select the weakest verbal prompt possible to still enable the learner to be successful.

VISUAL PROMPTS

Visual prompts include any visual aid (pictorial or textual; MacDuff et al., 2001) added to the S^D to increase the likelihood of the learner responding successfully. Visual prompts may include posters, picture sequences, and sample problems completed on a worksheet to illustrate the correct format for responses. Most classroom walls are covered with various examples of visual prompts. Although visual prompts may be provided to the whole class, you may create individualized visual prompts for students who need additional reminders to be successful. For example, one student may need a visual, or picture, schedule to assist with following the written schedule you post for others. Regardless of the type of visual prompt, your goal is to have learners respond to the naturally occurring S^D; therefore, you want a plan to fade the visual prompts so that your students are able to behave in the absence of a poster. (Plus, it will be nice to declutter your walls!)

GESTURAL PROMPTS

Gestural prompts include any motion or gesture (e.g., head nodding, pointing) provided in addition to the S^D to increase the likelihood of the learner responding appropriately. Gestural prompts stop short of fully demonstrating (i.e., modeling) the entire expected behavior. For example, when a teacher walks young students through the hallway, she may hold up two fingers (the schoolwide quiet symbol) as she walks. The teacher's quiet sign functions as a gestural prompt if students are more likely to walk quietly (behavior) in the hallway (S^D). Like all other prompts, gestures should be faded to ensure students know how to respond appropriately in their absence.

MODELING PROMPTS

Modeling occurs when an "expert" demonstrates the entire expected behavior. For example, a teacher may demonstrate (model) how to solve a complex math problem (S^D) before assigning students problems to complete (behavior) in small groups. Alternatively, a principal may ask a few high school seniors to show incoming first-year students (model) how to be respectful (behavior) during pep rallies in the auditorium (S^D). Research has demonstrated that models who are competent, "cool," and comparable to the learner(s) may be the most effective. In fact, research has shown that video self-modeling, which maximizes all three characteristics by editing videos of the learner ("cool" and comparable) successfully engaging in the desired behavior (competent), results in desired effects for many groups of learners (Alberto et al., 2021). To conclude, to be successful, models should (1) demonstrate the skill correctly (i.e., be competent); (2) have social "prestige" in the eyes of the learner (i.e., be cool); and (3) be similar to the learner (i.e., be comparable; Alberto et al., 2021), although similarity between the model and learner may not be critical to the success of modeling (MacDuff et al., 2001).

PHYSICAL GUIDANCE

When providing physical guidance, or manual prompts, a teacher physically assists a learner with moving through a skill to increase the likelihood of the learner responding successfully to an S^D. For example, when teaching a young student to use scissors correctly, a teacher may place his hand over a student's hand to guide the student through the first cuts. As this example illustrates, this type of prompting is sometimes called "hand-over-hand." To be clear, physical guidance is intended to teach or support skill development. Physical "assistance" intended to restrict movement or decrease unsafe behavior is called a physical restraint, and this should never be confused with physical guidance. For example, a teacher who holds a student's hands to keep the student from hitting herself is using a physical restraint, *not* physical guidance. Like all other prompts, physical guidance should be faded as quickly as possible to ensure that the learner responds to the S^D in the absence of prompting.

Fading Prompts

As we described, the goal is to fade prompts to ensure that the learner can respond successfully to the S^D without prompting; you want to avoid a situation in which the learner becomes dependent on prompts (e.g., Cengher et al., 2018; MacDuff et al., 2001). To effectively use prompts, you should plan your **prompt hierarchy,** or series of prompts you will use during your teaching and fading procedures (Riley, 1995), using student data to guide your decisions (e.g., Schnell et al., 2020). Although you may have a hierarchy within each type of prompt (e.g., more-to-less-intensive verbal prompts), you may also move through various types of prompts within your hierarchy (e.g., physical guidance to direct verbal prompts to indirect verbal prompts to gestures). Generally speaking, your goal is to start with the level of prompting required for the learner to respond successfully (i.e., with few or no errors) to the S^D, and then gradually but efficiently fade to less-intensive prompts until the learner successfully responds independently. In other words, the goal is to move from **most-to-least** prompting. In certain circumstances, you may want to ensure that you are not providing too intrusive a prompt, and you may gradually increase the level of prompting until the learner responds, providing **least-to-most** prompting. With both of these procedures, you may also use **time delay** procedures. Each of these fading strategies has merits (e.g., Alberto et al., 2021; Cengher et al., 2018; Cooper et al., 2021; MacDuff et al., 2001; Riley, 1995) and is discussed next.

MOST-TO-LEAST PROMPTING

By starting with the most intensive prompt needed to be successful, most-to-least prompting minimizes the likelihood of a learner making errors. In other words, you are progressively **decreasing assistance** provided for the learner to perform the skill (Riley, 1995). Depending on the type of prompt hierarchy used, most-to-least prompting may take a variety of forms. For fading *verbal or visual prompt*s, you may gradually **decrease information** provided by the prompt (Riley, 1995). That is, you may provide fewer and fewer details in your verbal or visual prompts, fading information that is easily recalled first so that the learner progresses toward independence.

When fading *visual prompts*, you may also use **stimulus fading,** which typically begins by exaggerating an aspect of the stimulus (e.g., increasing the intensity of color, increasing the contrast between stimuli), and then gradually fading the exaggerated aspect until the stimulus is the natural S^D (e.g., Cooper et al., 2021; MacDuff et al., 2001). For example, if you wanted a student to select her name when presented with two names, you might print her name on a black card with white lettering and print the other name on a white card with black lettering. Then, you would gradually "fade" the black background on her name (and darken the letters) until the two cards were both white with black lettering, and the student was appropriately attending to the differences in text (rather than other differences between the stimuli). An alternate approach is **stimulus shaping,** in which the instructional materials are gradually changed until the learner responds to the desired stimulus (e.g., Cooper et al., 2021; MacDuff et al., 2001). A popular example of this is the public television series *Word World*, wherein all characters and many objects are "drawn" from the letters comprising the word (e.g., a dog is drawn using the letters *D-O-G*). In this series, however, the stimuli are not shaped to the point where the letters become more prominent and the picture disappears; in instruction, you would want to gradually make the stimuli look closer and closer to the S^D, until the learner responds to the S^D in the absence of additional prompting.

For fading *physical guidance,* you may use a procedure called **graduated guidance,** in which you gradually decrease either (1) the level of *pressure* provided in physical guidance until you are only "shadowing" the learner or (2) the *proximity* of support provided by moving your hand(s) progressively away from the target part of the body (e.g., moving from hand-over-hand to hand on forearm, then elbow, then shoulder), eventually fading all support (e.g., Alberto et al., 2021; MacDuff et al., 2001). Again, regardless of form, the function of this type of fading is to minimize errors by ensuring the learner receives the level of prompting needed to be successful at the outset. Therefore, this is often called an **errorless learning** approach (Alberto et al., 2021).

LEAST-TO-MOST PROMPTING

In contrast, least-to-most prompting occurs when you present the S^D and gradually introduce more and more intensive prompts, as needed, until the learner responds successfully. Although this approach may be associated with more opportunities for a learner to make errors, it may also be more efficient (Doyle et al., 1988; Schnell et al., 2020). Least-to-most prompting ensures that the learner is not receiving unnecessary prompts that delay learning or progress toward independence. Therefore, this approach may be well suited for assessing a learner's current level of performance (MacDuff et al., 2001).

USING TIME DELAY WITH FADING STRATEGIES

For both categories of fading strategies, you may want to use a time delay to give the learner a chance to respond to the natural S^D before providing the first planned prompt. The time delay may be **constant** (e.g., 5 seconds every time) or **progressive** (i.e., increasing as the student gains fluency; Alberto et al., 2021). Most-to-least prompting with time delay may maximize the benefits of all prompt-fading strategies; it may result in the fewest errors while giving the learner a chance to respond independently (e.g., Libby et al., 2008), avoiding overreliance on unnecessary prompts for extended periods of time. For example, you may use the following sequence to teach a student to recognize a pentagon.

- Show the student a picture of a pentagon and say, "What shape?" (S^D). Then wait 5 seconds. If the student hasn't responded within 5 seconds, provide the most intrusive prompt (e.g., a verbal prompt: "A pentagon is a shape with five equal sides and five equal angles. This is a pentagon. When I ask what shape, say 'pentagon.'").
- Once the student responds correctly with the most intrusive prompt, present the same S^D and wait 5 seconds. Then present the next level of prompt (e.g., a verbal prompt with less information: "This shape has five equal sides and five equal angles. What shape has five equal sides and five equal angles?").

- Once the student responds correctly with the previous level of prompt, present the same S^D and wait 5 seconds. Then present the next level of prompt (e.g., an indirect verbal prompt: "Count the sides.").
- Repeat this process, continuing to fade prompts and using time delay after each time you present the S^D until the student responds immediately to the S^D.

Prompting is an effective way to increase the likelihood that a learner will respond effectively to an S^D by initially adding, and then efficiently fading, additional stimuli (verbal, visual, gestural, modeling, or physical) as the learner increases their independence in successfully responding to the S^D. (See Box 2.3 for additional examples of prompting in action.) Although prompting could be used as a stand-alone strategy, it is commonly part of a more comprehensive instructional approach. In the next section, we turn to three instructional approaches: (1) establishing stimulus control to bring existing behaviors under the control of the appropriate antecedent stimulus (e.g., saying "A" when shown the written letter *A* and asked, "What letter?"); (2) shaping to teach new and relatively simple behaviors; and (3) chaining to teach new and relatively complex (multistep) behaviors.

BOX 2.3. PROMPTING IN ACTION: INCREASING HOMEWORK SUBMISSION

As you think about your students, you can likely identify one or more students who have challenges with submitting their homework. When you consider the task of submitting homework, you realize there are multiple components involved, including recording what is assigned, bringing home all required materials, completing the task at home, bringing the completed work and materials back to school, and turning the work in to the appropriate place at the appropriate time.

First, you may teach each step in this sequence, as we describe in Box 2.6.

Second, to increase the likelihood of students completing each step, you may add prompts (i.e., additional stimuli to increase the likelihood that the S^D for each component occasions that response). For example, you may:

- Add a **verbal** instruction to prompt students to take out their planner and write their homework down at the beginning of that period/activity (added to the S^D of homework written on the board).
- Add a **visual** prompt (a picture of a planner, books, etc., going into a backpack) by the door students use to exit your classroom to remind them to bring needed materials with them (added to the S^D of the bell signaling the end of the period or day).
- Include a sample problem in the homework assignment or email families and guardians with instructions to **model** the skills required to complete the task (added to the S^Ds provided within the work).
- You may greet students at the door and point to the homework bin, **gesturing** for them to turn their homework in (added to the S^D of the bin by the classroom entrance).

After students begin to demonstrate success with each skill, you gradually but efficiently fade the prompts from each component until students are completing each step with the natural S^Ds.

Third, you may employ consequence strategies to reinforce homework submission, as illustrated for other behaviors in Box 2.2 and described for this sequence in Box 2.6.

Thus, prompts are one component of a comprehensive instructional approach to increase homework submission.

Stimulus or Antecedent Control

As you consider the various skills, concepts, and types of knowledge you teach in your classroom, you may come to realize that most of what you are doing is teaching learners to respond appropriately under the correct or desired stimulus conditions. For example, you want more novice learners to read, initially audibly and then privately (i.e., behavior), correct letters and words (S^Ds), and you want more advanced learners to string those words together in a coherent fashion to write a paragraph, essay, or even thesis (behavior) in response to a specific writing prompt or research question (S^Ds). Whether the content is related to literacy, language arts, mathematics, social studies, science, social behavior, or another relevant topic, the goal is for the learner to engage in the correct or contextually appropriate behavior(s) in the presence of particular stimulus conditions. In other words, the goal of much of your instruction is to establish **stimulus control.** Stimulus control builds on our knowledge of the three types of antecedents (S^D, S^Δ, and S^{D-}). This may be a good time to flip back and review those paragraphs if these symbols are not occasioning you to recite clear definitions of each type of antecedent (i.e., if the definitions are not yet under appropriate stimulus control!).

Establishing Stimulus Control

There are two basic steps in establishing stimulus control. First, you need to establish the link between the specific stimulus (S^D) and the desired response (which we will call response 1, or R_1). Then, you need to ensure that R_1 is under control of the relevant features of the S^D (and only the S^D). In our earlier example (saying "A" [R_1] when asked "What letter?" and shown a flash card with the letter A [S^D]), we would want to ensure that the learner was responding to the letter on the flash card and not just saying "A" when presented with any flash card (e.g., cards with letters B–Z). To accomplish this second part, you need to use discrimination training. Each step is explored next.

TEACHING THE ABCS (I.E., S^D–R_1–S^R CONTINGENCY)

The first step in establishing stimulus control is to explicitly teach the learner the contextually appropriate response (R_1) in the presence of the desired stimulus or context (S^D; Alberto et al., 2021; Cooper et al., 2021). When teaching your classroom norms, for example, you likely want your students to be considerate during a variety of your classroom routines. To accomplish this goal, you may define considerate (R_1) and model what it looks like in the context of one classroom routine, such as teacher-directed instruction (S^D). In a high school classroom where teacher-directed instruction may approximate a lecture, considerate may look like quietly sitting and listening to the instructor. Then, you may set up a classwide recognition system in hopes of reinforcing (i.e., increasing the future probability of) students being considerate within that classroom routine. In a high school class this may look like a group contingency: if students engage in considerate behavior during the lecture, they will be able to use extra minutes at the end of class to listen to music while starting their homework. (Otherwise, the lecture will extend through the end of class, and students will not have the opportunity to listen to music or start on homework.) Thus, you have started to teach the S^D–R_1–S^R contingency for considerate behavior within that classroom routine.

Consider a second scenario in which you are teaching a learner to cross the street at a crosswalk with a pedestrian signal (picture a signal with a green, yellow, or red stick figure with accompanying auditory signals). The desired response (R_1) is for the learner to move (e.g., walk, use scooter or wheelchair to roll) safely and efficiently across the street toward the pedestrian signal on the opposite side of the road, staying within the lines of the crosswalk. The S^D for this response is when the walk signal (stick figure) turns green and the appropriate auditory signal starts. Therefore, when the learner engages in R_1 in the presence of the S^D (i.e., moves across the street when the signal is green), you should provide access to pleasant stimuli (e.g., specific praise, access to desired item or activity on the other side of the road) to increase the likelihood of, or reinforce (S^R), the learner moving across the street when the signal turns green. (Of course, you only know if you have actually provided reinforcement if the behavior increases.)

DISCRIMINATION TRAINING

In addition to teaching the S^D–R_1–S^R contingency, it is critical to engage in discrimination training to ensure the learner is appropriately responding to the S^D, and only that S^D, with the target response (R_1), and only that response (Alberto et al,, 2021; Cooper et al., 2021). Returning to your classroom norms, you may have taught your students that considerate behavior looks like quietly sitting and listening (R_1) during teacher-directed instruction (S^D). However, you would also want them to know that (1) response 1 (R_1) may not be appropriate for different classroom routines (i.e., other antecedent stimuli) and (2) other responses (R_2_X) should not be used within that classroom routine (S^D). For example, sitting quietly at one's desk (R_1) would result in aversive and possibly punishing consequences (S^P) during a fire drill (S^{D-}). Similarly, other behaviors (R_2_X; e.g., talking with peers or walking out of class), which may be appropriate in different contexts (e.g., collaborative group work or fire drill, respectively), would not lead to reinforcement during teacher-directed instruction (S^D). Discrimination training is critical to ensuring that students know which behaviors are appropriate in which circumstances. And, because each behavior may be appropriate or inappropriate based on the context (the match between the response and the stimuli), you'll notice that we refer to behaviors as contextually appropriate and contextually inappropriate, as no behavior is inherently good or problematic—our goal is to use stimulus control to help students match the appropriate behaviors with the appropriate stimuli (context).

As a second example, again consider the scenario of teaching a learner to cross the street. In addition to teaching the S^D–R_1–S^R contingency, you must also ensure that the learner knows to move across the street (R_1) *only* in the presence of the S^D. In other words, you would want to explicitly teach that moving across the street in the presence of a red signal (S^{D-}; stick figure) could lead to punishment (S^P), and the learner should not pay attention to other irrelevant stimuli (S^Δ; e.g., birds flying by, other people running across the street when the signal is red, a dog barking), which do not have a direct bearing on a reinforcing or punishing outcome. In addition, you would want to ensure the learner did not engage in a different response (R_2_X; e.g., crawling, sitting, walking diagonally) in the presence of the S^D, as that situation could be equally dangerous. You would want to provide sufficient practice with each potential type of antecedent (S^D, S^Δ, S^{D-}) so that you had data to support the learner being able to respond appropriately (engage in R_1 and only R_1) in the presence of the specific S^D, and *not* in the presence of the S^{D-}. Without engaging in this discrimination training, you could not be sure that the appropriate

BOX 2.4. STIMULUS CONTROL IN ACTION: JEAN'S SPEECH

When I (Brandi) was 18 years old, I worked at a summer camp for youth and young adults with disabilities. One of the participants, whom I'll call Jean, was a 19-year-old young woman who repeated words, phrases, and dialogue she had previously heard at home, in movies, or in other contexts (known as echolalia); however, she did not use speech to communicate wants and needs. In other words, she had the ability to produce verbal language, but she did not use it purposefully or in the appropriate contexts—the behavior was not under appropriate **stimulus control.** (Of course, I did not have a clue what stimulus control was at that time. So, I'll continue with the story but insert the correct behavioral terms in parentheses.)

When the other camp counselors and I read more about Jean's history, we found out that she had used speech more purposefully when she was younger. However, she displayed echolalic speech patterns as she got older. So, we were interested to see if we could get her speech to once again become more functional—we wanted to see if she could use words to request items, communicate needs, and so forth.

One of Jean's favorite items was a red four-square ball, and it occurred to us that we might be able to get her to say "ball" if we said it repeatedly. We also thought that if she said "ball" when the ball was present, then we could give her the ball and celebrate with a lot of attention. But, if she said "ball" later, when it was not in the correct context, we would ignore it. And if she said anything else in the presence of the ball, we would also ignore that.

So, we had our plan (i.e., **discrimination training**):

- If the ball was present (S^D) and she said "ball" (R_1), then we would give her the ball and attention (S^{R+}).
- If other stimuli (S^Δ) were present and the ball was absent when she said "ball" (R_1), then we would not give her the ball (withhold S^{R+}).
- If the ball was present (S^D) and she said anything else (R_{2-x}), we would not give her the ball (withhold S^{R+}).
- To make it more likely for her to say "ball," we would hold up the ball and say, "Say 'ball.' " (That is, we would provide a modeling prompt.)

When we implemented our plan, a very surprising thing happened: Jean responded by saying "May I have the ball, please?" when we held up the ball and said, "Say 'ball.' "

By the end of the 6-week summer program, Jean was able to ask for desired items from an array of items presented to her, and she would occasionally request an item that wasn't included in the array. For example, if we asked her which color of paper she wanted to use and we showed her red, yellow, and blue papers, she occasionally requested orange. (Thus, we brought at least some of her verbal repertoire under appropriate stimulus control.) I was elated (reinforced) by her progress and only wished we could have continued to work with her beyond the 6-week program.

S^D–R_1–S^R sequence would occur; that is, you would not know whether or not stimulus control was established. (See Box 2.4 for an illustration of stimulus control in action.)

Programming for Stimulus and Response Generalization

Often, we want learners to respond to a group of stimuli that share one or more relevant characteristics (called a **stimulus class**), rather than one specific S^D, in a similar way. For example, we want learners to be able to identify a Yorkshire terrier, English springer spaniel, and Great Dane as members of the "dog" category, even though each animal has different characteristics. Responding similarly across a stimuli class is called **stimulus generalization** (Alberto et al.,

2021; Cooper et al., 2021). Returning to the street-crossing example, we likely want learners to respond to the class of pedestrian signals (e.g., signals with and without a tone, signals with a stick figure, the words "Walk" and "Don't Walk," an outline of a hand) in a similar way (i.e., move safely across the street when signaled). To promote stimulus generalization, we need to use sufficient *examples* that (1) illustrate the *sameness* among stimuli included in the class with regard to relevant features (e.g., all pedestrian signals on the opposite street corner that turn green and make a noise when it's OK to cross) and (2) highlight the range of *differences* across stimuli within the class with regard to irrelevant features (e.g., the various types of sounds and shapes of the signals). Further, we need to use *nonexamples* to demonstrate the "boundaries" of the stimulus class (e.g., a traffic signal for cars shares some similar features with a pedestrian signal, but it has a different shape and location) to ensure learners fully understand the class to which they should generalize their response (e.g., Horner & Albin, 1988).

In addition, learners occasionally need to adapt their responses to meet some of the unique features of members of the stimulus class. In other words, they need to tweak or adjust their responses by engaging in different behavior that has the same function as the initial response (i.e., a response that is a member of the same **response class**). This process is called **response generalization** or **adaptation** (Alberto et al., 2021; Cooper et al., 2021). Consider a simple situation in which you want learners to respond to a dark room and a light switch by turning on a light. Rather than teaching the learner how to respond switch by switch, you may choose several examples that represent the full stimulus class of "light switches," highlighting the sameness and differences within the class. Then you may teach the learner how to respond to those switches by selecting the appropriate response from the response class of "light-switch operating behaviors." For example, you may teach learners to turn on lights with a simple on–off flip switch (flick with finger), a dimmer knob (turn clockwise), and a pull cord (pull). Then you would want to test whether they generalized their skill use across stimulus and response classes (e.g., whether they could use a rocker switch, turn on a lamp, or operate a "clapper" switch). Selecting and using representative training examples to promote stimulus and/or response generalization is also known as **general case programming** (Alberto et al., 2021; Cooper et al., 2021; Horner & Albin, 1988; Stokes & Baer, 1977).

Consider once again the social skills context discussed previously. As we mentioned, you may want students to engage in considerate behavior during a variety of classroom routines (e.g., teacher-directed instruction, cooperative learning groups, fire drills). However, we also acknowledged that the same discrete "considerate" behaviors would not be appropriate across all contexts. Therefore, we would want to (1) teach the range of stimulus conditions in which considerate behavior is expected (i.e., all classroom routines); (2) teach the response variations that comprise the response class of considerate behavior; and (3) assess whether our students could generalize to other contexts in which considerate behavior is expected (e.g., an untaught classroom or nonclassroom routine) by adapting their considerate behavior to meet the new context. We will further discuss how to teach social skills using this approach in Chapter 6.

Thus, establishing stimulus control is the process of (1) teaching the ABC contingency, in which the S^D occasions the desired response (R_1) and explicitly teaching and systematically reinforcing R_1 in the presence of the S^D; and (2) using discrimination training to ensure that R_1 does not occur in the presence of inappropriate stimuli (i.e., stimuli that are not members of the same stimulus class as the S^D, including S^{Δ}s and S^{D-}) and that undesired responses (i.e., responses that are not members of R_1's response class) do not occur in the presence of the S^D.

Further, our goal is often to establish stimulus control between a class of stimuli (including stimuli functionally related to the S^D) and a class of responses that serve the same function as R_1. In this case, we would use the same procedures (teaching the ABC sequence and provide discrimination training) but apply them across a range of examples using general case programming. In each case, stimulus control is only possible once the response or responses are in the learner's repertoire. In other words, you can only build the ABC chain with behaviors that have already been learned. If a behavior has not yet been learned, then we can teach it with either shaping or chaining.

Shaping

When a behavior is relatively simple to perform, shaping is an ideal teaching strategy. With shaping, you identify (1) the desired behavior and (2) a behavior the learner can currently perform that is somehow related to the ultimate desired behavior. Then, you gradually reinforce the learner for engaging in behaviors that resemble the desired behavior more and more closely. In behavioral terms, you reinforce successive approximations of the desired behavior (Alberto et al., 2021; Cooper et al., 2021). You can shape along a variety of behavioral dimensions (described more fully in Chapter 4), as illustrated by the following examples. Shaping may be used to:

- Improve the *topography,* or form, of handwritten individual letters by providing specific praise as the student's letter formation becomes more and more legible (i.e., approximates correct letter formation).
- Increase the *frequency* with which a student submits homework on time by rewarding the student for submitting one, then two, then three (and so forth) assignments on time, until the student is submitting all assignments on time each week.
- Use shaping to increase a student's reading *rate* by reinforcing successive increases in words read correctly per minute until the student meets (or exceeds) age-appropriate benchmarks (i.e., desired behavior goal).
- Increase the *duration* of in-seat behavior by rewarding a student as they stay in their seat for longer and longer intervals (e.g., a student who is currently in their seat for 1–2 minutes may be rewarded when they stay in their seat for 3, then 4, then 5 minutes, then 7 minutes, 10 minutes).
- Decrease the *latency* (i.e., time between S^D and response) between the teacher giving an instruction to begin work and students starting the work by reinforcing shorter and shorter latency intervals.
- Decrease the *force,* or intensity, of voice volume by reinforcing students when their voices stay at lower and lower decibel levels for a specified period of time.

In each case, the learner should demonstrate fluency with the prior response level or form before trying to reinforce the next approximation of the desired response. As illustrated by the preceding examples, shaping can be used to teach, increase, or decrease a variety of behaviors along a variety of dimensions. (See Box 2.5 for an additional example of shaping in action.) However, if a behavior is complex (i.e., comprising multiple steps), then chaining is a better approach to instruction.

BOX 2.5. SHAPING IN ACTION: INCREASING YOUR RUNNING PERFORMANCE

You may already be an ultra-endurance marathon runner . . . but if you're like most of us, you're not quite at your desired performance in one or more fitness tasks, and you may want to consider shaping (reinforcing successive approximations of) your own performance.

Let's assume for a moment that you're not a runner at all—unless you're being chased, in which case you can run in short 1-minute bursts (initial behavior)—and you want to be able to run a 5K without stopping (terminal behavior). Rather than setting out to run the whole 5K on your first time out and falling on your face, you gradually increase the length of time you run (shift the criterion for reinforcement) before taking a walking break. You initially run for 3 minutes, then 5 minutes, then 8 minutes, and so on until you are running the entire 5K. After each increase, you celebrate your success by entering your milestone in a fitness app and posting it on your favorite social media site. As you hit different subgoals (e.g., running 1 mile without stopping), you may even buy yourself one piece of running gear. Before you know it, the 5K is easy and you're on to your next big goal!

Chaining

Chaining is used to teach complex, multistep behaviors (Alberto et al., 2021; Cooper et al., 2021). For example, it would be impossible to rely on shaping to teach long division, a problem-solving sequence, or how to follow a recipe to a novice learner. Instead, you would need to perform a **task analysis,** by identifying the component steps or skills required to perform the complex behavior and then teach the learner how to perform each step in the task sequentially using **chaining.** In the next sections we describe each of these procedures.

Task Analysis

Although there are many types of task analyses (TAs) in the literature (e.g., Carter & Kemp, 1996), we will focus on one type, the **component TA,** which is the most useful in the context of chaining. In this type of TA, your goal is to break a complex skill into the component steps required to perform the skill. It only takes a few experiences trying to assemble a child's toy, connect electronic equipment, or construct a piece of furniture using "easy-to-follow" instructions to realize that writing a TA (and following one) is not always easy! Your goal in performing this type of TA is to break a skill down into a "just right" number of steps: not so many that each step is too narrow and not so few that the learner needs to infer information that is not included in each step.

To determine the relevant steps in a sequence, it's usually necessary to (1) perform the skill yourself and note each behavior in which you engage to accomplish the task and (2) observe an "expert" performing the skill. If the skill is complex or if there is a range of response variations, you may want to watch multiple experts to identify critical skills required to perform the complex task and remove steps that may reflect personal preferences or idiosyncrasies and are not required to complete the task. For example, we asked a group of undergraduate students (future teachers) to write a TA for assembling a peanut butter (or sunbutter) and jelly sandwich. One student submitted a TA with 75 steps (seriously!), which reflected many personal preferences (e.g., exactly how to spread each ingredient, the specific placement of the bread, meticulous diagonal slice) in addition to the critical steps. When you are teaching a skill to a learner, especially a learner who requires intensive support, you want to focus only on the critical steps.

In addition to identifying the critical sequence of steps, you need to identify any prerequisite skills and materials the learner(s) will need to complete the task. For any prerequisite skills that are not yet mastered, you need to either teach those skills before beginning to teach the task with chaining or break those skills down further within the TA. For example, if you are teaching a student how to bake a cake but realize the student does not know how to measure ingredients, you can either teach the student how to measure or build detailed steps into your TA that will result in accurate measurement of cake ingredients. Once you have identified the steps in the task, prerequisite skills, and materials, you are ready to teach the student the task with chaining.

Types of Chaining

Chaining is teaching a sequence of steps from a TA. Stated differently, it's systematically teaching and reinforcing components of a complex behavior until the learner is able to perform the entire complex behavior. There are three ways to apply chaining. In **forward chaining,** you start by teaching the first skill (or step) that follows the S^D in the TA. You reinforce the learner when the initial step is performed fluently, and then you add the second step. Then, you reinforce only when the learner fluently performs the first step followed by the second step. You repeat this process, adding each step until the learner is performing the entire chain fluently to obtain reinforcement. For example, if you were teaching a learner to tie her shoe (complex response chain) when her shoes are untied (natural S^D), you would first teach her to pull her laces tight (step 1) and reinforce when she performs that step fluently. Then, you would teach her to cross her laces (step 2) and reinforce when she pulls her laces tight and then crosses them (steps 1 and 2). You would continue to build the chain (over days) until she was able to perform all the steps necessary to tie her shoe (response chain) each time it came untied (S^D) to be able to continue on to the next fun activity (S^R). Once the chain is built, the S^D occasions the entire response chain, and the learner accesses reinforcers only upon completion of the chain.

The same process can be applied in reverse, starting with the last step in the sequence and building the chain from back to front using **backward chaining.** Backward chaining may be appropriate when either (1) the skills at the end of the chain are easier or (2) the link to the natural reinforcer is so powerful that the learner may benefit from building the chain backward. For example, when teaching cooking, the last step in the chain leads to eating what was made. Because this is a primary and powerful reinforcer for most students (and teachers!), you may choose to teach cooking using backward chaining (i.e., starting with the last step, then the last two steps, then the last three, and so forth, working backward from the end to the beginning of the chain).

In other cases, it does not make sense for learners to practice any of the skills in isolation or out of context of the entire response chain. For example, in teaching a learner to cross the street, you would not want him to complete some, but not all, of the steps as that could lead to an unsafe outcome. Alternatively, it would be frustrating for a learner to learn to dress by putting an arm in and out of a jacket without ever putting the jacket on. In those situations, you would use **total task presentation,** which requires the learner to perform the entire chain each time the task is presented, with different levels of prompting for each component in the chain, until all prompts are faded and the chain is performed independently in response to an S^D.

BOX 2.6. CHAINING IN ACTION: INCREASING HOMEWORK SUBMISSION

Returning to the scenario presented in Box 2.3, assume you are working with your students to increase their homework submission. As we described, you realize that homework submission comprises a series of steps: recording what is assigned, bringing home all required materials, completing the task at home, bringing the completed work and materials back to school, and turning the work in to the appropriate place at the appropriate time. You recognize that anytime you can break a task down into a sequence of steps, you should consider using chaining to teach the skill. In fact, by identifying those steps, you've already begun your **task analysis, or TA**—the first step in chaining! You also know that to complete a TA, you need to watch expert learners (i.e., students who successfully submit their homework) complete the task to identify required steps.

After completing your TA, you realize that you need to consider prerequisite skills and materials required for students to complete the chain. In this case, your students have all mastered the identified prerequisite skills (e.g., writing, reading, carrying), and you'll identify specific materials required for each homework task on a daily basis.

Therefore, your next step is to determine whether to use forward or backward chaining or total task presentation as your approach to chaining. After thinking for a minute, you realize that you can work on each component skill, but you'd really like students to complete the entire sequence each time. Therefore, you explicitly teach each component (e.g., when and how to write their homework in their book). Then, you systematically add prompts for each step, as described in Box 2.3, and you identify a plan to fade prompts from one step at a time.

Finally, you decide to implement a reinforcement plan for homework submission. Initially, you reinforce students for accurately recording homework in their planner (step 1 in the identified sequence). Then, you do spot checks as students are leaving, and you reinforce students who have their homework accurately recorded and have the materials packed in their bag (steps 1 and 2). You continue to reinforce students for each step completed until they are completing the entire chain to earn reinforcement. You then gradually fade the added reinforcement so that the natural reinforcement (grades, learning, positive attention from the teacher) maintains homework submission.

By (1) completing a TA, (2) determining needed materials and prerequisite skills, (3) selecting your approach to chaining, (4) adding prompts for each step of the chain as appropriate, and (5) reinforcing students for completing each step of the chain as appropriate, you have successfully used chaining to teach homework submission. (How's that for a TA of chaining?)

In summary, to teach a complex skill it is critical to (1) break that skill down into its component parts by performing a component TA; (2) identify and teach prerequisite skills; and (3) teach the components of the complex skill using chaining, with chains that are built from front to back (forward chaining), back to front (backward chaining), or performed in total each time (total task presentation). Chaining can be used to teach complex academic tasks (e.g., long division), functional skills (e.g., tying a shoe, cooking from a recipe), or multistep social behaviors (e.g., problem solving, interviewing for a job, making a phone call, engaging in appropriate conversation, requesting assistance). Box 2.6 illustrates how chaining may be used to teach homework submission.

Learning History

By now, you can see how every person has learned countless behaviors that have been brought under stimulus control in the various contexts (e.g., home, school, community) over time. The behaviors we continue to engage in—including "private" behaviors, like thinking—have been (or are currently being) reinforced. And, we may behave differently in different contexts (e.g., how we talk with friends vs. colleagues vs. family members). Future experiences will continue to shape how we behave in current and new contexts. Upon reflection, you may also realize that some of your (and our) learning history is unique to each of us as individuals—no two people share the exact same experiences in the exact same context.

Additionally, we each share elements of our learning histories with other members of our family, school, community, religious, professional, racial, ethnic, gender identity, sexuality, (dis)ability, and other identity or cultural groups that share common experiences (i.e., antecedent and consequence stimuli) that have shaped similar behaviors (Sugai et al., 2012). Think, for example, about why someone may root for one sports team, pronounce certain words differently based on where they were raised, or respond to similar stimuli—like a police siren—in different ways based on their individual and shared learning histories. Throughout the rest of this book, we use the term "learning history" to describe an individual's unique and shared experiences (i.e., setting events, antecedents, behaviors, consequences) that help explain why we each behave in certain ways in certain contexts.

SUMMARY

In this chapter, we have highlighted the importance of becoming familiar with basic behavioral principles. As we stated at the beginning, the "tricks" that are often taught for classroom management occasionally fail; by understanding the principles behind the tricks, you can better understand when to apply them and how to adjust them. After reading this chapter (and completing the activities for each phase of learning), you should now have a basic understanding of the ABCs of behavior. That is, you should now be familiar with (1) the types of *antecedents* that explain when a behavior is most (and least) likely to occur, (2) the types of *consequences* that explain why a behavior is more (or less) likely to occur, and (3) the relations among those antecedents and consequences (i.e., the three- and four-term contingency). You should also be able to apply that knowledge to teach a variety of skills effectively through prompting, establishing stimulus control, shaping, and chaining. And, you should see how an individual's singular and shared experiences create a unique learning history that influences their future behavior. In the remaining chapters of this book, we discuss the applications of these basic principles schoolwide (Chapter 3) and in your classroom (Chapters 4–8), and we introduce advanced applications of these principles for students whose behaviors require targeted-group (Chapter 9) or individualized (Chapter 10) positive behavioral interventions and supports.

PHASES OF LEARNING ACTIVITIES: CHAPTER 2

Acquisition

1. Identify common ABC sequences (i.e., three-term contingencies) that explain one or more student behaviors in your classroom.

2. Identify visual prompts present in your classroom. For each one, remember when and how you introduced it and determine a plan for fading that prompt to ensure your students are responding to the "natural" S^Ds in your classroom, if appropriate.

Fluency

1. For each ABC sequence initially identified in Acquisition Activity 1, identify the type(s) of antecedents that predict when the behavior is most and least likely to occur (S^D, S^Δ, S^{D-}), identify the type of reinforcement maintaining the behavior (S^{R+} or S^{R-}), and consider whether a setting event explains any observed variations in behavior.

2. Use shaping to teach a learner a new skill (or increase/decrease use of an existing skill along one of the dimensions described).

Maintenance

1. For each three-term contingency identified in Acquisition Activity 1 and refined in Fluency Activity 1, practice describing those sequences (removing any identifying information) to a colleague using precise behavioral language. "Rinse and repeat" for additional colleagues until the behavioral language makes its way into your everyday speech.

2. Identify situations in which you use chaining to teach complex skills and behaviors in your classroom. For those skills supported by the curriculum, examine the TAs to determine whether they are appropriate (identify prerequisite skills, describe needed materials, and contain necessary steps). For skills that you have task analyzed, again consider the appropriateness of the TA. For both, adjust the TA as needed to improve the effectiveness and efficiency of instruction and consider the best approach to chaining (forward, backward, or total task presentation) for that skill.

Generalization

1. Once you are regularly using behavioral language (and identifying behavioral principles) in your professional work (i.e., following Maintenance Activity 1), see if you can apply the language and principles to other aspects of daily living (e.g., explaining a family's behavior when a toddler cries in a grocery store, analyzing your own behavior in response to specific antecedent stimuli).

2. Identify a range of social skills that you would like to emphasize in your classroom. For each skill, identify the best teaching strategy or strategies among those discussed in this chapter (i.e., establishing stimulus control, shaping, and chaining) and determine how you will use prompting in addition to the main teaching strategy. Choose one skill for each teaching strategy and develop a teaching plan for each skill. Implement that plan to teach the social skill and collect data to determine if your instruction was effective (i.e., if students' use of the social skill increased).

Other Skill-Building Exercises

1. Identify your typical classroom behavioral support strategies. Determine which behavioral principles (e.g., types of antecedents, types of consequences, teaching strategies) are represented in each, and consider whether each strategy is having the intended outcome (e.g., if your reinforcement strategies are actually resulting in increases in desired behaviors).

2. Challenge: If you are currently using negative punishment to decrease contextually inappropriate behavior (e.g., removing privileges contingent on problem behavior), see if you can "flip" the system so that students are able to earn the desired stimuli (e.g., privileges) contingent on contextually appropriate behavior. Collect and review data to determine which approach was more effective in your classroom.

CHAPTER 3

Tier 1 Schoolwide PBIS

CHAPTER OBJECTIVES

By the end of this chapter, you should be able to . . .

1. Identify the defining characteristics of PBIS.
2. Describe how outcomes, data, systems, and practices form the framework for school-wide PBIS—and how they center equity.
3. Integrate schoolwide PBIS within your classwide PBIS system.

Imagine This: *George is a first-year teacher at Rose High. When he arrives for the first day of school, he is instructed to bring his class to an assembly. At this assembly, the principal introduces members of the Schoolwide Positive Behavioral Interventions and Supports Team. The team members enthusiastically remind students of the school's norms ("Responsible," "Organized," "Careful," "Kind"), teach a few lessons (using students to role-play) to illustrate "ROCK" behaviors, and review the schoolwide reinforcement system (ROCK tickets that can be used as currency at the school store) with the student body. When he goes to his mailbox, George finds a stack of ROCK tickets for distribution. The ROCK tickets are preprinted with George's name, and they come with a list of student behaviors that are "ROCK-worthy."*

"Wow," George thinks. "It'll be easy to implement my classwide behavioral supports in a school that already has these systems in place. I picked the right place to work!" He whistles as he walks down the hallway, looking for students who are ROCK stars.

WHAT IS SCHOOLWIDE PBIS?

Schoolwide PBIS is a prevention framework for delivering social, emotional, and behavioral support to *all* students within a school setting. Schoolwide PBIS is a multi-tiered, preventive system based on the model for public health and disease control (Center on PBIS, 2023b; Walker et al., 1996). The public health model strives to prevent as much illness as possible by providing everyone in the population with proactive care, including preventive measures like vaccines, fluoride in the drinking water, foods enriched with folic acid to decrease the likelihood of neural tube defects in newborns, and public service campaigns (e.g., anti-tobacco advertisements, healthy lifestyle efforts). The logic is simple: keep everyone as healthy as possible by investing resources in prevention, and fewer people will need more intensive levels of care. Because this *universal* level of prevention is not enough to keep everyone from getting sick, the public health model offers other tiers of support. The second tier provides *targeted* interventions for members of the population who may be at risk. At the second tier, there are resources for people who have a history of a certain disease in their families, support groups for those prone to substance abuse, and community clinics for people who have limited access to health care. The third tier of support in the public health model provides *individualized* interventions for those members of the population who have chronic illnesses, serious injuries, or other pressing medical needs. By allocating resources to prevention, the public health model aims to keep as few people as possible from needing more intensive services. The model keeps more people healthy, and it makes economic sense.

In schoolwide PBIS, the multi-tiered prevention logic is applied to student behavior. There is a universal (i.e., Tier 1) level of prevention, which is designed to proactively support *all* students; meet the social, emotional, and behavioral needs of *most* students; and minimize the number of students who will need more intensive support. This level of prevention includes establishing positive expectations or norms, teaching those expectations or norms to all students, and having a schoolwide system for rewarding those expectations (all of which will be discussed later in this chapter). If universal supports are implemented with fidelity (i.e., all aspects of implementation are done effectively), more than 80% of the student body (higher in elementary, lower in middle and high schools) will receive one or zero office discipline referrals for the year (Educational & Community Supports, PBISApps, 2023; Spaulding et al., 2010). Schoolwide PBIS provides secondary prevention to students with elevated needs (i.e., those with a history of low-level, chronic social or behavioral mistakes or with unmet social, emotional, or behavioral needs) through targeted (i.e., Tier 2) prevention that could include a CICO system, specific social skills instruction, or intensified Tier 1 supports; about 15% of students will need secondary-level prevention. Some students who engage in highly unsafe behavior or whose social, emotional, and behavioral needs are consistently unmet will require more individualized, intensive behavioral support, considered Tier 3 prevention (e.g., functional behavioral assessment and behavioral intervention plans, wraparound services); these students make up approximately 5% of the student population. The multi-tiered prevention model is often represented as a triangle (to which we introduced you in Chapter 1; see Figure 3.1 for another version) and may also be known as a multi-tiered systems of support (MTSS) framework or similar (see I-MTSS Research Network, 2023). This chapter focuses on the Tier 1 (universal) level of prevention to support students' social, emotional, and behavioral needs.

WHY SCHOOLWIDE PBIS?

Why would schools want to commit to the schoolwide PBIS process? After all, the focus is on prevention, rather than on the immediate elimination of contextually inappropriate behaviors

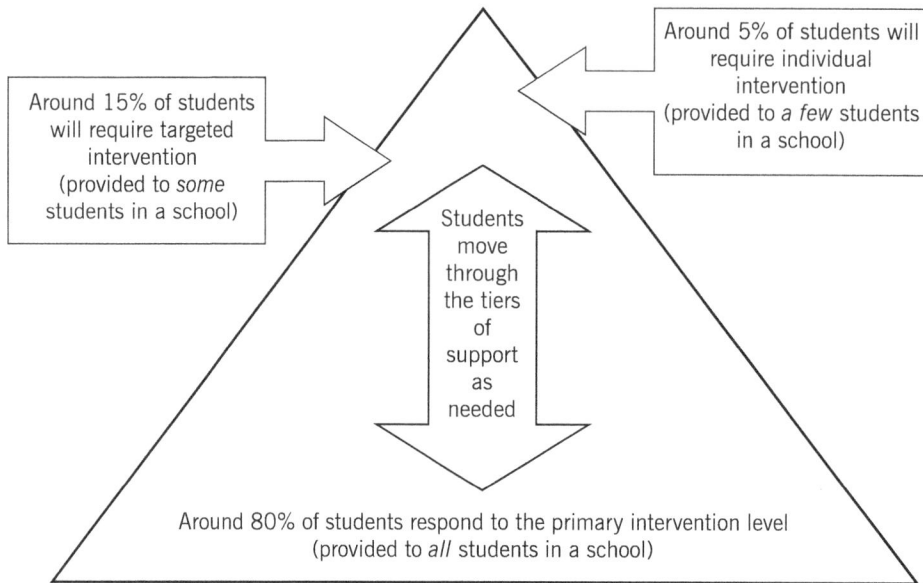

Around 5% of students will require individual intervention (provided to *a few* students in a school)

Around 15% of students will require targeted intervention (provided to *some* students in a school)

Students move through the tiers of support as needed

Around 80% of students respond to the primary intervention level (provided to *all* students in a school)

FIGURE 3.1. The multi-tiered support model of schoolwide PBIS. Approximately 80% of students need only the universal level of behavior support; the remaining 20% will require additional targeted and/or individualized behavioral interventions in order to demonstrate contextually appropriate behaviors. Adapted from *www.pbis.org.* Used with permission from the National Technical Assistance Center on Positive Behavioral Interventions and Supports.

(e.g., behaviors that interrupt learning or teaching). The training process is long—usually more than 1 year—and requires a sustained effort on the part of the school's designated schoolwide PBIS team. Data need to be collected and analyzed, contextually appropriate behaviors need to be taught, and all staff in a school need to be consistent in their response to both contextually appropriate and contextually inappropriate behaviors. It sounds like a lot of work—is it worth it?

As of this writing, more than 27,000 schools in the United States would say, "Yes, it's worth it" (the National Technical Assistance Center on Positive Behavioral Interventions and Supports continuously updates this number on its website, *www.pbis.org*). We summarized the research for you in Chapter 1 so will include just a few highlights here. Schools have been implementing schoolwide PBIS since the 1990s; schools that implement schoolwide PBIS with high fidelity are likely to continue implementation over the years and outperform schools that implement with lower fidelity (e.g., McIntosh et al., 2010; Simonsen, Eber, et al., 2012). Schoolwide PBIS implementation has been associated with various positive outcomes, including lower rates of office discipline referrals (ODRs), increased attendance, higher test scores, a decreased discipline gap between students of color and white peers, and overall improvement in school climate (e.g., Bradshaw et al., 2010, 2012; Lassen et al., 2006; Santiago-Rosario et al., 2022, 2023). When fewer students are sent out of the classroom or to the office due to behavioral mistakes, administrators and support staff have more time to provide instructional, social, emotional, and behavioral leadership at the school. Schoolwide PBIS focuses on *all* systems within a school, including classroom settings (the focus of this book), nonclassroom settings, and individual student settings. Whether schools have high rates of ODRs or other indicators of frequent behaviors that challenge the staff, schoolwide PBIS provides a system for supporting all students' social, emotional, and behavioral needs and can support all staff as they make the effort to encourage contextually appropriate behaviors throughout the school.

ELEMENTS OF SCHOOLWIDE PBIS

When schools implement schoolwide PBIS, their efforts are driven by a culturally conscious focus on five essential elements: equity, outcomes, data, systems, and practices. These elements are often represented as four concentric circles (i.e., data, systems, and practices, encircled by outcomes) with equity in the center, which you saw in Chapter 1. We've included them again for you in Figure 3.2. The circles are concentric and center equity because the five elements cannot exist independently within schoolwide PBIS; all are critically important to the implementation, success, and sustainability of schoolwide PBIS.

Equity

As we mentioned in Chapter 1, equity is a throughline that connects the other essential elements of schoolwide PBIS (i.e., outcomes, systems, data, and practices, which we discuss below). By centering equity, teams identify relevant outcomes, develop sustainable systems, and select contextually appropriate practices that reflect the learning histories of their students, their families, and their staff. (We provide an in-depth look at centering equity in your classroom in Chapter 4). A multi-tiered prevention model like schoolwide PBIS is grounded in equity; its inclusive design promotes all students getting evidence-based support to meet their unique social, emotional, and behavioral needs. As the field of PBIS has grown, so has its focus on enhancing equity, particularly in relationship to exclusionary discipline practices (e.g., suspension, expulsion, ODRs; Leverson et al., 2021; Santiago-Rosario et al., 2022).

In order to enhance equity, our approach to universal social, emotional, and behavioral supports must be culturally responsive. Being "culturally responsive" means that we hold high

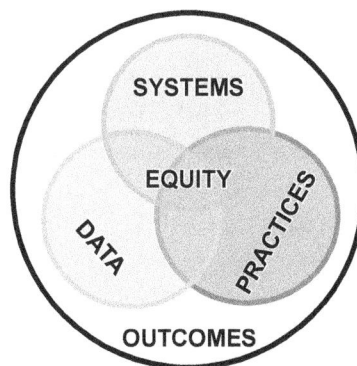

FIGURE 3.2. The five essential elements of schoolwide PBIS. Adapted from *www.pbis.org*. Used with permission from the National Technical Assistance Center on Positive Behavioral Interventions and Supports.

expectations—social and academic—for all students, we consider students' unique learning histories to increase their likelihood of success, and we provide all students with access to effective supports and access to learning (Leverson et al., 2021). Cultural responsiveness within schoolwide PBIS includes five core components: "identity, voice, supportive environment, situational appropriateness, and data for equity" (Leverson et al., 2021, p. 7). Throughout this chapter, we highlight ways we can center equity and the core components of cultural responsiveness as we explore the other core elements of schoolwide PBIS.

Outcomes

Before beginning schoolwide PBIS implementation, a school team must determine *why* they wish to implement schoolwide PBIS. Do they want to decrease ODRs? Increase teacher and student attendance? Decrease referrals for more intensive behavioral supports? Increase cultural responsiveness? Increase test scores? Build a more positive school culture? Close an existing discipline gap or reduce exclusionary practices? Whatever the reasons for implementing schoolwide PBIS, the school team must be able to identify measurable, culturally responsive **outcomes** that reflect the voice, values, and agency of all partners: students, families, the community, educators, and support staff. How will you know if schoolwide PBIS is working if you aren't sure where it should be taking you? Any identified outcomes should be observable, measurable, specific, and achievable. In addition, all members of the school community—regardless of their unique learning history—should experience the same improved results with the implementation of schoolwide PBIS. For example, research indicates that students of color experience more exclusionary discipline than their white peers do (e.g., Gage et al., 2021; Santiago-Rosario et al., 2022); if an outcome targets a reduction in exclusionary discipline, the result should be experienced by *all* students in the school. And, if students of color are experiencing greater exclusionary discipline, an outcome focused on closing the "discipline gap" (i.e., ensuring students of color experience a greater decrease in exclusionary discipline) would be appropriate (in addition to an overall decrease in exclusionary discipline).

Examples of Outcomes
- After 1 year of implementation, our ODRs will have decreased 10% from the previous year.
- After 2 years of implementation, we will be implementing with fidelity, as measured by a score of 70 on the Tier 1 subscale of the Tiered Fidelity Inventory (TFI, a research-validated and reliable instrument for measuring implementation fidelity of schoolwide PBIS; Algozzine et al., 2019).
- After 3 years of implementation, we will see a 60% improvement in attendance at monthly family-inclusive events.

Nonexamples of Outcomes
- The school will feel like a nice place to work and attend. (How would we know? Instead, you could write an outcome about increasing perceptions of positive school climate, as measured by a reliable and valid staff school climate survey, by 20%.)
- Students will be happier. (Again, you could make this measurable by including an out-

come about increasing perceptions of positive school climate, as measured by a reliable and valid student school climate survey, by 20%. Even better, given that different student groups have different experiences of school climate [see La Salle, 2023], you could plan to look at results for each student population separately—disaggregating findings by race/ethnicity, gender identity, sexual orientation, and ability status—and write an outcome that ≥80% of students in each subgroup have positive perceptions of school climate.)

The outcomes should be decided and agreed upon by the schoolwide PBIS team and reflect the identity and voice of all partners (as mentioned above). In addition to being observable and measurable, outcomes should be contextually relevant. For example, in a school where expulsions are higher than average, a contextually specific outcome would be a reduction in the number of expulsions. In a school where it is difficult to retain substitute teachers, a contextually specific outcome would be an increase in the number of substitute teachers who have a positive experience and wish to return to the school. To ensure that the outcomes reflect the identity and voice of all partners, teams can use surveys (e.g., Feedback and Input Surveys; Center on PBIS, 2022c) to get input from students, families, community members, and all staff in the educational setting. The outcomes need to be locally determined, meaningful, and contextually and culturally relevant if they are to be valued by the entire school and used to shape the implementation of schoolwide PBIS.

Data

Once the schoolwide PBIS team has selected measurable outcomes, the team must determine how to collect data to gauge progress toward these outcomes. Remember, one of the five core components for cultural responsiveness within PBIS is "data for equity" (Leverson et al., 2021). Data for equity means that school personnel take responsibility for the outcomes for each student at the school—regardless of a student's circumstances. If the data show inequitable outcomes (e.g., students from certain groups outperform others), the team should examine these data from a systems perspective first, *before* thinking about individual interventions. That is, are these data indicative of practices that may be culturally irrelevant or unresponsive? Did we include the voices of all partners when determining outcomes? Do the supports we provide to achieve these outcomes center equity and account for unique learning histories? By asking and answering these kinds of questions, we increase the likelihood of culturally responsive behavioral support and improved outcomes for all members of the school community. (See Center on PBIS, 2023c, for further guidance.)

Collecting Data

In deciding which data to collect, remember that data serve two purposes for the schoolwide PBIS team: (1) data are used to monitor fidelity and progress toward outcomes, including any performance discrepancies between groups in the disaggregated data, as mentioned above; and (2) data are used to make decisions about revising the schoolwide PBIS action plan or to tweak aspects of the system that do not seem to be effective. Thus, schools collect and routinely use outcome data, fidelity data, and perception data (e.g., input, climate).

Some student outcome data are fairly simple to collect; most schools have a way to track grades, student attendance, and exclusionary discipline (e.g., ODRs, suspensions, expulsions). In addition, schools are beginning to value and use additional data sources, including universal social, emotional, and behavioral screeners; school climate surveys; requests for mental health support; visits to the school nurse; and other school and communitywide data sources that indicate strength and need among members of the school community. Schoolwide PBIS trainers encourage schools to use an efficient system to track and analyze the data (see *www.pbisapps.org* for an example of a web-based ODR collection system and free-access school climate data suite).

To center equity, teams collect, monitor, and use data to make decisions in an equitable and culturally responsive manner (Center on PBIS, 2023c; Leverson et al., 2021; Santiago-Rosario et al., 2022; Vincent et al., 2011). Teams can set the stage for this by first ensuring that the site's contextually appropriate expectations or norms are operationalized as much as possible—which helps, by default, to operationalize behaviors that are contextually inappropriate. For example, "being disruptive" is not operational and may look and sound different to staff members (and students) based on their own unique learning history; "being out of your seat without permission" is a discrete, measurable behavior that can be seen and measured. When establishing operational definitions, be aware of the potential for cultural bias: for example, "talking out" may be a problem behavior in a school's dominant culture, but it may be a culturally appropriate, expected, and possibly rewarded behavior for some students outside of school. As mentioned earlier, schoolwide PBIS teams should examine disaggregated data to determine if students' grades, attendance, rates of exclusionary discipline, perceptions of school climate, and other important indicators are the same across all groups within a school; our data can confirm that students are having equitable experiences or provide us with valuable information to revise our current practices as needed.

In addition to collecting data on student outcomes, school leadership teams collect data on the fidelity of schoolwide PBIS implementation. Some schools start by gathering staff opinions of implementation locally (i.e., within the school) by using the PBIS Self-Assessment Survey (SAS; available at *pbisapps.org*). The schoolwide PBIS team uses the initial SAS results to see which aspects of schoolwide PBIS staff perceive are in place, partially in place, and not in place; the survey asks about behavioral supports in schoolwide, classroom, Tier 2, and Tier 3 systems. In addition to rating the current status of PBIS features as "in place," "partially in place," or "not in place," the SAS asks respondents (all staff in the school) to assign a priority level of "high," "medium," or "low" to each aspect of implementation. Teams can use the results from the SAS to help with action planning and ensure that the entire team has the opportunity to weigh in on the most critical needs related to behavioral support. The fidelity of PBIS implementation can also be evaluated through use of the TFI (available at *pbisapps.org*), which can be facilitated annually by an external coach (i.e., someone who does not work in the school). The schoolwide PBIS team can use the results of the TFI to conduct an initial assessment of behavioral support, guide schoolwide PBIS implementation and action planning across tiers, assess implementation across tiers, or report out (e.g., to district or state stakeholders) on the status of their schoolwide PBIS implementation (Algozzine et al., 2019).

To supplement the quantitative data collected on discrete behavioral events and fidelity of implementations, teams should ensure they're capturing perception, or "customer satisfaction," data from students, families, educators, and other partners; this also drives equity across behavioral support initiatives by including the voices of the community. For example, the Feedback and Input Survey suite (Center on PBIS, 2022c) provides opportunities for open-ended responses from students, families, and school personnel who may have valuable insights into how the current behavioral supports can be enhanced and more culturally responsive.

Developing Effective Routines for Data

In order to facilitate the collection and use of data, the schoolwide PBIS team must establish effective routines. For example, the team determines how and by whom the data will be collected and analyzed. Maximizing the efficiency of data input and output will increase the likelihood that the team will have data to use for decision making at each meeting. Schools should consider having a dedicated data entry person, whether a member of the schoolwide PBIS team, an administrator, or an administrative assistant for whom data entry is a primary responsibility. If the school does not make data entry, aggregation, and disaggregation (by subgroup) a priority, the team will find themselves without data to review and use at meetings; without data, the team cannot track progress toward outcomes, make decisions to improve current performance, or use data to examine equity. After all, if you do not have evidence that what you are doing is working, how will you convince your colleagues to sustain the effort? In addition to web-based systems like the School-Wide Information System (SWIS; Educational & Community Supports, PBISApps, 2023) and other applications that can track data (see *www.pbisapps.org*), sometimes a simple Excel spreadsheet or a district-created data dashboard can provide schoolwide PBIS teams with some relevant information. Whatever data collection system a school selects, it must be efficient, reliable, and sustainable.

Once efficient and effective data collection systems are in place to measure student outcomes, fidelity of implementation, and the experiences of students, staff, and families, the team can begin using data to facilitate and improve schoolwide PBIS. If schools collect data but do not use the data for any ostensible purpose, the staff will (rightfully) grumble about the expectations for data collection, and the likelihood of reliable data collection will decrease.

Examples of Using Data Effectively

- The schoolwide PBIS team reviews the monthly ODR numbers and creates a graph to post in the school foyer that shows a decreasing trend.
- The schoolwide PBIS team reviews the ODR data and determines that a high number of referrals are generated from the cafeteria; the team decides to increase supervision in the cafeteria.
- The schoolwide PBIS team reviews the number of schoolwide tickets distributed by staff members and evaluates equity of delivery across staff and students and shares insights during a faculty meeting.
- Attendance data show a decrease in student attendance on half days; the team suggests that teachers schedule tests or due dates on those days and incentivize attendance.
- The results from the Feedback and Input Survey for students indicate that multiple students have witnessed bullying or been harassed during the past week; the team suggests that the upcoming professional development day be devoted to this topic.

Nonexamples of Using Data Effectively

- ODRs are collected and put into a file cabinet in the principal's office.
- Suspension rates are reported to the state but not shared with the schoolwide PBIS team.
- The SAS is handed out, but the team does not prompt for its completion and very few surveys are collected from the staff.

Yes, collected data can and should be used to revise the schoolwide PBIS action plan based on any identified for improvement, but data should also be used to celebrate successes. Teams can consider setting a goal (e.g., 100 fewer ODRs in a quarter) and then having a schoolwide reward contingent on meeting that goal (e.g., music playing for everyone at lunch). Successes should also be shared with families and the community to bring attention and visibility to the schoolwide PBIS efforts. Data can be posted at family–teacher conference nights, sent home in newsletters or daily agendas, communicated through email or other family-facing applications in use at the school, posted to a school web page, and shared with the local newspaper.

Systems

The "systems" component of schoolwide PBIS drives the schoolwide PBIS process. Within a schoolwide PBIS framework, the systems are the structures that support staff behavior; without adequate staff support, the framework cannot stand. A systems approach ensures that if there is a personnel change (e.g., the assistant principal, who was heading up the schoolwide PBIS team, wins the lottery and retires immediately), schoolwide PBIS is sustainable because the underlying structure is in place. Though the moving parts may change, the system itself remains stable and established within the school culture.

One critical system in schoolwide PBIS is the schoolwide PBIS **leadership team.** Team membership should be voluntary, and the team should represent all partner groups (i.e., school personnel, students, families, and the community). Roles, expectations, and time commitments for all members should be clearly outlined. The team should include an administrator and general and special education teachers from a range of grade levels. In addition, the team should include representation from paraprofessionals, clinical staff (e.g., guidance counselors, social workers), custodians, bus drivers, families, students, and anyone else who can provide insights and ideas about how to support student behavior in a culturally responsive way. Because the team will make decisions, keeping it relatively small is most efficient; using a subcommittee approach (e.g., grade-based team, community partnership team) can help ensure inclusivity and voice.

Every schoolwide PBIS team requires a coach (and some schools opt for two co-coaches, which is a great idea to be sure that coaching expertise and experience is shared and doesn't leave the team if one person leaves). The coach should be someone who has attended (or will attend) all PBIS trainings and has the skill set to deliver the training information to the team and to the school staff. They must be willing to delegate tasks and follow up (we've heard the term "polite nagging" to describe situations where persistence is warranted) to ensure that those tasks are completed. The coach should be someone who has established positive relationships within the school and who gets along with their colleagues, with students, and with members of the community; while these traits are more subjective than we would like, if you think about the people you know, surely you can think of some excellent examples. At least one PBIS coach should be internal (i.e., works at the school), and they may receive support from an external coach (i.e., someone who works for the district or an organization outside the school). An external coach must have regular access to the school, the team, and the data to ensure they can effectively support the PBIS effort at the school.

The schoolwide PBIS leadership team, with the coach's facilitation, should meet regularly (at least monthly; likely more often during the initial planning and implementation phases). Meetings should be efficient, with a clear agenda and established roles, including a timekeeper to ensure that discussions remain on topic and on schedule. During meetings, the team should review any available data and use those data to make decisions regarding any necessary tweaks to the action plan or to current implementation efforts. Tasks to be accomplished before the next meeting should be assigned and successes should be acknowledged and shared with the rest of the school staff.

A second critical system within schoolwide PBIS is **data management.** As we have described, data collection needs to be efficient and consistent and, like the other elements of schoolwide PBIS, center equity. Once the team determines the types of data to be collected and reviewed, they should immediately designate someone to enter and aggregate the data for review purposes. Data review should be on the agenda at every schoolwide PBIS team meeting, and any schoolwide PBIS presentation to the staff should include data to demonstrate progress toward outcomes, fidelity of implementation, or how concerns (e.g., inequity shown in disaggregated data) or suggested improvements have been addressed.

Another critical system in schoolwide PBIS is the **training received by staff.** All staff members need to be trained in the various aspects of schoolwide PBIS, including (1) teaching the school expectations or norms, (2) prompting contextually appropriate behaviors, (3) acknowledging contextually appropriate behaviors, (4) using an established continuum of responses to contextually inappropriate behaviors, and (5) how cultural responsiveness and self-awareness impact behavioral support. Any schoolwide PBIS-based professional development should address a specific need or challenge. "Booster sessions" can be scheduled if staff members need more support to practice using a schoolwide PBIS practice fluently or consistently (e.g., prompting students about contextually appropriate behaviors). Professional development should be purposeful, outcome-oriented, and culturally responsive (i.e., accessible to all learners, multimodal, reflective of learning histories, differentiated as needed) to most efficiently and effectively meet the school's needs. In addition, professional development should be ongoing and based on the phases of learning. When staff members are in the acquisition phase of learning schoolwide PBIS, they will need frequent feedback and support as they apply newly learned skills. As they become more fluent, staff members will need opportunities to practice their schoolwide PBIS skills; professional development sessions should include role-playing and problem-solving scenarios. To ensure that staff members are able to maintain their schoolwide PBIS skill set, all professional development sessions should begin with a review of previously taught material, and "booster sessions" and prompts should be given after breaks (e.g., the coach could say the following during morning announcements: "Welcome back, everyone! Remember to look for students who demonstrating the norms and reward them with a ROCK ticket!").

Because the staff training system is vitally important to the success of all behavioral support efforts across the school (including support at the classroom level), it warrants another paragraph. In addition to the guidelines above, effective administrators model the behaviors they expect from their teachers and other school personnel. Administrators should define their expectations and explicitly teach staff members how to engage in behaviors that meet those expectations (i.e., through professional development and even targeted or individualized support, if necessary; see Simonsen, MacSuga-Gage, et al., 2014, for a description of how an MTSS model can be applied to teacher training and Myers et al., 2020, for a deep dive into training teachers in classwide PBIS). Administrators should provide prompts, follow-up, and feedback when staff members begin implementing newly learned skills to ensure acquisition of and fluency with those skills. In addition, administrators should be actively reinforcing staff behaviors that enhance the fidelity, cultural responsiveness, and success of schoolwide PBIS implementation; ideas for staff reinforcement are described in the next paragraph.

Last, there must be a system in place to **recognize staff members' efforts** in developing schoolwide PBIS. While much of the emphasis is (and should be) on acknowledging student behavior, the schoolwide PBIS team should establish a system to reward staff members whose behavior helps the team's implementation effort and effectively supports students. Some schools reward staff members who have the highest number of positive referral tickets; other schools reward staff members who consistently show up at extracurricular functions (e.g., basketball games, concerts). These rewards can be social (e.g., announcing over the loudspeaker that Mr. Smith has shown incredible school spirit by organizing a parking-lot cleanup) or tangible (e.g., a gift card to a coffee shop contingent on a bus driver regularly prompting students to follow the bus norms). Some schools have shown incredible creativity in their staff reward systems, including awarding "The Golden Plunger" (i.e., a plunger painted with gold spray paint) to the cleanest classroom at the end of the day and awarding a prime parking space to a staff member nominated by colleagues as the "PBIS Exemplar of the Month" for going above and beyond in the implementation of schoolwide PBIS. By reinforcing staff behavior that contributes to the viability of schoolwide PBIS, the team can increase the likelihood of that behavior continuing in the future—exactly what schoolwide PBIS systems are designed to do.

Examples of Schoolwide PBIS Systems in Place

- The schoolwide PBIS team meets on the first Wednesday of every month and reviews fidelity data, aggregated student outcome data, and disaggregated data for key student subgroups (i.e., race/ethnicity, gender identity, and disability), which they then report at the monthly staff meeting; graphs are included in the follow-up summary email, and they may drill down in outcome data to identify patterns (e.g., when and where students are making behavioral mistakes and receiving ODRs, when and where there are the greatest/least inequities between student subgroups).
- After any PBIS-based professional development, members of the team survey staff members to solicit feedback, see if there are questions, and send out links to relevant resources or materials.
- During the monthly raffle, when a ROCK ticket is drawn to determine which student wins the schoolwide PBIS prize, the staff member who issued the winning ticket is given a gift certificate to use at a local coffee shop.

Schoolwide PBIS is not about changing student behavior; it's about changing the environment to increase the likelihood of contextually appropriate behavior and decrease the likelihood of contextually inappropriate behavior. Any necessary environmental changes are enacted by staff and include (as needed) changes in staff behavior. The success of schoolwide PBIS depends on the feasibility, appropriateness, cultural responsivity, and sustainability of the systems in place at the school.

Practices

Once the schoolwide PBIS team has determined outcomes, identified relevant data sources, and established systems to support staff behavior, the team needs to select evidence-based practices to support student behavior. As mentioned previously, schoolwide PBIS is not a magic wand to change student behavior; schoolwide PBIS rearranges the environment to make certain behaviors more likely and other behaviors less likely. Schoolwide PBIS does this through a series of evidence-based, culturally responsive practices that are cornerstones of schoolwide PBIS implementation and can be adjusted in intensity based on students' needs and tweaked to ensure relevance across all settings.

First, the schoolwide PBIS team must develop a **behavioral vision** for the school that reflects common beliefs, values, and behavioral expectations or norms. This practice includes establishing a schoolwide approach to behavioral support, meaning that all staff members are committed to the schoolwide PBIS process. The outcomes determined by the schoolwide PBIS team should serve as the basis for the school's vision. For example, if the school's outcomes include reducing ODRs and increasing test scores, those goals could be reflected in a vision statement that reads: "Here at Rose High, we maintain high expectations and standards for our students to ensure their academic and social success as young adults." Good leaders know where they're going; the vision statement should reflect the desired direction of the school and the values of all partners—students, staff, families, and the community.

After the behavioral vision of the school has been established, the schoolwide PBIS team should determine the **behavioral expectations or norms** for the school. These should be few in number (i.e., between three and five), easy to remember, and positively stated (i.e., "Be kind" rather than, "No name-calling"). The expectations or norms are stated positively in order to remind students what *to* do, rather than what *not* to do. The expectations should be age appropriate and context specific, and they should be broad enough to include all expected student behaviors. The expectations or norms should be culturally relevant, serving "a legitimate purpose within the setting, as opposed to simply school tradition or maintaining the status quo" (Leverson et al., 2021, p.15). They should focus on high standards for *all* students in the setting and be reflective of and respectful toward all cultures (Leverson et al., 2021). All expectations or norms should be posted and taught in all languages spoken by all students and their families, which may require involving adults with culturally and linguistically diverse backgrounds (Vincent et al., 2011). Students with distinctive, unique learning histories may need multiple examples and applications of the norms to clarify the how they are relevant in the school setting. Figure 3.3 shows examples of schoolwide behavioral expectations.

Once the expectations or norms are determined, the next step is to **explicitly teach expected behaviors** across all schoolwide routines. Specific social skills instruction is an evidence-based practice consistently associated with increases in contextually appropriate student behavior and decreases in contextually inappropriate student behavior (Alberto et al., 2021; de Mooij et al., 2020). In order to determine what to teach, the schoolwide PBIS team

> At Cooper Middle School, we are:
>
> *Caring*
> We are kind to each other.
>
> *Responsible*
> We are accountable for our actions.
>
> *Prepared*
> We are ready to learn.

FIGURE 3.3. Example of schoolwide norms at the middle school level.

must first define the expected behaviors in the context of school routines. For example, if one of the schoolwide norms is "We are Responsible," the team would define what "being responsible" looks like in the hallway (e.g., going directly to your destination), in the cafeteria (e.g., having your lunch money ready), on the playground (e.g., wearing a coat when it's cold), in the library (e.g., return books on or before the due date), and in any other context within the school. One easy way to do this is in a matrix format; see Figure 3.4 for an example of what a school's matrix could look like.

Contextually appropriate behaviors should be taught in the natural context whenever possible; expected bus behaviors should be taught on the bus, and expected dismissal behaviors should be taught in the classrooms and hallways where dismissal occurs. The schoolwide PBIS team should develop lesson plans to teach the schoolwide expectations or norms within routines, and these lesson plans should be taught by the staff members responsible for monitoring and reinforcing expected behaviors whenever possible. If it is not feasible to have cafeteria staff teaching cafeteria expectations, the cafeteria staff should at least be available for the practice part of the lesson.

	Hallway	*Cafeteria*	*Assemblies*	*Library*	*Bus*
Caring	Travel quietly. Keep hands and feet to self.	Greet cafeteria workers. Say "please" and "thank you."	Keep eyes on the speaker. Keep feet on the floor.	Remain quiet. Handle materials carefully.	Greet driver. Keep hands and feet to self.
Responsible	Have a pass. Stay to the right.	Dispose of trash in bins. Remain with your class.	Raise hand to ask questions. Pay close attention.	Return materials on time. Clean up area before leaving.	Know your bus number. Check for belongings before leaving the bus.
Prepared	Go directly to destination. Arrive on time.	Listen for staff directions. Have money and choice ready.	Arrive on time. Remain seated until conclusion.	Ask for help if needed. Check out books prior to end of class.	Be at the bus stop on time in the morning. Be ready when it's your turn to get off the bus.

FIGURE 3.4. Example of a schoolwide matrix that defines contextually appropriate behaviors across school routines.

Each lesson should define the contextually appropriate behavior being taught and give examples and nonexamples of the expected behaviors (e.g., "Being safe in the hallway looks like walking and keeping hands to yourself"; "Being safe in the hallway does not look like running and slamming lockers"). Lessons should include modeling of the behavior being taught to ensure that students know what the expected behavior looks like, and students should be given ample opportunity to practice the expected behavior through role-playing, discriminating between examples and nonexamples, or any other activity that will build fluency. Students should be given feedback and reinforced for engaging in newly taught behaviors; those teaching the expected behaviors should approach instruction as they would approach an academic lesson (i.e., modeling the new skill, having students practice, offering feedback, "testing" by asking students to perform the skill independently, and acknowledging when students perform the new skill correctly—and offering helpful, specific feedback when they don't). Staff should also ensure that their process for teaching expected behaviors helps students be successful regardless of their learning history and is respectful to families' beliefs; if some expected behaviors differ between home and school, staff should provide a clear rationale for the difference and offer ample opportunities for practice and feedback as students build fluency with the new skill (Leverson et al., 2021).

After the expected behaviors have been taught, staff members should provide opportunities for students to engage in and receive reinforcement for demonstrating the new behaviors. In addition, all staff members should be prompting for contextually appropriate behaviors whenever possible. For example, while students line up on the playground to return to class, the recess monitors can say, "Remember what it looks like to be safe in the hallway! Walk and keep your hands at your sides!" (We revisit strategies to teach expectations within your classroom and provide a lesson plan format in Chapter 6.)

When new staff members and new students come to a PBIS school (or return after an extended absence), they should be oriented (or reoriented) to the expected behaviors and universal practices as soon as possible. For example, some schools use a "passport" strategy, where new students receive a booklet and are "stamped" (or given a staff signature) upon completing lessons about contextually appropriate behaviors across each of the school routines. This might look like a new student traveling from the gym to the cafeteria to the locker area to the bus and being explicitly taught what the expected behaviors look like in each area. For new staff members, the schoolwide PBIS leadership team can prepare a "Welcome" packet that describes the expected behaviors, staff responsibilities related to behavioral support, the reinforcement system, and any other PBIS-related practices within the school. All new staff members also should receive any overt recognition tools (described shortly) with an explanation of how they should be used.

Once expected behaviors have been established and taught, staff members must actively and positively **reinforce** those behaviors. We learned about reinforcement in Chapter 2 (if you need a refresher, just flip back!), so we know actions followed by pleasant consequences tend to be repeated and thus learned; therefore, when students engage in expected behaviors, those behaviors should be followed by a pleasant consequence to increase the likelihood of the behavior occurring in the future. At a minimum, school staff should recognize expected behaviors with specific and contingent praise statements (see Chapter 7 for a full description of specific, contingent praise and other reinforcement strategies). Praise statements should use behavior-specific language, for example, "Bernie, that is exactly how we demonstrate responsibility in the gymnasium, by putting equipment back where we found it" or "This class really understands what it means to be engaged! Look at how you are all watching the speaker attentively!" These statements not only have the potential reinforce the learner(s) engaging in the appropriate behavior (if those learners enjoy praise and adult attention); these specific praise statements also serve as verbal prompts to any student within earshot.

Most schoolwide PBIS schools select a more overt reinforcement system to acknowledge behavior that meets expectations. Research has demonstrated that token economies can be effective with learners of all ages and abilities (Alberto et al., 2021; Kim et al., 2022), and schools can apply the principles of a token economy at the schoolwide level. Although token economies will be discussed in detail later in Chapter 7, we provide a brief summary here. In a token economy, the target behavior (in the case of schoolwide PBIS, any contextually appropriate behavior that has been taught to students) is contingently reinforced with the distribution of a token. In other words, when a student engages in a behavior that we'd like to see again in the future, we present the student with a "token" (i.e., generalized conditioned reinforcer, as we explain in Chapter 7), while explicitly stating the behavior we intend to reinforce (e.g., "Way to help a peer pick up their belongings, Roman! Here's a ROCK ticket for your efforts."). These tokens can then be exchanged for something of value (i.e., a backup reinforcer) at a later date.

Schools often select tokens that relate to the expectations, if possible; in our example school, ROCK is the acronym for the schoolwide expectations of Responsible, Organized, Careful, and Kind, and the students can earn "ROCK tickets" for expectation-following behavior. A school with a tiger mascot could use "Tiger Paws" as tokens; other schools opt for simple "Caught Meeting Norms Cards." See Figure 3.5 for examples of schoolwide tokens. In a schoolwide acknowledgment system, all staff members should have easy access to tokens for distribution. This can be achieved by putting a stack of tokens in each staff member's mailbox on a weekly or monthly basis (pro tip: putting each staff member's name on their tokens increases efficiency and the likelihood that they will be distributed). Schoolwide PBIS team members can remind colleagues to distribute tokens through emails, announcements, or verbal prompts at faculty meetings. If administrators wish to increase the number of tokens being distributed, they should be conspicuous models, reinforcing displays of expected behaviors with tokens of their own.

Tokens can be adjusted as the context dictates. If the schoolwide PBIS team knows that a certain setting or antecedent is more likely to occasion contextually inappropriate behaviors (e.g., the bus, a substitute teacher), they can increase delivery of tokens in these settings or perhaps create a special token (e.g., a ROCKStar ticket worth 10 regular tickets) that can be distributed by the staff member in that setting. When paired with thoughtful prompting (e.g., "Remember, finishing all of your work when there's a substitute teacher can earn you a Giant Tiger Paw"), a quantitative relationship between the number of tokens and the degree of difficulty for engaging in expected behaviors can increase the likelihood of contextually appropriate behaviors in even the most challenging settings. Further, all students should be able to earn schoolwide tokens. Schoolwide expectations should be inclusive of students with individualized or intensive social, emotional, and behavioral needs, and schools should ensure their method for recognizing student behavior is differentiated to ensure each student is recognized for their own efforts and improvements in meeting (or exceeding) schoolwide expectations or norms.

After selecting a schoolwide token, the leadership team needs to set up an exchange system. Students should be able to exchange their tokens for items of value to them or collectively

Congratulations!

You showed us how it's done at
Cooper Middle School!

Student name: _____

You were spotted being:

☐ Caring

☐ Responsible

☐ Prepared

Staff initials: _____
Date: _____

You're a
STAR!

Safe

Thoughtful

Active

Ready

FIGURE 3.5. Examples of tokens from schoolwide reinforcement systems.

pool tokens toward a school community priority; some schools distribute surveys to students to get more information and ideas about the kinds of rewards students prefer. In addition, the team should engage with families and communities to create reinforcement options that are meaningful, authentic, and reflective of important cultural values (Leverson et al., 2021). To facilitate the exchange of tokens for backup reinforcers, some schools opt for a school store model, where students have certain times of day (e.g., morning, dismissal, lunch) when they can visit the "store" and exchange tokens for items (e.g., pens, pencils, notebooks, toys) of varying values. Having a range of values for the backup reinforcers ensures that all students—even those who earn minimal tokens—will be able to access reinforcement for their appropriate behavior. Other schools choose to use a raffle method, in which students' tokens (usually tickets that include their name, the behavior for which the ticket was given, and the name of the staff member who awarded the ticket) are put into a receptacle, and there is a drawing for prizes on a daily, weekly, monthly, or quarterly basis. These prizes can be tangible items donated by local business (e.g., ear buds, gift certificate for a nearby store, school sweatshirt) or activity rewards (e.g., board game party for class, movie tickets). Another option is to host "pay-to-play" events (e.g., school dances, staff–student basketball games, field days) for which students must "pay" with a certain number of earned tokens—these options can be budget-friendly and have the added benefit of providing additional opportunities for community building at the school, especially if families and community members can participate.

Some schools choose to use a nontangible reinforcement system. We described behavior-specific praise statements previously; another option is to have students' rewards tied to a charitable contribution. A school partnering with a service-learning program like Pennies for Peace (see *www.penniesforpeace.org*) may provide students with the opportunity to convert their tokens to "money" that can be donated to support education in central Asia. A school partnering with Heifer International (see *www.heifer.org*) may reinforce expected behavior with a donation to help international families who experience hunger and poverty. Many schools use a combination of these tangible and nontangible reinforcement systems; the most important aspects of any system are its cultural relevance and consistency of implementation (including pairing any token with specific praise!).

Even with the most carefully taught rules and a consistent reinforcement system, some students will make mistakes and engage in contextually inappropriate behaviors. When this happens, all staff members should be using a consistent **continuum of strategies and evidence-based practices to discourage contextually inappropriate behaviors** in an instructional manner that sets students up to be successful in the future. The first response to a minor behavioral mistake should be an error correction, similar to correcting an academic error. Think about the following scenarios:

- *A teacher sees a student running in the hallway. "Don't run," the teacher yells. The student stops running. When the teacher turns away, the student begins running again.*
- *A teacher sees a student running in the hallway. "That doesn't look like being safe in the hallway. Can you show me what being safe looks like?" The student begins walking. "Great, that's exactly what being safe looks like. Thank you," says the teacher. The student walks away.*

In the first scenario, the teacher's response is what we call a "no, stop, don't" response to contextually inappropriate behavior. This is intended to positively punish the student's behavior by adding an aversive stimulus (i.e., the "Don't run" statement) to the environment. In the second scenario, the teacher corrects the error, reminds the student of the expectation, and praises the student when they engage in the appropriate behavior. The second scenario provides the student with an opportunity to practice and receive feedback on the expected behavior; we would treat an academic error similarly. If a student spelled a word incorrectly, we wouldn't tell him, "Don't spell that word that way." We would (hopefully!) say something like "That's not the correct spelling; can you try again?" and perhaps increase our level of prompting (e.g., "Can you sound it out?" or "the word is spelled _____."). When the student did spell the word correctly, we would say, "That's right."

Usually, when a "no, stop, don't" statement is issued, there is no contingent feedback when the student stops the contextually inappropriate behavior. Also, it doesn't set the student up to recall/learn, practice, and receive positive feedback for the contextually appropriate behavior. Coaching staff members to respond to minor behavioral mistakes as they would respond to academic errors is the first practice on the continuum of responses to problem behavior.

Of course, simple error corrections are not always going to be enough, nor are they appropriate for more disruptive or unsafe behaviors. For more intensive behavioral mistakes, responses need to be consistent, predictable, and documented. Most schoolwide PBIS schools use a flow-chart to depict their system for responding to behavioral errors or contextually inappropriate behaviors (see Figure 3.6 for an example). One critical role of the schoolwide PBIS team is to determine which contextually inappropriate behaviors should be managed by teachers in their classrooms and which behaviors should be handled by the office. Usually, minor contextually inappropriate behaviors like not responding to teacher directions, being tardy, and low-level disruption to instruction are handled in the classroom, while major behavioral mistakes like fighting are handled by the administration.

All staff must be aware which behavioral mistakes are to be handled in the classroom, and the schoolwide PBIS team needs to ensure that the teachers have the requisite skills to handle contextually inappropriate behaviors when they happen in class. The schoolwide PBIS team

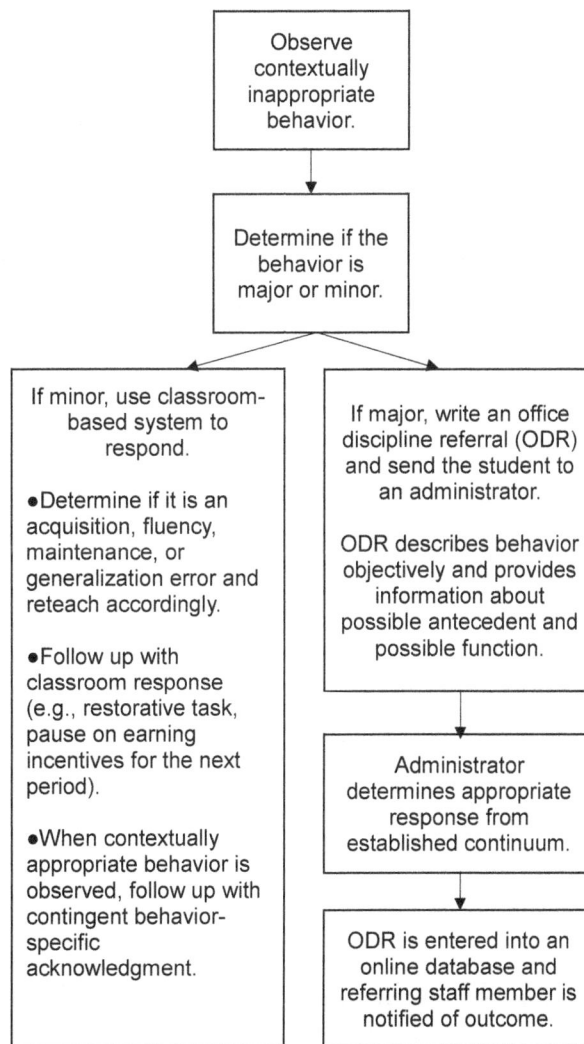

FIGURE 3.6. A flowchart illustrating how staff members should respond to contextually inappropriate behaviors.

should arrange ongoing professional development for teachers that allows them opportunities to practice and receive feedback on their handling of contextually inappropriate behaviors in the classroom; unless teachers have read a book like this one (which we highly recommend!) or taken a course on classroom behavioral support, the likelihood of them receiving any formal training in handling students' contextually inappropriate behavior is very low.

Embedded in this training should be an understanding of the basics of behavior, including the function of behavior. Remember from Chapter 2 that understanding behavioral basics helps us avoid inadvertently reinforcing behavioral mistakes (e.g., sending a student away from instruction, when their contextually inappropriate behaviors were functioning to escape instruction, could reinforce those behaviors). More importantly, it helps us think about why the student is making a mistake and respond accordingly. Do they have an unmet need (e.g., want attention, need a brief break)? Is there something that is preventing them from engaging in the contextually appropriate behavior (e.g., perhaps they are tardy because they had to care for a sibling in the morning). Rather than rushing to "give a consequence," teachers can strive to understand the why and respond in a supportive and instructional manner.

Thus, the schoolwide PBIS team must provide support if they intend to have teachers handling minor behavioral errors in the classroom. Some schools choose to document minor behavioral errors on an ODR and consider three minor behavioral errors to equal a major one, so the student is sent to the office after the third violation; like all other practices within schoolwide PBIS, the response to contextually inappropriate behavior should be supportive, instructionally focused, culturally responsive, and shaped by the needs of the school community.

Examples of Using Practices to Support Student Behavior

- When the school opens its new computer lab, all students circulate through for a lesson on what "being responsible" looks like in the new lab. Prior to their first class in the lab, all students are prompted with "Remember, being responsible looks like using the computer for classwork and turning it off when you're done."
- When the schoolwide PBIS team notices that fewer students are redeeming their tokens at the school store, they open a "suggestion box" at the store and ask students for input about items they'd like to see stocked at the store. They also send a questionnaire to families soliciting ideas.
- When Mrs. Guerra notices that her class is louder than expected during dismissal, she takes a few minutes the next day to reteach dismissal procedures and tells the students that she will be looking for the contextually appropriate (i.e., quieter) behavior that afternoon and distributing tokens accordingly.

Nonexamples of Using Practices to Support Student Behavior

- The schoolwide PBIS team establishes expectations and makes posters of the expectations. After hanging the posters, the team waits to see if there is a change in ODR numbers. (They missed the critical step of explicitly teaching expectations across school contexts!)
- When a new teacher arrives at the school and asks about the expectations she sees on a poster, another teacher tells her, "Don't worry, you'll pick up on the rules as you go

along." (Remember, adults also need explicit and supportive professional development to be successful.)

- When Mrs. Guerra notices that her class is louder than expected during dismissal, she yells, "Stop making noise!" When the class quiets down, she leads them out the door. (She missed the opportunity to set the students up for future success!)

SUMMARY

Schoolwide PBIS provides schools with a preventive framework to deliver culturally responsive behavioral support to all students in a school. This chapter described the universal level of intervention, which schools use to proactively teach contextually appropriate behaviors and to prevent as many contextually inappropriate behaviors as possible. Schoolwide PBIS is composed of five essential elements: **outcomes** that support social, emotional, behavioral, and academic competence; **data** that support decision making and evaluate progress toward outcomes; **systems** that support staff behavior and provide structure for schoolwide PBIS implementation; **practices** that support student behavior by teaching, prompting, and reinforcing contextually appropriate behaviors; and a focus and center on **equity** that connects the other four elements. When schoolwide PBIS is implemented with fidelity, schools can expect to see improved outcomes.

So, why is there a chapter about schoolwide behavioral interventions and supports in a book about supporting teachers' *classroom* practices? The main reason is that classroom supports are more easily implemented and sustained in an environment that systematically and intentionally supports all students' social, emotional, and behavioral needs. Teachers can model their classroom norms after the schoolwide expectations, and they can adapt the schoolwide reinforcement system for use in their classrooms. The schoolwide PBIS team should be working with administration to provide professional development that enhances teachers' classroom behavioral support skills, focusing on evidence-based practices like using behavior-specific praise, providing opportunities to respond, and responding to minor behavioral errors like academic errors. The conceptual framework behind schoolwide PBIS (i.e., the science of behavior) is also the framework behind our strategies for effective classroom behavioral support; we rely on the same principles (e.g., prompting, reinforcing, antecedent stimulus control) to encourage contextually appropriate behavior at the schoolwide, classroom, and individual student levels. Although classroom behavioral support is often easier in a schoolwide PBIS school, you can use these techniques in any environment. If your colleagues and administrators are impressed with how you support students' behavior in your classroom, you could tout the benefits of a schoolwide model and volunteer to head up the schoolwide PBIS implementation effort!

PHASES OF LEARNING ACTIVITIES: CHAPTER 3

Acquisition

1. Your school has recently decided to implement schoolwide PBIS, and you volunteer to serve on the schoolwide PBIS team. Describe what the first training session might look like, with specific examples of materials and content provided.

2. Identify and describe the key features of schoolwide PBIS, including the five key elements and the basics of implementation.

Fluency

1. You have been asked to introduce schoolwide PBIS to your colleagues at a faculty meeting. What content will you include in your presentation?

2. You are charged with planning the back-to-school assembly where schoolwide PBIS will be introduced to the student body. Create an agenda for the day that will ensure students understand schoolwide PBIS and how it will affect their daily experiences in the school.

Maintenance

1. How do the behavioral principles you learned in Chapter 2 apply to schoolwide PBIS?

2. How can you use data to sustain schoolwide PBIS implementation? Give at least three specific examples in your answer.

Generalization

1. Describe which aspects of schoolwide PBIS would be the same and which would be different for implementation in the following settings: (1) an urban elementary school, (2) a suburban high school, and (3) an alternative middle school for students with challenging behavior.

2. How does schoolwide PBIS support effective classroom behavioral support? Make specific connections between the features of schoolwide PBIS and behavioral support in the classroom.

3. How can you ensure that your site includes family and community voices across all aspects of schoolwide PBIS implementation? Create a presentation on how you would solicit input from these critical partners to improve effectiveness and cultural responsiveness of behavioral support in your school.

4. You volunteer to go to the school board to request resources for schoolwide PBIS implementation. Describe the rationale you will use to make the case for your request, citing specific examples of how schoolwide PBIS will affect your school. In addition, make a list of the resources you will need and offer reasons for each.

CHAPTER 4

Introduction to Classwide PBIS
Focus on Equity, Outcomes, Data, and Systems

CHAPTER OBJECTIVES

By the end of this chapter, you should be able to . . .

1. Center *equity* in all essential elements of implementing classwide PBIS.
2. Identify *outcomes* of implementing PBIS for your classroom.
3. Collect and use *data* to make decisions in your classroom.
4. Identify *systems* to support, enhance, and sustain your implementation over time.

Imagine This: *Mr. Stott approaches you and says that his classroom is falling apart. You ask him to describe what he means, and he stares blankly. Then you ask him what he would like his classroom to look like. Again, your question is met with a blank stare. You quickly realize that he is not sure what he hopes to achieve in his classroom, he is not sure how to describe the current problems or assess progress, and he is looking to you for support. You start by emphasizing that it is essential to center equity to create a classroom environment that supports each and every student. You describe the importance of identifying outcomes for your own classroom and provide some examples of outcomes you hope to achieve this year for your students and yourself (more blank staring). You also mention how critical it is to have data to inform your practice (his eyes are now starting to glaze over and roll backward). You are already on multiple committees, mentoring three new teachers, and feeling a bit overwhelmed yourself. Therefore, you would like to find systems to support Mr. Stott in centering equity, developing outcomes, identifying efficient data systems, and implementing classwide PBIS practices to meet his outcomes. You hand him this chapter as a starting point for understanding those elements for his classroom, as you work to identify additional school-based supports.*

OVERVIEW OF CLASSWIDE PBIS

Various terms are used to describe behavioral support in a classroom, including *classroom management* and/or *behavioral management*. In this book, we use the term *classwide PBIS* to indicate that this approach is consistent with the broader PBIS implementation framework and signal our emphasis on positive and proactive strategies. As you read in Chapter 1, there are five essential elements of PBIS implementation: equity, outcomes, data, systems, and practices (Center on PBIS, 2023b). In Chapter 3, we described what these essential elements look like when implemented schoolwide. We also mentioned that implementation of schoolwide PBIS is associated with a variety of positive outcomes, including decreases in contextually inappropriate behaviors and exclusionary discipline (i.e., ODRs, suspensions, expulsions, reported bullying) and increases in desired outcomes (i.e., contextually appropriate behaviors, academic performance, school climate, or organizational health) for students and staff (e.g., Bradshaw et al., 2008, 2009, 2010, 2012; Horner et al., 2009; Waasdorp et al., 2012).

In this chapter, we present an overview of the same essential elements for your classroom. If you teach in a school where the majority of staff members are effectively implementing schoolwide PBIS or a similarly proactive and positive schoolwide approach to support student behavior, you should align the essential elements in your classroom with the broader school context. If you teach in a school environment where student behavior is not supported at the schoolwide level, you can still establish and effectively implement PBIS in your classroom. Now that you understand the concept of stimulus control (discussed in Chapter 2), you realize that you can bring desired student behavior under stimulus control of the antecedents unique to *your* classroom. Even if the rest of your building is "managed" with punitive or reactive practices, you can greet students at your door; remind them of your shared norms or expectations; center *equity*, elevating and celebrating diverse student histories and experiences throughout your classroom; implement culturally relevant, empirically supported, positive, and proactive *practices*; collect *data* to see what is working for whom; and create a welcoming and supportive environment that results in desired *outcomes* in your own classroom!

CENTER EQUITY IN CLASSWIDE PBIS

In Chapter 3, we described centering equity in the context of schoolwide PBIS. Now, we turn our focus to centering equity in classroom PBIS implementation. Consider the students with the greatest needs in your classroom—these may be students with identified disabilities, students who have experienced trauma, or students who require intensive support for any number of reasons. How would you design a classroom to ensure that each and every student, including students with the most intensive needs, is set up for success? How would you engage your students (and their families) in collaboratively designing your classroom community to be welcoming and inclusive, so each student feels they belong? How would you honor your students' unique backgrounds when designing engaging and relevant instruction throughout the year? How would you maintain high expectations for each student, and provide the necessary support to enable them to meet these expectations? How would you know if each student was benefiting and adjust your support if they were not? How would you celebrate effort and steps toward achieving important outcomes together?

These questions are the start of a conversation about centering equity in your classroom PBIS implementation—a conversation that should continue to evolve as you meet your students and their families and consider your broader school community. At this point, you may be wondering what we exactly mean by centering equity in your classroom. Centering equity in PBIS is . . .

- . . . more than just a conversation, as it requires intentional, inclusive, and culturally responsive implementation of the PBIS framework (Leverson et al., 2021; Santiago-Rosario et al., 2022; Simonsen, Putnam, et al., 2020).
- . . . based on an understanding that students may need different levels of support to be successful in your classroom. (Luckily, that's what this whole book is about—using the PBIS framework to implement support in your classroom so that everyone is set up for success . . . including you!)
- . . . *not* a current trend or politically motivated idea. As educators, our jobs are ensuring each and every student has opportunities to access, engage in, and benefit from high-quality learning environments.
- . . . critical, as decades of research have demonstrated that students with disabilities and students of color are more likely to experience reactive and exclusionary discipline (Fabelo et al., 2011; Sullivan et al., 2014; U.S. Department of Education, Office of Civil Rights, 2018, 2022). When schools implement PBIS, all students—including students with disabilities—can benefit (Center on PBIS, 2022d; Santiago-Rosario et al., 2023); and when schools intentionally center equity in PBIS, students of color may experience greater benefit (Santiago-Rosario et al., 2022).

Leverson et al. (2021) defined core components of cultural responsiveness in PBIS: "identity, voice, supportive environment, situational appropriateness, and data for equity" (p. 7). Consistent with their definition, we emphasize centering *equity* by (1) working to understand our own and our students' individual and cultural learning histories (or identities); (2) engaging students in designing and implementing *practices* (voice) to create a welcoming, positive, and proactive classroom (supportive environment) where contextually appropriate behaviors are explicitly taught, prompted, and celebrated (situational appropriateness); (3) using *data* to monitor implementation and outcomes for each of our students; and (4) ensuring that each student is benefiting from or adjusting supports to better meet students' needs to make progress toward meaningful *outcomes*. Throughout this chapter and the remaining chapters in this book, we highlight ways to center equity in the other essential elements (i.e., outcomes, data, systems, and practices), and we reference important guidance on how to implement PBIS in a culturally responsive manner (e.g., Hollins-Sims et al., 2022; Leverson et al., 2021).

OUTCOMES OF CLASSWIDE PBIS

Outcomes are data-based goal statements that describe what you and your students hope to achieve to support students (e.g., increases in contextually appropriate behaviors and academic performance, decreases in contextually inappropriate behaviors) or yourself (e.g., consistent implementation of positive and proactive PBIS strategies in your classroom, reductions in reactive classroom practices). Generally, research suggests that when you implement empirically supported classwide PBIS practices with fidelity, you can expect students to increase contextually appropriate social behavior, improve academic behavior (e.g., on task, academically engaged, correct responding), and decrease contextually inappropriate behavior (e.g., off-task or disruptive behavior; see review provided by Simonsen et al., 2008).

To identify appropriate outcomes for your classroom, consider specific areas you would like to see yourself (e.g., implementation of practices) and your students (e.g., social behavior, academic performance, or both) improve with respect to classwide PBIS. Like all good goal statements, develop your outcomes collaboratively with your classroom community by identifying the (1) *conditions* under which the outcome will be achieved, (2) *individual(s)* expected to meet the outcome (students and/or teacher), (3) specific *behaviors*, and (4) *criteria* for success (Alberto et al., 2021; Cooper et al., 2021). The following examples demonstrate possible outcomes for students (examples 1–2) and a teacher (examples 3–4) that include these four components.

1. Given regular social skills instruction, ongoing review and supervision, and regular recognition (*conditions*), students (*individuals*) will demonstrate kindness in the classroom by actively listening, using nice words to talk with their peers and their teacher, and otherwise taking care of themselves and others (*behaviors*) across 80% of sampled opportunities during the first quarter (*criterion*).

2. Given actively engaging instruction that includes high rates of opportunities to respond (*conditions*), 90% of students (*individuals*) will demonstrate academic success (i.e., stay on task, complete the majority of assignments, and apply knowledge and skills accurately; *behaviors*) as indicated by earning 90% of points possible on academic assessments during the second semester (*criterion*).

3. During teacher-directed instruction (*conditions*), I (*individual*) will provide all students with ≥3 opportunities to respond per minute (*behavior*) across 80% of sampled lessons (*criterion*).

4. Across all classroom routines (*conditions*), I will provide at least five positive acknowledgments for students' appropriate behavior (i.e., behavior-specific praise) for every one negative or corrective statement (*behavior*) across 90% of sampled opportunities (*criterion*).

Before reading the remaining sections of this chapter, draft a few outcome statements for your classroom (see Acquisition Activity 1). To assist in determining specific criteria for success and monitoring progress toward outcomes, it is necessary to collect and use data. In the next section, we describe a variety of strategies for collecting data on behavior in your classroom.

DATA: SUPPORTING DECISION MAKING IN CLASSWIDE PBIS

To measure progress toward your identified classwide PBIS outcomes, it is critical to use data to inform your decision making. You are probably used to collecting a variety of types of data in your classroom related to students' academic performance. However, we have found that it is less common for teachers to collect data on students' social behavior beyond ODRs. Although ODRs are a useful source of data for schoolwide decision making, they are rarely sensitive enough to inform your own implementation of classwide PBIS practices. ODRs also fail to capture the contextually appropriate behaviors (i.e., the skills students should be learning) and other indicators of social, emotional, or behavioral needs (e.g., visits to a nurse, concerns about a students' physical and/or mental health). Thus, it is critical to collect additional data on your implementation of and students' responses to classwide PBIS practices. As the saying goes, teaching (or implementing interventions) without data is like driving in the dark without headlights: you *can* do it, but it's dangerous!

To make your data collection feasible, you should always start by identifying the purpose or guiding questions for your data collection. Within your classroom, you may collect data for a variety of purposes, including monitoring your implementation, assessing students' current performance (e.g., social skills use, levels of contextually inappropriate behavior), identifying or defining a problem, informing selection of an intervention, monitoring progress, and evaluating the effects of an intervention. Once you have identified the purpose of your data collection, you will want to identify an efficient approach to data collection. Although it is possible to design incredibly complex approaches to measuring behavior, we believe that simple is better! In this section, we describe a variety of strategies to operationally define; identify relevant dimensions of; and design a system to measure, summarize, and use data to make decisions related to behavior (e.g., your practices, students' social behaviors) in your classroom.

Operationally Defining Behavior

Before you can collect and use data, it is critical to know what you are going to collect data on and how you plan to use those data to inform decision making. The first step is operationally defining the behavior(s) of interest, including the behaviors you would like to increase (e.g., your use of PBIS practices; students' social, emotional, and behavioral skills) and the behaviors you would like to decrease (e.g., contextually inappropriate behaviors) in your classroom. As the name implies, an **operational definition** is a description of the "operations" that comprise a behavior, or a detailed account of what the behavior "looks like." A good operational definition starts with a general description of the behavior and includes examples and nonexamples to further illustrate what the behavior does and does not look like. For example, consider the operational definition of "on-task behavior" provided in Figure 4.1. After reviewing the general description, examples, and nonexamples, the teacher, students, and outside observers should all be able to tell when a student is on task.

Although some operational definitions may apply more generally (e.g., shared definition of specific praise) or be collaboratively agreed upon as a classroom norm (e.g., shared definition of

General Description	
A student who is on task is performing the appropriate task for the context. In other words, they are engaging in behaviors that are specified and desired by the teacher at that time.	
Examples of Behavior	**Nonexamples of Behavior**
• Looking at the teacher when the teacher is speaking • Performing assigned task • Focusing attention on appropriate person or activity • Holding correct materials in hand (e.g., pencil)	• Staring at the wall when teacher is speaking • Talking with a peer during seatwork • Focusing attention on activity that is not assigned (e.g., playing with crayons in desk) • Playing inappropriately with materials

FIGURE 4.1. Example of the operational definition of on-task behavior.

respect), there may be times when you need to define a more unique behavior for an individual student (e.g., a specific contextually inappropriate behavior that is interfering with their learning). To develop an operational definition of a student-specific behavior, it is typically necessary to directly observe the student a few times. Even if you know the student well, it is likely that you are focused on so many things while teaching that it will be hard to describe exactly what the behavior looks like. Therefore, you may need to set aside a few minutes to observe or ask a colleague to observe in order to generate an accurate description of the behavior. Once you have your detailed description of the behavior, it is often necessary to refine your initial definition by considering the relevant dimensions of behavior.

Identifying Relevant Dimensions of Behavior

After you have drafted your initial operational definition of a behavior, you are often left with additional questions: Exactly what does the behavior look like? How often does it occur? How long does it last? Where does it occur? How intense is it? Each of these questions points to a different dimension of behavior. In the next sections, we (1) define and provide examples of each dimension and (2) discuss the importance of dimensions in operationally defining and ultimately measuring behavior.

Dimensions of Behavior

The key dimensions of behavior describe what (topography), how often (frequency, rate, and celeration), how long (duration, inter-response time, and latency), where (locus), and how intense (force) a behavior is (Alberto et al., 2021; Cooper et al., 2021). Each of these dimensions represents a different aspect of behavior and each may be important given the context in which the behavior occurs.

WHAT: TOPOGRAPHY

The **topography** of a behavior is a clear and rich description of its "shape" (think topographic map) or what it looks like. Therefore, topography is always included in a good operational definition. For example, instead of just labeling a behavior "self-injury," you would describe that the student "grasps his right wrist with his left hand, pulls his right wrist toward his mouth, and bites the inner side of his right forearm just above the wrist." With that clear description, an outside observer (or substitute teacher) would know exactly what self-injury looks like for a particular student. Likewise, instead of just telling students to "be considerate," you would explain that being considerate looks like "being kind to others by using nice words, actively listening, and showing caring actions." In short, the topography describes the behavior and is a critical component of all operational definitions.

HOW OFTEN: FREQUENCY, RATE, AND CELERATION

The **frequency** of a behavior is simply how often a behavior occurs. However, a pure count (e.g., the behavior occurred 50 times) is hard to interpret without also knowing how long it took to reach that count. For example, if a student talked out 50 times in a 50-minute period (one talk-out per minute), we would consider that behavior more frequent (and more disruptive to their learning!) than if the behavior occurred across 50 class periods (one talk-out per period). Considering the frequency in the context of time requires you to (1) record the length of each observation or data collection period and (2) calculate **rate** by dividing frequency (count) by time observed (in minutes, hours, or another relevant time period). In our example, 50 talk-outs divided by 50 minutes results in a rate of one talk-out per minute (i.e., 50/50 = 1). Thus, when you are interested in how often a behavior occurs, rate is the more meaningful dimension to consider and report. You may also be interested in documenting changes in rate, or **celeration,** over time. For example, you may want to know if a student's rate of words read correctly per minute is increasing (accelerating) or if her rate of talking out is decreasing (decelerating).

HOW LONG: DURATION, INTER-RESPONSE TIME, AND LATENCY

When examining "how long," we may be interested in either (1) how long a behavior lasts from beginning to end (the **duration** of a behavior); (2) how long the student works between contextually inappropriate behaviors (the **inter-response time**); or (3) how long it takes for a behavior to begin after the discriminative stimulus (S^D) is presented—the **latency** of a behavior. For example, you may have three students in your classroom who engage in "off-task" behavior. You may be concerned with how long one student spends off task throughout the day (cumulative duration), how long the second student works between episodes of off-task behavior (inter-response time for off-task behavior) during independent seatwork, and how long it takes the third student to start on a task (latency to on-task behavior) after you give the students their assigned classwork (the S^D). Thus, duration (time elapsed between start and end of behavior), inter-response time (time elapsed between behaviors), and latency (time elapsed between S^D and behavior) are different ways to represent "how long."

WHERE: LOCUS

The **locus** of a behavior is where it occurs. Locus may be described as the location in the *environment* (e.g., students are expected to demonstrate safety in the hallway by walking, with hands, feet, and objects to self, on the right side of the hallway) or the location on the *body* involved (or injured) in the behavior (e.g., the student was hit by a peer in his right upper arm, which resulted in a light-colored bruise). The bruise is actually an indicator of force, described next.

HOW INTENSE: FORCE

The **force** of a behavior refers to its intensity. For example, in a cafeteria setting (locus), school administrators may be concerned with the volume of students' voices and other noises. In a day care setting, providers may be concerned with the intensity of a young child's biting behavior (e.g., extent of skin damage—from no mark to broken skin). Voice volume and biting intensity are examples of force.

Importance of Dimensions

Dimensions of behavior are important for two key reasons. First, by understanding and describing behavior in terms of relevant dimensions, you are able to achieve a more complete and accurate description of the behavior. For example, is a student off task if she looks out the window for 2 seconds and immediately returns to the assignment? Or, is a student only off task if she looks out the window for 10 or more seconds? Second, it may be one (or more) dimension(s) of the behavior, rather than the behavior itself, that results in a behavior being contextually inappropriate. For example, everyone (including you!) is off task a small amount of time during a class period; however, when a student is routinely off task for 60–80% of the class time (duration), the behavior is likely interfering with their learning. Similarly, we want students to talk, interact, and practice their social skills during lunch; however, when they practice them at a high voice volume (force), the behavior is not appropriate for the context. (In contrast, talking at high volume may be appropriate on a playground or at a sporting event.) Therefore, it is critical to understand which dimensions are the most important for a particular student, a particular behavior, and/or a particular setting or context, as you will need to select one (or possibly a few) dimension(s) of behavior when you design a system to measure that behavior.

Selecting or Designing a Measurement System

Now that you have operationally defined the target behavior and identified the relevant dimensions of behavior, you are ready to measure. In this section, we review types of measurement systems, highlight resources to identify existing measurement systems, and present guidelines for selecting and designing your own appropriate approach to measurement.

Types of Measurement Systems

Whether you are designing your own system or selecting a published tool, it's important to be familiar with the various approaches to measuring behavior. There are five main approaches to describing or measuring behavior: anecdotal reports, permanent products, event recordings, time-based estimates or sampling, and timings (e.g., Alberto et al., 2021; Cooper et al., 2021). In addition, there are other strategies that may be employed to measure one specific dimension of behavior or hybrid systems that may capture multiple dimensions of behavior. As stated, your selection of measurement system should be guided by (1) the purpose (or guiding questions) of your data collection, (2) the operational definition of the behavior, and (3) the relevant dimension(s) of that behavior and its context. In the following paragraphs, we describe each measurement system, provide examples of its use, and highlight when it may be appropriate (i.e., for which types of behaviors and dimensions).

ANECDOTAL REPORTS

Anecdotal reports are narrative descriptions of behavior. To generate a clear operational definition, it may be helpful to write a narrative description of exactly what a behavior looks like (i.e., topography) using an anecdotal report. Teachers sometimes use anecdotal reports to describe the context in which a behavior occurs by writing streams of ABC sequences. Anecdotal reports may also be used to describe other dimensions of behavior, such as locus (noting where the behavior occurred) and force (describing intensity of behavior). Because anecdotal reports are difficult to quantify, they should be considered a descriptive, rather than a true measurement, system.

PERMANENT PRODUCTS

When a behavior produces a physical change in the environment that remains after the behavior has stopped, then you may use that **permanent product** to measure the behavior. Permanent products can be used to measure frequency (e.g., number of errors or correct answers on a quiz) and describe topography (e.g., letter formation), locus (e.g., location of property destruction in environment, location of bruise or injury on body), and possibly force (e.g., size of hole in wall, extent of injury).

EVENT RECORDINGS

To measure how often a behavior occurs, perhaps the simplest measurement system is **event recording,** which is also known as a **tally** or **frequency count.** To use event recording, you simply count (using paper and pencil, a counter, or an application on a smart device) each occurrence of a behavior in a specified period of time. As previously mentioned, to convert frequency to rate, you divide your frequency count by units of time observed; and to describe celeration, you summarize changes in rate (i.e., slope of a line graphing rate) over time. For this system to be an accurate reflection of behavior, each tally mark (or count) needs to represent a similar amount of behavior. In other words, it is appropriate to count behaviors that are (1) *low rate* or "countable," (2) *discrete* (i.e., have a clear beginning and ending), and (3) *similar* in duration, intensity, and other relevant dimensions. For example, it is typically appropriate to count spoken swear words, as most students use swear words at a low enough rate to be countable, and each swear word is discrete and similar in length (good old four-letter words!). In contrast, it is inappropriate to count off-task behavior, as the beginning and ending are often less clear, and a student may be off task for 10 seconds during one incident and 10 minutes during the next. Likewise, it may seem appropriate to tally how often a student hits himself (hits are typically discrete and similar), but if the student hits himself at a high rate (e.g., 45 hits per minute), it would be difficult, if not impossible, to accurately count his hits.

TIME-BASED ESTIMATES OR SAMPLING

When you are interested in how often a behavior occurs (frequency or rate) but event recording is not appropriate (i.e., behavior is not low rate, discrete, or similar), it is best to use a time-based estimate. **Time-based estimates (or sampling procedures)** allow you to estimate (sample) how often a high-rate, less discrete, or variable behavior occurs. There are three types of time-based estimates: partial-interval recording, whole-interval recording, and momentary time sampling. For all three methods, you start by dividing your observation period into a number of equal time intervals (typically ranging from 10 seconds to 2 minutes). The shorter intervals (e.g., 10 seconds) allow for more precise estimates, but longer intervals (e.g., 2 minutes) are easier and more practical if you are collecting data while teaching. For example, if you observed for 10 minutes and used 10-second intervals, you would have a data sheet with sixty 10-second intervals (see Figure 4.2).

After you have a data sheet divided into intervals, your next choice is how to estimate the behavior. With **partial-interval recording,** you mark the behavior as having occurred if it happens during any *part* of the interval, regardless of how long it lasts or how often it occurs. That

Codes		
Antecedents (A)	Behaviors (B)	Consequences (C)
1. *Teacher* attention 2. *Peer* attention 3. Independent *seatwork* (no attention) 4. *Transition*/interruption 5. *Other* (specify in additional observations)	1. *On*-task (attending to teacher, performing assigned task, focusing attention on appropriate person or activity, etc.) 2. *Disruptive* off-task behavior (verbal and nonverbal) 3. *Nondisruptive* off-task behavior 4. *Other* (specify in additional observations)	1. *Teacher* attention 2. *Peer* attention 3. *Work* removed 4. *Access to* other stimuli (e.g., activity, item) 5. *Other* (specify in additional observations)

Date: _____   Time started: _____

Event	0:10	0:20	0:30	0:40	0:50	1:00	1:10	1:20	1:30	1:40	1:50	2:00	2:10	2:20	2:30	2:40	2:50	3:00	3:10	3:20	3:30	3:40	3:50	4:00	4:10	4:20	4:30	4:40	4:50	5:00
A																														
B																														
C																														

Additional Comments

Date: _____   Time started: _____

Event	5:10	5:20	5:30	5:40	5:50	6:00	6:10	6:20	6:30	6:40	6:50	7:00	7:10	7:20	7:30	7:40	7:50	8:00	8:10	8:20	8:30	8:40	8:50	9:00	9:10	9:20	9:30	9:40	9:50	10:00
A																														
B																														
C																														

Additional Comments

FIGURE 4.2. A data sheet for conducting a 10-minute observation using a time-based estimate procedure with 10-second intervals. This data tool has options for noting antecedents (A) and consequences (C) in addition to behaviors (B).

is, you would mark a "plus" (or other symbol used to represent occurrence) whether the behavior (1) lasts for 1 second during the interval or throughout the entire interval and (2) occurs once or multiple times. With **whole-interval recording,** you mark the behavior as having occurred only if the behavior lasts throughout the *whole* interval. In other words, if you were using 2-minute intervals, you would only mark that the behavior occurred if the behavior was occurring (or started exactly) at the beginning of the interval and lasted throughout the entire interval. With **momentary time sampling,** you mark whether the behavior is occurring at the *moment* the interval ends. That is, if the student was out of seat during most of the interval but returned to their seat at the end of the interval, you would mark that the behavior did not occur, as you would only track what occurred at the end of the interval.

To illustrate how these estimate procedures work, consider a situation in which you have divided your data sheet into 30-second intervals. Your timer is running from the beginning of the observation through the end. The student begins to engage in the target behavior at second 15 and stops the behavior at second 45. If you were using partial-interval recording, you would mark that the behavior occurred during the first and second intervals, as the behavior occurred during seconds 15–30 of the first interval, which spans 0–30 seconds, and seconds 30–45 of the second interval, which spans 30–60 seconds. If you were using whole-interval recording, you would mark that the behavior did not occur during either the first or second interval, as the behavior did not last throughout either interval. If you were using momentary time sampling, you would mark that the behavior was present at the end of the first interval. In other words, you would record that the behavior occurred during two (partial-interval recording), zero (whole-interval recording), or one (momentary time sampling) intervals depending on which time-based estimate you selected. Therefore, it is critical that you clearly describe your measurement procedures (if including these data in a report for others), summarize data as "percent of intervals" rather than a count or duration, and use the shortest time interval feasible to increase the accuracy of your estimate. (As a challenge, calculate the difference in how you would record the same behavior if you used 10-second intervals instead of 30-second intervals.)

TIMINGS (DURATION, INTER-RESPONSE TIME, AND LATENCY RECORDINGS)

Although time-based estimates are good for estimating the frequency of behaviors, they do not yield a specific measure of how long a behavior lasts. To accurately measure duration, inter-response time, or latency, it is necessary to time either from the beginning to the end of the behavior (**duration recording**), from the end of one behavior to the start of the next (**inter-response time**), or from the presentation of the S^D to the beginning of the behavior (**latency recording**) using a stopwatch, timer, or other application on a smart device. See Figure 4.3 for a sample data collection tool to record duration, which you can easily adapt to record inter-response time or latency. Duration and latency recording are feasible only when a behavior is discrete (i.e., has a clear beginning and ending). If the behavior is not discrete, then time-based estimates are the best approach.

OTHER STRATEGIES TO MEASURE DIMENSIONS OF BEHAVIOR

The systems just discussed are probably the most common approaches to measuring behavior; however, there may be other strategies or devices to measure specific dimensions of behavior.

Observation Date:	Observer:
Behavior:	
Operational Definition:	

Event	Start	Stop	Duration	Details
1				
2				
3				
4				
5				
6				
7				
8				
9				
10				

Total Duration: _____	Average Duration: _____
Sum the durations for each incident to calculate the total duration.	*Divide the total duration for the observation by the number of behavioral events recorded to calculate average duration of each behavior.*

FIGURE 4.3. A data sheet for recording duration of a behavior.

For example, if you want to measure the volume (force) of voices, you could use a decibel meter. These devices have been used in research (e.g., Kartub et al., 2007) and are commercially available as "stoplights" that signal when volume exceeds certain levels. Further, it is possible to combine aspects of different measurement systems to simultaneously track multiple dimensions (c.f., Alberto et al., 2021; Cooper et al., 2021). To note the frequency, locus, and topography of a behavior, for example, you may use a "descriptive analysis card" (see Figure 4.4). Each card represents one behavioral incident (frequency), and the card prompts you to note the duration of the incident; the location (locus) and contextual features that came before and after the behavior (antecedents and consequences, which were discussed in Chapter 2); the discrete behaviors that comprise the incident (topography); and any additional notes (where you could also record subjective impressions of force). Thus, in one data tool, it is possible to capture a great deal of information about a student's behavior.

Selecting a Published or Existing Measurement System

Now that you understand the various approaches to measuring behavior and when each approach may be appropriate, it is time to select an approach. To do that, you may first consider published or existing measures. There are a variety of instruments that are already available for measuring student behavior. For example, direct behavior ratings (DBRs; *https://dbr.education.uconn.edu*) provide a flexible, efficient, and effective approach to rating student behaviors using simple (one item per behavior) rating scales. DBR has established psychometric properties (e.g., Chafouleas et al., 2012) and online training and tracking applications. As another example, consider the Behavior Observation of Students in School (BOSS; Shapiro, 2013), which has an app you can use on your smartphone or device. The BOSS allows you to track frequency of specific target behaviors and also allows you to track engagement (passive and active) during your observation. In addition to these examples, you can find other tools reviewed in the professional literature (e.g., Riley-Tillman et al., 2005), online (e.g., National Center on Intensive Intervention; *https://charts.intensiveintervention.org/bprogressmonitoring*), and in app stores for smart devices.

Considerations in Designing a Measurement System

Although published measurement systems may have advantages (e.g., available, established psychometric properties), we often find that it is helpful to design a measurement system that specifically captures the contextually appropriate (i.e., PBIS practice; social, emotional, or behavioral skill) or contextually inappropriate behavior you are trying to support or address, respectively. Given the variety of options for describing and measuring behavior, consider the following guidelines to help you select the most appropriate approach as you design your own measurement system. First, consider the operational definition of the behavior(s) of interest. Note whether the described behavior is discrete (i.e., has a clear beginning and ending), has a low or high rate (i.e., generally how often it is observed to occur), and whether each instance of behavior is similar. These aspects of the behavior will begin to point you toward (or help rule out) specific measurement systems. For example, event, duration, and latency recording are only feasible when behaviors are discrete.

Second, consider the most relevant dimensions of behavior for the context. Return to the questions presented to refine your operational definition (i.e., How often? How long? Where?

Student Name: _____

Date/Time	Antecedent(s)	Behavior(s)	Consequence(s)
	☐ Demand or request	☐ Inappropriate verbal behavior	☐ Demand or request removed or avoided
	☐ Difficult task	☐ Physical aggression	☐ Difficult task removed or avoided
Duration	☐ Transition	☐ Property destruction	
	☐ Peer conflict	☐ Elopement	☐ Teacher attention
			☐ Peer attention
	☐ Preferred item or activity removed	☐ Self-injury	☐ Get/obtain tangible item
	☐ _____	☐ _____	☐ _____

Staff Reporting: _____

Comments: _____

_____
_____
_____
_____
_____
_____
_____
_____
_____
_____
_____
_____
_____
_____
_____
_____
_____
_____
_____

FIGURE 4.4. A descriptive analysis card. Such cards allow recording of frequency, duration, locus, topography, and other aspects of a behavior in an efficient tool.

How intense?). Consider which dimensions are the most critical for the behavior you are working to increase (e.g., shaping the topography of on-task behavior in the classroom) or decrease (e.g., reduce duration of out-of-seat behavior). Once you have identified the relevant dimension(s), it should become clear which measurement system(s) would be appropriate. For example, if you were interested in the frequency of a low-rate and discrete behavior, which is similar each time it occurs, event recording would be the simplest strategy.

Third, consider who will be collecting the data and what else they will be doing at the time. If you are planning to collect data on an entire classroom to examine how often any student talks out relative to how often any student raises their hand while you are teaching, you will need to use a really simple system to record data (e.g., sticky note with a line down the middle, where you record talk-outs on one side and hand raises on the other side) as you will be multitasking. Similarly, if you want to track your use of specific praise to corrective feedback, you will need a simple way to record your statements, like the free Be+ App (*www.pbis.org/announcements/track-positive-reinforcement-with-our-be-app*). In contrast, if you ask a specialist to come in and observe a student to gather in-depth information to guide development of a support plan, the specialist may be able to use a complex 10-second partial-interval recording system that estimates the frequency of multiple behaviors and also notes aspects of the context (e.g., locus, antecedent and consequence events, as in the example shared in Figure 4.2). Regardless of how you choose to collect data, your goal is to summarize your data and then use those data to inform decision making.

Summarizing and Graphing Data

When measuring any behavior, you want to be sure that you have a representative sample of behavior to make decisions. As everyone can have good and bad days, you want to be sure that your data collection samples behavior (e.g., 10- to 30-minute observations) on several days (a minimum of 3–5 days) and occurs in or during relevant contexts or routines. Once you have a sufficient amount of data, the next steps are to summarize the data and present them in a graph to facilitate decision making.

Summary Scores

Each observation or data collection opportunity should be summarized into one main **summary score,** or number that quantifies the entire observation. For example, if you used event recording to measure the rate of a behavior, your summary score for that observation would be the rate of behavior (i.e., behavior per units of time). If you used duration recording, your summary score could be the cumulative duration of behavior throughout the observation (sum of the recorded durations of each behavioral incident) or the average duration of each behavioral incident (cumulative duration for that observation divided by the number of behavioral incidents observed). To determine which summary score is best, return to the purpose of data collection. For example, if your goal was to increase a student's on-task behavior, you may be most interested in how long a student is on task throughout an activity (cumulative duration). As illustrated by these examples, data obtained through each measurement system may be summarized in a variety of ways (see Figure 4.5 for a list of potential summary scores for each measurement system). When you succinctly summarize each observation or data collection opportunity with one summary

Measurement System	Summary Score(s)
Anecdotal report	• Narrative description
Permanent product	• Number of events • Number/time (rate) • Percent of total
Tally/count	• Number of events • Number/time (rate) • Number or percent of events per category
Duration or inter-response time recording	• Total time (cumulative) • Percent of time • Average time per event (beginning to end) or between events (end to beginning)
Latency recording	• Total time (cumulative) • Percent of opportunities on time • Average time (between S^D and behavior)
Partial-interval recording	• Percent of intervals
Whole-interval recording	• Percent of intervals
Momentary time sampling	• Percent of intervals (or opportunities)

FIGURE 4.5. Alignment among measurement system and appropriate summary scores.

score, it becomes easy to create a meaningful visual display of your data. You may use tables to summarize your data, but the old saying "a picture is worth a thousand words" applies: graphs are the easiest and most effective way to summarize your data to facilitate decision making.

Types of Graphs

Although there are numerous ways to graph or visually represent data, there are two main types of graphs that will be the most helpful for summarizing your data: line and bar graphs. **Line graphs** are useful for showing patterns in levels or trends of behavior across time. In other words, line graphs are useful at illustrating how often or how long a behavior occurs across observations. In general, line graphs should have a descriptive title, units of time (e.g., observation, date) represented along the x-axis (horizontal), and units of behavior (i.e., one of the types of summary scores presented in Figure 4.5) represented along the y-axis (vertical). If you represent more than one behavior on the graph, be sure to use different shapes for data points and different weights or patterns for the lines representing each data path. (Excel and professional graphing programs will do this by default.)

You can use more advanced graphing conventions to convey additional information within your graph. For example, if you make a change (e.g., implement or modify an intervention), you can note that by drawing a vertical line on the graph when the change is made. This vertical line is called a **phase line,** and you should label what was occurring before and after each phase line (e.g., baseline, intervention) using text boxes. In addition, if something happens that interrupts your data collection for one or more days (e.g., school vacation, student illness), you should represent the interruption by deleting the line connecting the data points before and after the disruption. This **continuity break** indicates that a disruption occurred, and you can describe the nature of the disruption below the graph. (Figure 4.6 presents a line graph illustrating the various graphing conventions described.)

Bar graphs are useful at illustrating categories of events or behaviors. In other words, bar graphs may be used to compare the relative occurrence of different types of behavior (topography), different locations in which behaviors occur (locus), or other features of the context that may be categorized (e.g., common antecedent and consequence events). Like line graphs, bar graphs should have a descriptive title and units of behavior (i.e., appropriate summary score) represented along the *y*-axis (vertical). However, bar graphs have categories (rather than time) presented along the *x*-axis (horizontal). Bar graphs are easy to read and interpret, as a quick scan reveals which bar(s) are highest or lowest.

Presenting Data

As you prepare your graph(s) to address each purpose or guiding question, consider the following tips. When you present data, keep your presentation simple. Although professional graphing programs give you countless options for making your graph "pretty," a clearly labeled, black-and-white graph is often easier to understand and interpret than a graph containing multiple

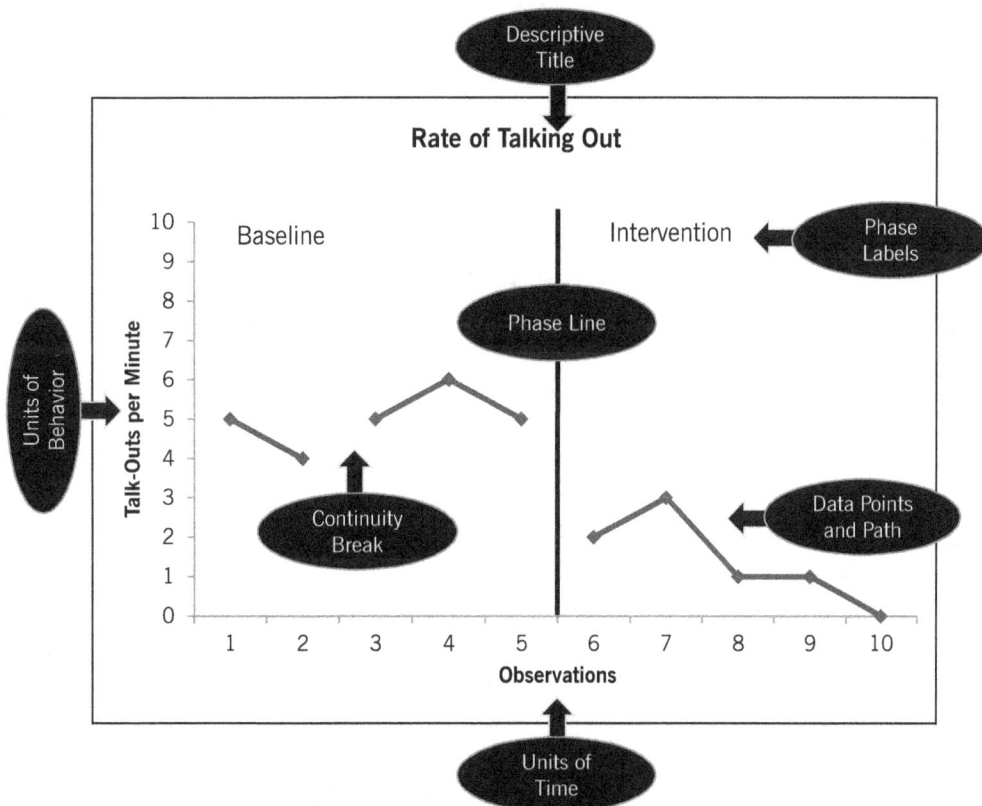

FIGURE 4.6. Line graph illustrating (1) levels of behavior (*y*-axis) across time (*x*-axis), (2) changes in behavior before and after intervention (phase line), and (3) minor disruptions in data collection due to school vacations (continuity breaks).

colors, streams of data, or other frills. If you are sharing your data with others (e.g., colleagues, families, students), aim to showcase the data, not your ability to create fancy graphs! Similarly, plan to present your data clearly and succinctly, using common language (as opposed to professional jargon) so that everyone can access the information and participate meaningfully in the conversation. By effectively presenting data, you will increase the likelihood that your data will effectively facilitate decision making.

Using Data to Guide Decision Making

As we described at the beginning of this section, you may collect and use data for various purposes. You may use data to monitor what's going well or to inform a problem-solving process (Riley-Tillman et al., 2005). In the context of classwide PBIS, you may collect data to (1) monitor your implementation of specific classwide PBIS practices (e.g., opportunities to respond, specific praise); (2) evaluate the effectiveness of instructional programs (e.g., academic curriculum; social, emotional, and behavioral skills instruction); (3) identify the scope of a problem or concern (e.g., whole class, targeted group, individual); (4) describe and measure the dimensions of contextually inappropriate behaviors for one or more students; or (5) use a solution-oriented process to select (based on scope and dimensions of contextually inappropriate behaviors) and evaluate the effectiveness of additional intervention strategies. Each purpose of data collection in classwide PBIS should guide your selection of target behaviors, relevant dimensions, measurement systems, appropriate summary scores, and effective visual displays. Then data should be used to guide decision making to maintain what is working and adjust what is not working in your classroom. See Boxes 4.1 and 4.2 for examples of outcomes and data related to your behavior and your students' behavior, respectively.

SYSTEMS: SUPPORTING TEACHERS' IMPLEMENTATION OF CLASSWIDE PBIS[1]

If you are feeling a little overwhelmed with the idea of centering equity, setting outcomes, and collecting and using data, then you have arrived at the right section! We know that effectively implementing all elements of classwide PBIS may feel like a challenge, especially early in your career. Unfortunately, many of us enter the field with limited, if any, training in effective classroom behavioral support practices from our preservice programs (Begeny & Martens, 2006; Freeman et al., 2014). If you are lucky, you may receive some training once you are in the field; however, most teachers report (1) receiving little professional development in classroom behavioral supports (Wei et al., 2010); (2) feeling unprepared to meet students' social, emotional, and behavioral needs (Gable et al., 2012; Reinke et al., 2011); and (3) having ongoing concerns with student behavior (Bushaw & Lopez, 2010; Harrison et al., 2012). However, there is hope! Recently, researchers, practitioners, and policymakers have begun to take a serious look at strategies to support and respond teachers' practices, including classwide PBIS (e.g., Center on PBIS, January 2023a; Hirsch et al., 2021; Wilkinson et al., 2020). We even wrote a book on it! (See *Implementing Classwide PBIS: A Guide for Supporting Teachers;* Myers et al., 2020.)

---

[1]We would like to thank our colleagues, including Susan Barrett, Chris Borgmeier, Kate Dooley, Jen Freeman, Laura Kern, Kristine Larson Terry Scott, and George Sugai, for contributing to many discussions that shaped this section.

BOX 4.1. TRACKING SPECIFIC PRAISE RATES

The following sequence illustrates how a teacher may select an outcome and use data to track their progress toward that outcome, using the process described in the text.

Outcome (with required parts of goal in parentheses):

During teacher-directed instruction (*condition*), I (*individual*) will deliver an average of one **specific praise statement** (*behavior*) per minute during 90% of sampled opportunities (i.e., 10-minute samples of instruction) across the first quarter (*criterion*).

Data (including suggested steps for designing a measurement system):

1. **Operational Definition of Specific Praise**
   Teacher provides specific positive feedback to one or more students, contingent on behavior.

   Examples
   - During teacher-directed instruction, a student raises her hand. **The teacher says, "Thank you for raising your hand."**
   - A student enters the class during teacher-directed instruction; the student quietly walks to his seat. **The teacher walks over to the student and whispers, "Thank you for coming in the room quietly."**
   - After the teacher points to the consonant blend /th/, which is underlined in the word *though*, and says, "What sound?" a student responds by correctly pronouncing /th/. **The teacher says, "Nice pronunciation."**

   Nonexamples
   - During teacher-directed instruction, students are talking over the teacher. The teacher rolls his eyes and says, "Gee, thanks for listening." (This is sarcasm, and not specific praise.)
   - A student enters the class during teacher-directed instruction; the student quietly walks to her seat. After about 90 seconds, the teacher gives the student a "thumbs up." (This is a delayed nice gesture, and not specific praise.)
   - During a direct-instruction lesson, the teacher points to the consonant blend /th/, which is underlined in the word *though*, and says, "What sound?" (This is an opportunity to respond, and not specific praise.)

2. **Relevant Dimension(s)**
   Rate (frequency of specific praise divided by minutes observed).

3. **Measurement System**
   Event recording, using a counter (either a golf counter or an app that tracks frequency). Specifically, the teacher will identify 10-minute samples and use the counter to track specific praise rates during those 10 minutes.

4. **Summary and Graph**
   Following data collection, the teacher will enter their data into an Excel spreadsheet that automatically updates a line graph, displaying rate across time.

5. **Use Data to Make Decisions**
   After collecting data during five sampled opportunities, the teacher will review the data, determine the average rate, and determine whether they are close to meeting the outcome. If not, the teacher may set a goal to increase the rate and/or implement a self-reinforcement plan (i.e., self-delivering a privilege after school on each day the goal rate was achieved). Once the outcome level is reached and maintained, the teacher may fade supports or frequency of data collection to promote skill maintenance. The teacher may also sample other classroom routines to promote generalization of skill use.

BOX 4.2. TRACKING STUDENT TALK-OUTS AND HAND RAISES

The following sequence illustrates how a teacher may collect data on talk-outs and hand raises during teacher-directed instruction.

Outcome (with required parts of goal in parentheses):

During teacher-directed instruction (*condition*), students (*learners*) will **raise hands**, in lieu of talking out (*behavior*), during 80% of sampled opportunities (i.e., 10-minute samples of instruction) across the first quarter (*criterion*).

Data (including suggested steps for designing a measurement system):

1. **Operational Definitions**
   Hand Raise: Students elevate one hand calmly above shoulder level and wait until called on to speak.
   Talk-Out: Student speaks loudly enough to disrupt the learning of self and others without being called on (during instructional routines when quiet listening is expected).

   Examples of Hand Raises (Nonexamples of Talk-Outs)
   • During teacher-directed instruction, a student lifts her hand, waits for the teacher to call her by name, and then speaks to participate.
   • When a student needs to take care of personal business (e.g., go to the restroom, get a drink), he raises his hand and waits for the teacher to call on him (or approach him) before requesting to use the appropriate facility.

   Nonexamples of Hand Raises (Examples of Talk-Outs)
   • During teacher-directed instruction, a student waves her hand quickly in the air and shouts, "Call on me! Call on me!" Then she quickly says the answer, all before the teacher has called on her.
   • A student gets up, announces he needs to go to the restroom, grabs a pass, and leaves the room.

2. **Relevant Dimension(s)**
   Rate (frequency of hand raises and talk-outs divided by minutes observed).

3. **Measurement System**
   Event recording, using a tally on a sticky note or an app that tracks frequency of multiple behaviors. Specifically, the teacher will identify 10 minutes of teacher-directed instruction and tally each time a student in the class talks out or raises their hand.

4. **Summary and Graph**
   Following data collection, the teacher will enter their data into an Excel spreadsheet that graphs rate of each behavior (as illustrated in Figure 4.6).

5. **Use Data to Make Decisions**
   After collecting data during five sampled opportunities, the teacher will review data for both skills. If data indicate that students are already raising hands rather than talking out (i.e., meeting outcome), then the teacher may maintain the current approach and collect data to ensure levels are maintained. If the data indicate that students are talking out rather than raising their hands during some/all of the sampled opportunities, the teacher may implement an intervention (e.g., social skills lesson and group contingency for hand raising) and continue to collect data to determine if the intervention had the desired effect (i.e., increased hand raising and decreased talking out).

Approaches to Supporting Teachers' Implementation of Classwide PBIS

In both research and practice, there are three main approaches to supporting teachers: self-management supports, peer supports, and expert supports. In this section, we describe these three general approaches, and we note that each may be intensified to support all teachers (as we describe in the following section). Additionally, regardless of approach, research suggests that effective professional development is job-embedded, focuses on content (e.g., evidence-based practices), is explicit (modeling, active opportunities to practice with feedback), and is supportive (e.g., includes opportunities for peer or expert support; Darling-Hammond et al., 2017).

Self-Management

Self-management occurs when we manage our behavior the same way we would manage someone else's—by changing the environment or antecedents, learning and using new behaviors or skills, monitoring or evaluating our own behavior, and providing contingent consequences to increase our use of desired behaviors or decrease our use of undesired behaviors (e.g., Skinner, 1953). For example, you may set a bag of materials you need for school the next day by the door (antecedent strategy) to increase the likelihood that you will bring the materials with you (desired behavior). Similarly, you may use a to-do list (antecedent prompt and monitoring system) to increase the likelihood that you complete the items on your list (desired behaviors) and reward yourself when you complete the items on your list (consequence). As these simple examples illustrate, you are likely already using self-management strategies in real life, and research suggests that similar strategies can be used to increase teachers' use of simple classwide PBIS practices (Chalk & Bizo, 2004; Layden et al., 2023; Rispoli et al., 2017; Simonsen et al., 2013, 2017; Simonsen, MacSuga-Gage, et al., 2014; Simonsen, Freeman, et al., 2020; Sutherland & Wehby, 2001; Sutherland et al., 2000; Zoder-Martell et al., 2019). In the absence of any external supports, you can use self-management strategies to enhance your use of classwide PBIS practices. Like all strategies, self-management may be intensified based on need, as we describe in the next section.

Peer Supports

In our field, peer supports have become increasingly popular. We see schools using various teaming (e.g., grade-level teams, discipline-specific departments, professional learning communities) and partnering (e.g., "buddy" teachers) structures to facilitate peer-based support among teachers. Although the research on the effectiveness of these structures is limited in the area of classwide PBIS, we believe that peer-based supports may have the potential to inform and enhance your implementation. These supports may range from informal supports (e.g., asking a peer for suggestions on classroom management) to more formal supports (e.g., asking a peer to observe and collect data on your implementation of specific practices), and may be intensified based on need, as we describe subsequently.

"Expert" Supports

Perhaps the most "typical" or traditional type of support is relying on an outside expert to provide "sit and get" professional development. Although research demonstrates that this type of "train-and-hope" approach, when used in isolation, may be less effective (Allen & Forman, 1984; Fixsen et al., 2005; Stokes & Baer, 1977), expert support can be a critical part of a professional development—especially when the experts are school-based or local and when support is matched to teacher need (see Hirsch et al., 2021, for an example of intensive, high-quality, and expert-led professional learning to enhance teachers' use of effective classroom practices).

First, experts can provide brief, explicit didactic training in specific classwide PBIS skills. This type of training may be a necessary, but not sufficient, expert support. In addition, many schools use experts (e.g., senior teachers) as mentors for new teachers—through either established induction programs or informal school-based mentoring approaches. When carried out well, research suggests that these supports can assist new teachers with implementation of classwide PBIS (e.g., Briere et al., 2015). We have also seen an increased emphasis on coaching or consultation supports in schools (see Reinke, Herman, et al., 2011, for a useful discussion of the Classroom Check-Up, a teacher consultation model that can be used to increase teachers' use of evidence-based classroom behavioral support practices). Evidence supports expert coaching or consultation approaches for classwide PBIS (e.g., Wilkinson et al., 2020), and these supports may be especially important for assisting teachers who require intensive supports to succeed with their implementation (e.g., MacSuga & Simonsen, 2011; Reinke et al., 2008).

Overview of an MTSS Framework for Classwide PBIS

As a field, we have also begun to realize that, when designing supports for teachers, one size does not fit all. Thus, researchers have suggested adopting an MTSS framework to support teachers' implementation of classwide PBIS (e.g., Center on PBIS, 2023a; Myers et al., 2011; Simonsen, MacSuga-Gage, et al., 2014). In alignment with other multi-tiered approaches discussed in Chapter 1 (i.e., PBIS, MTSS), all teachers should participate in high-quality and supportive professional development in Tier 1, teachers who continue to experience new or minor implementation challenges with classwide PBIS may participate in targeted professional development in Tier 2, and teachers who experience chronic or significant implementation challenges with classwide PBIS may receive intensive and individualized professional development in Tier 3. In this section, we present an overview of an MTSS framework for teachers (see Figure 4.7).

As you read, consider your current level of need in implementing the critical elements of classwide PBIS and identify appropriate supports for your own implementation. Because this framework is not fully tested, we emphasize that it is a way to organize evidence-based professional development supports—much like PBIS for students—and we share a range of potentially effective strategies that you can use on your own (self-management), with colleagues (peer support), or with expert support across three tiers within an MTSS framework. We also emphasize how the three types of support (self, peer, and expert) may be combined to create a range of flexible support options for teachers. (Again, see the Center on PBIS, 2023a, resource on *Supporting and Responding to Educators Needs* and our book [Myers et al., 2020] for more detail on an MTSS approach to supporting educators.)

Tier 1 Professional Development: Support for All Teachers

As teachers, we can all benefit from ongoing reminders and support in centering equity, identifying outcomes, collecting and using data, and implementing effective classwide PBIS practices. Tier 1 professional development support should be effective (i.e., employ empirically sup-

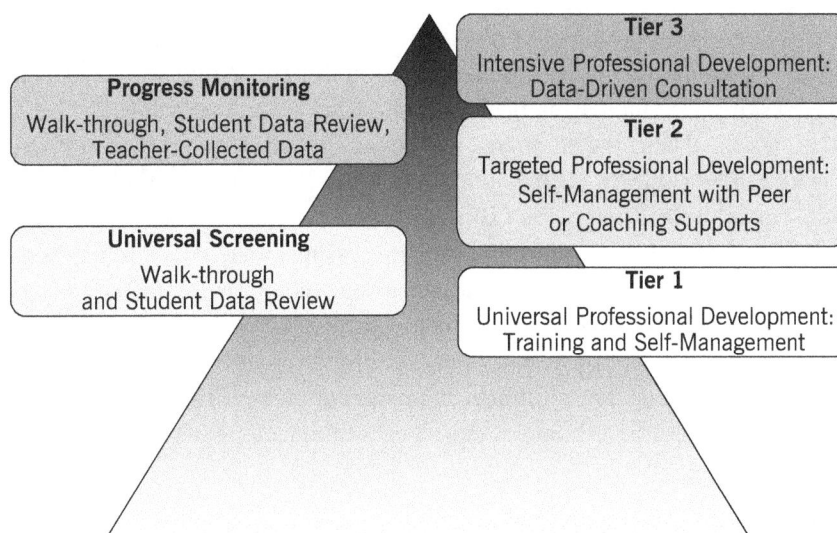

FIGURE 4.7. A multi-tiered system of support framework to support teachers' implementation of classwide PBIS. Adapted from Simonsen et al. (2014). Copyright © 2014 Sage Publications. Adapted by permission.

ported features that result in desired outcomes), efficient (brief), and universal (provided to all teachers). Each approach to supporting teachers (self, peer, and expert) has features that may be implemented, in isolation or in concert, within Tier 1. For example, an "expert" (administrator, school-based behavior coach, school psychologist, mentor teacher) can provide a brief and explicit didactic training to all teachers on one classwide PBIS skill during 10–15 minutes of a faculty meeting. Because this training is necessary but likely insufficient, teachers may supplement it with self-management and/or peer supports. For example, teachers may use Tier 1 self-management strategies by selecting 15 minutes of their day when they monitor (i.e., count or track) their use of the skill presented by the expert. Then they may set a goal for increasing their performance, evaluate whether they meet their goal daily, and reward themselves on days they meet their goals (return to Box 4.1 for an example related to behavior-specific praise). Alternately, teachers may choose to brainstorm strategies to enhance their implementation within existing peer groups (e.g., grade-level teams, departments) in their building, implement the identified strategies, and report back to the group about successes and challenges. Teachers may also choose to use all three approaches (i.e., attend the training, self-monitor and evaluate skill use, and share their data to celebrate or brainstorm improvements with colleagues) in Tier 1.

Tier 2 Professional Development: Targeted Support for Some Teachers

For teachers who experience minor implementation challenges (e.g., need to increase use of positive feedback relative to negative) or new implementation challenges (e.g., difficult class in a particular year, first year teaching), Tier 2 professional development supports should be considered in addition to the supports provided in Tier 1. Tier 2 supports should be effective (i.e., empirically supported), streamlined (i.e., require minimal time and effort to implement beyond Tier 1), and targeted (i.e., match specific needs identified by staff). Again, all three approaches to delivering support (expert, peer, and/or self) may be implemented within Tier 2. For example, an expert may meet with teachers who require Tier 2 and provide brief training on specific targeted skills (e.g., increasing behavior-specific praise). Alternately, a school may form a skill-based professional learning community to engage in learning and peer-support activities related to the identified skill. As a third option, a teacher may intensify their self-management plan by focusing on additional classwide PBIS skills, intensifying their current self-management approaches for the previously identified skill (e.g., increasing antecedent strategies, monitoring, criterion for self-recognition, available rewards), or some combination of the two approaches. Finally, a teacher may combine strategies from all approaches, creating additional possibilities for Tier 2 supports. For example, a teacher may request to meet with an expert to review her self-management plan and ask for additional implementation tips, then the teacher may share her data and plan components with one or more peers to recruit peer support.

Tier 3 Professional Development: Intensive Support for Individual Teachers

Teachers who (1) continue to struggle with chronic implementation challenges after participating in Tier 1 and 2 supports or (2) experience significant implementation challenges may require intensive and individualized Tier 3 supports. Like the other tiers, Tier 3 supports should be effective (i.e., empirically supported), but they should be individualized to the specific teacher and intensive enough to assist the teacher in improving their implementation. All three approaches (expert, peer, self) may be intensified at Tier 3, but it is more likely that a combination of the approaches will be required to effect desired change. For example, expert support in Tier 3 likely includes ongoing coaching or consultation support that incorporates performance feedback on specific skills targeted for improvement. **Performance feedback,** which includes regular data-based updates on current performance and specific suggestions for improving practice, is an effective strategy to increase teachers' implementation of various interventions (e.g., Noell et al., 1997). Although coaching or consultation may be expert driven (i.e., where the expert determines needed skills, collects data, and provides performance feedback), it can also be combined with other support approaches. For example, the expert may work with the teacher to review their self-monitoring data, develop a detailed action plan that enhances strategies already included in the self-management plan, and continue to meet with the teacher and provide feedback based on teacher-collected data. Regardless of the specific features, Tier 3 supports should be continued and refined until sufficient improvement is observed.

Thus, all teachers receive the type (self, peer, and/or expert) and level (Tier 1, 2, and/or 3) of support required to achieve success within an MTSS framework. Although additional research is needed, we believe this is a promising approach for improving the experience and outcomes of professional development for classwide PBIS.

PRACTICES: BRIEF INTRODUCTION TO PART II

The fourth critical element of classwide PBIS is **practices,** or interventions and supports for students' social behavior in your classroom. In this section, we provide a brief overview of the classwide PBIS practices, which are described in detail in Parts II (Classwide PBIS Practices) and III (Additional Tiers of Support for Students) of this book. Specifically, there are five empirically supported, critical principles that should guide your implementation of Tier 1 classwide PBIS (Simonsen et al., 2008):

1. Create an inclusive, predictable, and safe classroom environment by establishing routines and effectively arranging your classroom.
2. Actively engage students in developmentally appropriate and culturally relevant instruction.
3. Collaboratively select, define, teach, prompt, monitor, and review a few positively stated expectations or norms for your classroom community.
4. Implement a continuum of strategies to recognize and increase contextually appropriate behavior.
5. Implement a continuum of strategies to supportively respond to and decrease contextually inappropriate behavior.

We present these principles, along with examples of practices for each, in Chapter 5 (features 1 and 2), Chapter 6 (feature 3), Chapter 7 (feature 4), and Chapter 8 (feature 5). For students whose behaviors continue to require more support, we present strategies to (1) enhance and target these practices for groups of students requiring Tier 2 support (Chapter 9) and (2) develop individualized practices for students who require intensive Tier 3 support (Chapter 10).

SUMMARY

To implement classwide PBIS, teachers center equity, identify outcomes, collect and use data to drive decision making, and identify systems to support their implementation of culturally relevant and empirically supported practices. As we have emphasized throughout this chapter, the key is to keep it simple! First, center equity by considering your students' unique needs and background and actively engaging students and their families when designing your shared classroom community. Second, review data to develop outcomes that are meaningful to you, your students, and their families and document those outcomes using a four-part (conditions, individuals, behaviors, and criteria) outcome or goal statement. Third, adopt efficient measurement systems that allow you to collect data to monitor progress toward outcomes and inform your decisions about implementing, adjusting, or discontinuing intervention strategies. Fourth, select and implement culturally relevant and empirically supported practices (discussed in detail in the next section of this book) that are aligned with your outcomes and indicated by your data. Last, and most important, identify systems to support your implementation based on (1) the approaches (self, peer, or expert) that you prefer or have access to and (2) your level of need (Tier 1, 2, or 3).

PHASES OF LEARNING ACTIVITIES: CHAPTER 4

Acquisition

1. In collaboration with your students and their families, identify *outcomes* of successful implementation of classwide PBIS for you and for the students in your classroom.
2. Identify relevant *systems* or support structures available in your school and your district for teachers at your level (preservice, induction, tenured, etc.) for implementing classwide PBIS.

Fluency

1. Select a student who engages in contextually inappropriate behavior, operationally define their contextually inappropriate behavior, identify the relevant dimensions of the behavior (related to why it should not occur in the classroom context), design a measurement system, collect 3 days of data, and summarize the data in a graph.

2. Select a self-management strategy, as discussed within the "systems to support teachers" section, and use it to monitor, evaluate, and/or reinforce your use of specific classroom PBIS practices related to achieving your outcomes.

Maintenance

1. Repeat Fluency Activity 1 with two or more additional students this year.

2. Fade your use of the strategies you implemented in Fluency Activity 2, and then use periodic checks to examine whether your skill use is maintained in the absence of the self-management strategy. If you have maintained your skill use, celebrate! If not, reinstate the strategies included in Fluency Activity 2.

Generalization

1. Develop a *data* or measurement system to track your performance and/or your students' performance related to one or more of the outcomes you identified in Acquisition Activity 1 for your classroom.

2. Once you have become fluent and maintained your skill use, work with a peer to support them in an identified area of need with respect to classwide PBIS.

Other Skill-Building Exercises

1. After reading Chapter 5, apply concepts learned in this chapter to (1) identify outcomes and (2) design and implement a data collection system related to increasing students' opportunities to respond and improving academic outcomes.

2. After reading Chapter 6, apply concepts learned in this chapter related to data to measure students' acquisition, fluency, maintenance, and generalization of key social, emotional, and behavioral skills (i.e., being kind to a peer, asking for help or support) in your classroom.

PART II

CLASSWIDE PBIS PRACTICES

CHAPTER 5

Create an Inclusive, Predictable, Safe, and Engaging Classroom

---

CHAPTER OBJECTIVES

By the end of this chapter, you should be able to . . .

1. Intentionally connect and foster positive relationships with and among your students.
2. Create an effective classroom environment by (a) collaboratively defining, teaching, and practicing predictable classroom routines and (b) thoughtfully arranging the physical classroom environment to promote access and to encourage contextually appropriate behavior.
3. Design relevant instruction and engage students in learning by increasing the rate and variety of relevant opportunities to respond that you provide to students.

Imagine This: Mr. Jericho, a middle school general educator, was often heard yelling at his students. After the principal received multiple complaints from teachers on Mr. Jericho's hallway, she asked you, one of her teachers with experience and expertise in positive and proactive approaches to supporting students' behavior, to observe his classroom and share some helpful strategies. When you walk into Mr. Jericho's classroom for your first observation, you are struck, not by the yelling you hear or by the students' behavior (which is largely off task), but by the appearance of his classroom. You look toward the whiteboard to see what the students are working on during the period. Other than some vocabulary words and (hopefully) student doodles you do not see anything on the board. Trying to get some idea of the routines or schedule of the class, you scan all of the walls and the students' desks. Still, you do not see anything resembling a schedule, a teaching objective, or any kind of routine.

As you continue to scan the room, you notice that the only organized spots in the room are the students' desks. Mr. Jericho's desk is covered in heaps of paper, and there are even piles of paper on the floor. Almost every horizontal surface, except student desks and some walkways between desks, *is covered in paper and nonessential materials. You notice that one of the students uses a wheelchair, and has limited access to many spaces in the room given the clutter. You realize that before you can address anything else, you have to help Mr. Jericho with the physical arrangement in his classroom!*

At this point, you also begin to process what he is saying to his students. You hear what you assume is a lecture on states and capitals, but you hear Mr. Jericho identifying the wrong pairs of states and cities. (You hear him say that Tallahassee is the capital of Georgia and Raleigh is the capital of Virginia.) As he goes on (and on) with his lecture, you notice that students are staring blankly out the window, doodling on their papers, or even sleeping. Thus, not only is he teaching inaccurate information, his delivery of the information is so ineffective that the students are not listening to his instruction. (You then decide that may be a good thing; at least, you hope, they are not learning the wrong states and capitals!)

You close your eyes and picture your own classroom, where you have your typical routines posted next to your whiteboard, your learning objective written at the top of your whiteboard, and a "Do Now" activity waiting for students when they first arrive in your classroom. You picture your walls, which have sections that showcase exemplary student work and contain posters that prompt appropriate academic behaviors (e.g., the writing process, how to format a paper) and contextually appropriate social behaviors (e.g., kind to self, others, and environment). You picture the gleaming metal bins where students turn in their homework upon entering the room and the materials you have neatly organized to help them complete the various tasks for the day. You picture the top of your desk, which does have some stacks of papers to be graded, but is largely organized with bins and trays. You picture your lesson plan book, the binders of evidence-based curriculum, and your other instructional materials, and you hear yourself effectively using various strategies to engage your students in your instruction (e.g., unison responding, response cards). You open your eyes, take a deep breath, and decide that you will take Mr. Jericho on a field trip to the local office supply store and, as you drive, talk with him about the importance of creating a safe space that all students can navigate to access instructional materials and activities, teaching predictable routines, finding his district-approved curriculum, and actively engaging students in relevant instruction.

OVERVIEW OF FOUNDATIONAL CLASSROOM PRACTICES

As the "Imagine This" scenario illustrates, connecting with students and creating an inclusive, predictable, and safe classroom environment where you deliver actively engaging instruction is foundational to fostering both student learning and contextually appropriate behavior (Center on PBIS, 2022a). First, we have found that taking time to get to know and connect with our students and other members of our classroom community (staff, families, volunteers) is critical to being able to (1) create a setting where everyone feels welcome and like they belong and (2) plan a classroom environment that meets each student's unique needs.

We have also seen that the classroom environment—both the physical space and the routines that support the activities in the space—is the foundation for implementing the remaining principles of classwide PBIS. When we are asked to support a teacher who is struggling with classwide PBIS, like Mr. Jericho, we always start by working on the classroom environment. Without an inclusive, predictable, and safe classroom environment, it is difficult to establish and teach expectations, deliver instruction, or consistently implement any other social, emotional, and behavioral support strategy.

Further, it is difficult to imagine a classroom where there is effective social, emotional, and behavioral support in the absence of good instruction. Although most teacher preparation programs emphasize good teaching pedagogy and content expertise, instruction should also be delivered in a way that is developmentally and culturally relevant and actively engages students in meaningful learning opportunities. In this chapter, we provide an introduction to connecting with students, creating an effective classroom environment, and actively engaging students in instruction.

CONNECT AND FOSTER POSITIVE RELATIONSHIPS WITH AND AMONG YOUR STUDENTS

As the foundation for a successful school year, take time to get to know and maintain connections with each of your students and their families. Although we see positive relationships as an outcome of the many effective practices you will implement throughout the year (i.e., everything in this book, as we'll describe in Chapter 11), there are intentional steps that you can take before the school year even starts (and throughout the year) to connect with your students. And your intentional efforts to connect may lead to better relationships with (Wilson-Ching & Berger, 2023) and outcomes for (e.g., Allday & Parkurar, 2007; Cook et al., 2018) your students.

To intentionally and positively connect with students and families, the Center on PBIS (2022a) suggests that teachers purposefully communicate, build in regular communication opportunities to connect throughout the year, learn about their students, and "validate and affirm students' and families' personal and cultural learning histories" (p. 12). Consider, for example, sending out a communication to students and families before the school year begins to introduce yourself (e.g., provide a QR code to a video introduction) and invite them to introduce themselves (e.g., upload a video to an electronic classroom/platform, respond to a survey, send an email) and share any information that would be important for you to consider in designing your classroom environment and instruction. Then, during the first week, plan activities to get to know more about each student's learning history, unique needs, preferences, and other details that can help you connect with them throughout the year. Getting to know your students—and understanding their individual and collective learning histories—will enable you to better anticipate your students' needs and adjust your classroom supports to set each student up for success.

Beyond the start of the year, consider ways to stay connected with students and families in addition to the typical school routines (e.g., conferences, back-to-school events). For example, sending regular positive emails, sharing a weekly or monthly newsletter, or using apps that facilitate communication can all be simple strategies to maintain connections throughout the year. In addition, consider how you can intentionally foster positive relationships through your classroom practices. One simple strategy is to positively greet your students at the door, which provides an opportunity to positively connect with each student ("Good morning, Jamar. How was your evening?"), prompt classroom norms or expectations ("Remember to kindly greet your peers as you enter the room."), and direct students to engage in their first instructional activity ("Check the board for our 'do now' activity"). This simple strategy can set students up for success—increasing the likelihood they are engaged in academic activities and other contextually appropriate behavior (Allday & Parkurar, 2007; Cook et al., 2018). After greeting students, you can continue to foster positive relationships by ensuring the classroom environment supports all your students.

CREATE AN INCLUSIVE, PREDICTABLE, AND SAFE CLASSROOM ENVIRONMENT

An effective classroom environment—one that is inclusive, predictable, and safe—includes both the physical and the organizational elements (i.e., predictable routines) of the classroom. Research indicates that structured classrooms and other environments where crowding and distraction are minimized result in desired outcomes for students and are preferred by teachers (see Simonsen et al., 2008). However, research does not neatly prescribe one way to create an effective physical space. (Unfortunately, there is not one magical seating arrangement that will set all future students up for success in your classroom!) Instead, the goal is to be thoughtful about the physical environment and organizational elements of your classroom and adjust both based on data (as emphasized in Chapter 4). In this section, we present considerations for (1) establishing and teaching predictable classroom routines and (2) arranging your classroom environment to prioritize safety, promote access and engagement, and prompt contextually appropriate behavior.

Establish and Teach Predictable Classroom Routines

Having effective classroom routines is critical to creating a safe, positive, and predictable experience for your students (and yourself!) in the classroom. When teachers and students establish, practice, and consistently use routines, we have seen that students know what to expect, and they are able to progress through the class activity, period, or day with minimal prompting. In other words, by allocating time to (1) establish, teach, and practice routines at the beginning of the year and (2) provide periodic reviews throughout the year, you save yourself (and your students) from losing instructional time to constant reminders and behavioral mistakes related to typical classroom routines (e.g., how to transition between activities, distribute and collect materials, turn in and collect assignments, and other daily activities). Thus, it is important to identify, describe, post, teach, and differentiate your classroom routines.

Identify and Describe Consistent Classroom Routines

To identify your classroom routines, consider how students will successfully engage in their classroom from the moment they walk through the door at the beginning of the period or day until the moment they leave. Consider student routines for:

- Entering the classroom
- Turning in homework or in-class assignments
- Putting away materials (upon entering the room or transitioning between activities)
- Getting started (consider providing an opening "warm-up" or "do now" activity to get students immediately engaged in an academic task)
- Accessing materials (e.g., writing materials, books, manipulatives) when needed
- Distributing materials (e.g., returning student work, passing out response cards) at specified times
- Participating in or actively listening to teacher-directed instruction
- Requesting assistance from the teacher or a peer
- Engaging in cooperative learning group activities
- Completing independent assignments or tests

- Working with a partner, when assigned
- Taking care of personal needs (e.g., bathroom, drink of water, calming routine)
- Handling a visitor in the classroom
- Adjusting to a substitute teacher (or student teacher)

As you considered the various routines we suggested, you likely also thought of many other routines that are specific to your classroom, grade level, or school setting. For each activity that occurs, consider what you expect students to do during each routine and engage your students in describing what the routine should "look and sound like" in your classroom community. For example, you and your students may develop a routine for entering the room that includes (1) a positive greeting at the door (you stand by the door, welcome students into the classroom, they greet you kindly, and you provide a brief reminder of positive classroom norms or expectations), (2) checking the smartboard (or whiteboard) for any announcements, (3) walking to the homework bin, (4) turning in their homework from the previous night (if assigned), (5) walking by materials and picking up anything they need for the period (e.g., pencil), (6) walking to their desk, (7) hanging their bag on the back of their chair, (8) getting out needed materials, and (9) beginning the warm-up activity. By collaboratively developing, explicitly teaching, and practicing your beginning-of-class routine, you will start each day or class period with a positive connection and set students (and yourself!) up for success.

ENSURE STUDENT ROUTINES ARE CONTEXTUALLY APPROPRIATE

As you identify student routines, be sure you consider the age, ability, learning history (i.e., individual and shared cultural experiences that influence how they respond in certain contexts; see Chapter 2), and content taught in your classroom. Routines are important in all contexts, but they should clearly look different based on learner characteristics (e.g., age, ability, preferences, learning history), teacher characteristics (e.g., preferences, teaching style, learning history), and content (e.g., language arts vs. science vs. industrial arts). For example, in a kindergarten classroom, a teacher may need to be even more explicit with what each step in a routine looks like, as some students may not have experienced things like lining up, gathering in a circle, or other common activities. In contrast, teachers in a high school science lab should be even more explicit with routines around various lab activities and equipment, as those activities and materials present very real safety risks to students if routines (and expectations) are not established and followed. Even in our university courses, we have to establish clear routines for in-class activities, including quizzes, group work, and lectures; communicating with students outside of class (e.g., expectations about email; for example, "Students can expect a response within 1 business day, but not within an hour—especially if you send your email at 3:00 A.M.!"); and managing course assessments (e.g., how students will turn in, receive, and respond to feedback on assignments and quizzes).

Further, students with elevated social, emotional, and behavioral needs, including those who have experienced individual or collective trauma (e.g., students returning to school after a crisis), may need even more explicit predictable routines, proactive communication about changes in routines, and opportunities for healthy breaks (e.g., engaging in a calming routine, connecting with peers) interspersed among academic activities (Center on PBIS et al., 2022). Similarly, students with some disabilities (e.g., autism, emotional or behavioral disabilities) benefit when educators teach, practice, and prompt predictable routines in an accessible way (e.g., visual schedule; Bennett et al., 2011). As you can see, it's important to design predictable routines to support all students in a range of contexts, and predictable routines are especially critical for students with unique or elevated social, emotional, or behavioral needs.

EMBED CHOICE WHENEVER POSSIBLE

Although you want routines explicitly defined and consistent, consider opportunities to build in student choice within and across routines. Providing choice is a great antecedent strategy to promote academic engagement and prevent or decrease contextually inappropriate behaviors (e.g., Dunlap et al., 1994; Royer et al., 2017). For example, you may have a routine for independent seatwork, and one component of that routine may be that students choose the order in which they do tasks. Other choices you may want to build into your routines include:

- Which activity will be completed first (i.e., order of activities).
- What materials students will use to complete the task (e.g., type and color or writing utensil).
- Whether to work independently, with a small group, or with a partner (and choice of partner, if appropriate).
- Where students will complete the activity (e.g., desk, rug area, close to teacher).
- How students will respond (i.e., response modality: handwritten, typed, verbal, etc.).
- What students will receive or earn.
- Other similar opportunities for students to select how they will complete or participate in various routines.

EMPLOY BEHAVIORAL MOMENTUM

Within and throughout routines, also create opportunities to build "behavioral momentum" (e.g., Cooper et al., 2021). Consider beginning each activity, or at least each major part of the day, with activities that are likely to result in student success (i.e., lead to reinforcement) so that momentum (i.e., recent history of frequent reinforcement for engaging in academic tasks) increases the likelihood that students will attempt and engage in more difficult tasks. Similarly, throughout the day, intersperse routines and tasks that are easier (i.e., lead to more frequent reinforcement with less effort) among those that are harder. For example, if you have students all day long, don't pack all of your difficult content into 3 consecutive hours of instruction. Instead, intersperse (1) difficult content with fun review activities and (2) preferred subjects with less preferred subjects to increase the likelihood that your students will be more likely to stay engaged throughout the day.

CONSIDER STAFF ROUTINES

In addition to student routines, consider routines for yourself and the staff in your classroom. If you are an experienced educator, you may recognize that these are the things you wish you had known in your first year. Consider, for example:

- When you will plan your lessons, especially if you need to arrange time for collaborative planning with a co-teacher or your grade-level or subject-area team.
- When and how you will review, provide feedback on, and return student work.

- How you will communicate with volunteers, instructional assistants, various special or related service providers, and other individuals who enter your classroom, and how you will do so in a manner that does not interrupt instruction.
- When you will take care of your personal needs (e.g., going to the bathroom, having lunch, getting drinks of water, or procuring your favorite caffeinated beverage).
- When and how you will communicate with families and guardians, ensuring that you have multiple positive contacts with all of your students' families throughout each quarter.
- How you will keep track of committee meetings, duties, and all other "nonteaching" tasks assigned to you.
- How you will ensure that you continue to participate in meaningful professional development activities; to stay current and effective, teachers are lifelong learners.

Again, you can likely identify countless other routines in your day in addition to those mentioned above. Although you may eventually figure out how to manage your routines by trial and error, it would be better to talk with experienced teachers to gather ideas about how they organize their day and develop a consistent plan for how to manage the recurring routines in your day. That way, you can better deal with any disruptions and exceptions to your routines, as the majority of your routines will be on "autopilot."

Post Classroom Routines

Once you have collaboratively identified and described your classroom routines with students and staff, document them. For your students, post your daily schedule in a prominent location (e.g., on your whiteboard) and review it at the beginning of each class period, activity, or day. Again, consider the age and ability level of your students as you determine how and where to post routines. For some students, a detailed schedule on the board will be effective. For other students, a picture schedule may be more appropriate and useful. Depending on the diversity of ability and languages spoken within your classroom, you may need to consider posting in a variety of ways. For example, you may post your general schedule on the whiteboard for all students in one or more languages. Then, you may provide one student with a detailed written plan for the day that includes her personal schedule for any pull-out services or other activities she attends. For another student, you may tape a Velcro board to his desk that depicts a picture sequence of the activities for that day. You may ask his instructional assistant to review the student's schedule at the beginning of each day, work with him to complete each activity, assist him in removing the picture corresponding to that activity when he's done, and review the schedule to identify the next activity. For another student, you may provide the written schedule in Braille and provide additional verbal direction for anything presented visually.

In addition, post directions for specific routines in visible and meaningful locations in the classroom. For example, you may want to have a poster of the steps for entering the classroom within students' line of sight (e.g., on the door, by the whiteboard) as they enter the room. Clearly label materials and locations related to your routines (e.g., label the "in-box" where students turn in their homework or class assignments for your review) and post routines related to those materials and locations in appropriate places. For example, if you set up a station for students to pass through as they enter the room, you may post step-by-step instructions for students to (1) put homework in the in-box, (2) pick up any needed materials for the day, and

(3) walk to their seats and begin the warm-up activity. For students who cannot access visual content, ensure that there are auditory prompts or other strategies to prompt routines (see Center on PBIS et al., 2023). Again, consider how to differentiate posting routines to meet students' unique needs and ensure all students have access to the information.

For you and your staff, document your routines in a personal schedule using a calendar (perhaps one in your lesson plan book or accessible on your smart devices) or other self-management system that works for you. We find that electronic reminders are helpful, even for recurring tasks, and scheduling time to accomplish various activities (e.g., setting aside 2 hours per week to call or email families) is critical to staying on top of our personal routines.

Teach and Differentiate Classroom Routines

After you have collaboratively identified and described your classroom routines and developed strategies for posting them (e.g., writing on whiteboard, hanging posters, labeling locations and materials related to routines, making labels in Braille) in an accessible manner, it is critical to engage your students in explicit instruction and practice on what each routine looks and sounds like. To begin, introduce each routine, **model** what you expect students to do within each routine (or have "expert" students model for each other), and introduce where a poster or other strategy prompts the routine. Engage (or **lead**) students in an activity where they identify examples and nonexamples of what the routine looks like. Then "**test**" students by providing an opportunity to practice the routine (e.g., pretend it's the beginning of the day and practice entering the classroom) and provide specific feedback on what they did correctly (and incorrectly). Then be sure to provide ongoing reminders and monitor students as they engage in that routine in the future. (If you supervise staff, use a similar process to train and practice clear routines for the adults in your room.) Use data (i.e., observations of students' engaging in the routine) to guide your instruction. As we describe in the next chapter, you also want to explicitly teach students the classroom norms, or positively stated expectations, within each of the routines. This explicit social skills instruction—using a model–lead–test format—will further refine your students' understanding of shared norms or expectations within and across the classroom routines.

Arrange Your Classroom Environment to Promote Access and Contextually Appropriate Behavior

In addition to having clear predictable routines in your classroom, consider the physical arrangement of your classroom. As we mentioned, there is no one perfect floor plan or seating arrangement that will set all students up for success. However, there are some general guidelines that will promote access and contextually appropriate behavior in your classroom: minimize crowding and distraction, ensure adequate supervision, consider transitions and movements, match seating arrangements to your instructional approach, and use effective design to prevent predictable mistakes.

Minimize Crowding and Distraction

To the extent possible, consider strategies to minimize crowding and distraction in your classroom. Ensure visual displays are meaningful, instructionally relevant, and timely. For each object you consider posting on a wall or hanging from the ceiling, consider the purpose of posting and length of time you will display it. Posters that prompt expected academic and social behavior are clearly meaningful and instructionally relevant in your classroom. Displaying student work to celebrate effort and accomplishment is also important, but you should rotate work displayed so that work completed in September is not still on the wall in May. If your visual displays are purposeful, they are less likely to lead to distraction and more likely to prompt (or recognize) contextually appropriate behavior. In contrast, if you display everything students ever create or produce, you can imagine your classroom would look fairly distracting within the first month of school and be hard to navigate by winter break.

Similarly, arrange and select your furniture to minimize crowding (if possible). First, consider any object or piece of furniture you introduce into your classroom. Some things will assist with overall classroom organization (e.g., bins to organize materials, folders for lessons and assignments) and improve structure, but other things are just things. Wherever possible, remove excess clutter from your classroom and ensure that all students have access to relevant classroom spaces and activities. Consider students with unique physical (e.g., wheelchair users, students who use a cane), academic, social, emotional, or behavioral needs when designing the space. For example, if students would benefit from an opportunity to "take space," create a planned area in your room that supports students' use of calming routines. Second, consider arranging the furniture in your classroom to match your classroom routines. For example, if you routinely use centers or carpet activities in an elementary classroom, ensure that you have those zones set up in your classroom. Third, once you have observed students across the first couple of weeks of school, consider revising your arrangement if you or your students encounter challenges with accessibility (e.g., areas where some students do not have easy access to instructional materials), crowding (e.g., areas where students cluster during transitions), or distraction (e.g., students not able to focus on instruction because of proximity to materials).

Ensure Adequate Supervision

Regardless of the specific design or layout of your classroom, it is critical that you can actively supervise all areas. If existing structures (e.g., coat closets, lab tables) prevent you from seeing all portions of your classroom at the same time, consider where you need to stand and how you need to move during each activity or transition to ensure that you can adequately and actively supervise your students. At times, simple adjustments can improve your ability to supervise and support your students. For example, rather than having your back to the rest of your class if you are meeting with individual students, ensure that (1) you are facing the rest of the students, (2) you periodically scan your classroom, and (3) you take opportunities to provide positive (or corrective) behavior-specific feedback to the class regarding their ability to work independently throughout the time you are engaging in individual meetings.

Consider Transitions and Movement

As you plan your classroom layout, also consider how students will move throughout your classroom. Consider students' unique mobility needs as you plan the paths they will take as they enter and exit the room and move among classroom locations and activities. Ensure that you arrange furniture to create clear and easy movement paths, use visual or tactile prompts (e.g., tape on the floor, soft material on corners of desks) to facilitate effective "traffic flow," and adjust as needed after observing your students in the classroom.

Match Seating Arrangements to Instructional Approach

As you design your seating arrangements for students, consider your typical instructional approach. If you typically deliver teacher-directed instruction, having desks arranged in rows or columns facing forward may make sense. If you use a lot of cooperative learning group activities, arranging desks in clusters may be the most effective arrangement. If you have students who struggle to keep their bodies and materials to themselves, ensuring that desks are spaced more than an arm's length apart would be prudent. If your classroom is set up for flexible seating (e.g., different types of chairs, table sizes and heights, work spaces), consider how students will use these spaces and teach predicable routines (see the last section of this chapter!) and expectations (see the next chapter!) for how to engage in these spaces. Again, there is not a one-size-fits-all approach to seating arrangements. So, start with a thoughtful arrangement that matches the instructional activities you have planned and adjust as necessary.

Use Effective Design to Prevent Predictable Mistakes

Think about common mistakes that have occurred in your classroom in the past, and consider environmental strategies to prevent predictable mistakes. For example, rather than getting frustrated that students play with materials when they are supposed to be focused on other instructional activities, a teacher may hang a small curtain in front of the materials, which they can open when materials are available (or use another visual signal to remind students to pause before playing with materials).

Also be thoughtful about any unique circumstances your classroom presents. For example, you may not actually have your own classroom—you may move among classrooms or be assigned to an unconventional space (e.g., stage) to teach. In these circumstances, consider the best way to organize your materials to promote appropriate behaviors and prevent problems. For example, an itinerant teacher may arrive with an organized cart that has his expectations posted on the front of the cart, needed materials for students on the top shelf of the cart, and his personal teaching materials on the bottom shelf. A music teacher who is assigned to the stage may (1) use colored tape to create different "zones" for instruments, sheet music, and other materials (and tape can also define classroom boundaries if they are not clear) and (2) post and teach routines for each zone.

To summarize, the first principle of implementing effective classwide PBIS is to create an inclusive, predictable, and safe classroom environment. Specifically, we described guidelines for connecting with students and for identifying, describing, posting, teaching, and differentiating predictable routines with the students (and staff) in your classroom. We also discussed how the physical arrangement of your classroom should be carefully planned with your students in mind, considering their unique needs and learning histories, and adjusted according to your observations of student behavior and other data indicating a need. An effective classroom environment sets the stage for effective, actively engaging instruction.

ACTIVELY ENGAGE STUDENTS IN RELEVANT INSTRUCTION

We often say that good teaching (i.e., effective instructional design and delivery) is one of the best social, emotional, and behavioral support tools. A teacher can have clear routines, positive classroom norms or expectations, a well-executed recognition system, and other social, emotional, and behavioral supports to help students sit in their seats and appear ready to learn. However, if that teacher's instruction is not relevant, engaging, and effective, the other social, emotional, and behavioral supports will not be sufficient to facilitate learning or maintain contextually appropriate behavior. Effective instruction can also be an important protective factor that supports students' social, emotional, and behavioral needs (Simonsen, Goodman, et al., 2021).

Consider your students' interests, abilities, and unique learning histories when planning instruction to engage your students (Chaparro et al., 2015). Students should see themselves represented in the curriculum—in the authors and content of selected stories and texts, in the historical events and narratives prioritized in class, in the scientific discoveries, and in all other elements of the curriculum—throughout the school year (that is, not only during women's history, black history, disability awareness, pride, or other designated months; Leverson et al., 2021). Additionally, consider the prerequisite skills and knowledge students need to engage with the curriculum, and plan to preteach and provide additional differentiated support, as needed, to enable all students to access and participate in instruction. For example, ensure all instructional materials are available in accessible formats (e.g., Braille, large print, audio) and supported with appropriate assistive technology (e.g., communication devices set up to enable students to participate in instruction).

For all age groups, ability levels, and content areas, promoting active engagement is critical to increasing students' academic, social, emotional, and behavioral outcomes (Simonsen et al., 2008). Although there are a variety of content- or discipline-specific strategies to actively engage students, we focus on two general principles that are supported by extensive evidence and can be implemented in all contexts: deliver high rates of relevant **opportunities to respond (OTRs)**, and ensure that you provide a variety of OTRs. An OTR is any stimulus (e.g., teacher asking a question, peer making a request, computer presenting a task) that solicits an observable response from a student (e.g., verbal answer, written response).

Deliver High Rates of OTRs

Beyond the curriculum and content, consider culturally and developmentally relevant ways to engage students in meaningful instruction. One key way to ensure your instruction is actively engaging for your students is to provide high rates of instructionally relevant OTRs. Research indicates that increasing the rate of OTRs during instruction results in desired outcomes for students (e.g., increases in correct responding and desired behaviors and decreases in undesired behaviors; see MacSuga-Gage & Simonsen, 2015; Van Camp et al., 2020). Research is less clear about exactly what constitutes a "high rate" of OTRs across student characteristics (i.e., various age and ability ranges), instructional activities (e.g., teacher-directed instruction, independent seatwork), and academic content areas. For example, early recommendations for OTR rates during teacher-directed instruction suggested four to six OTRs per minute for new or initial learning and eight to 12 OTRs per minute for drill-style practice (Council for Exceptional Children, 1987). More recent descriptive studies suggest that effective teachers typically provide three to five OTRs per minute during teacher-directed instruction for simple responses (e.g., quick verbal or gestural responses) and as few as one OTR per minute if the responses are more complex (e.g., solving a math problem on a whiteboard; MacSuga-Gage & Simonsen, 2015). Further, if students are engaged in a prolonged task, like writing an essay, a teacher may provide only one OTR (writing prompt) every 10–30 minutes, but this OTR could still be effective if students are accurately and actively engaged in the task. Therefore, our general recommendation is to increase OTRs throughout your instructional activities, but do not sacrifice quality for quantity. In other words, do not rely *only* on drill-and-practice activities to increase OTRs. Instead, as we describe in the next section, we suggest providing a variety of OTRs, which may result in fluctuations in OTR rates. As always, use data on students' academic, social, emotional, and behavioral skills to monitor the effectiveness of your instructional practices and adjust the rate with which you present OTRs based on your data.

Use a Variety of OTRs

As you plan the types of OTRs you will use during instruction, consider both the ways you will provide the OTRs (your behavior) and the various types and modes of responding (student behavior). In general, research suggests that OTRs that (1) are presented to most or all students (e.g., mixed or unison responding) and (2) allow the teacher to determine the accuracy of student responding (e.g., response cards) are more effective than other types of OTRs (e.g., MacSuga-Gage & Simonsen, 2015). However, research is still emerging, and we recommend using a variety of strategies to increase OTRs.

Strategies for Providing OTRs

There are numerous ways, discussed below, that you can provide students with OTRs. During teacher-directed instruction, you may consider strategies to provide teacher-directed OTRs to students individually (individual responding; e.g., Haydon et al., 2009), all at once (unison responding), or some combination thereof (mixed responding). In addition, there are other strategies to provide OTRs during other types of instructional activities (i.e., partner or cooperative learning activities, computer-based instruction).

INDIVIDUAL RESPONDING

As the name implies, individual responding occurs when an OTR is presented to an individual student. Perhaps the most typical approach to individual responding is traditional hand raising, in which a teacher asks a question and calls on an individual student who raises their hand. The challenge with this approach is that the same students often raise their hands to participate while other students become disengaged. However, there are other alternatives to individual responding. Some teachers will ask a question, provide wait time, and then randomly call on a student (by pulling a name out of a container) to respond to the question. Thus, all students have an equal opportunity of being called on and are held accountable for being actively engaged in instruction. Other teachers insert a step after they ask a question wherein students have an opportunity to discuss their response with a partner before the teacher calls on someone to provide a response.

If you choose to use an individual-responding approach, be sure that you set up all students for success. For example, you may need to plan your questions ahead of time and preteach the questions and possible responses to students who struggle with the content or participation skills. That way, all students have a chance to give a "right" answer. You may also ask opinion questions, which do not have a right or wrong answer, and encourage participation from a range of students. In addition, consider employing other classwide PBIS strategies discussed in later chapters to (1) teach expectations for supporting peers during individual responding (Chapter 6) and (2) recognize efforts to participate using classwide reinforcement approaches (Chapter 7). With any type of solicited response, be sure you are accounting for the unique needs of your students. For example, students who are impacted by anxiety, who have receptive language disorders, or who react negatively to public attention may freeze when asked to respond in class; be sure to provide these students with additional support and strategies as needed.

UNISON RESPONDING

In contrast to individual responding, unison responding (e.g., choral responding, call and response) requires that all students respond simultaneously to the OTR. In other words, the teacher presents an OTR to the whole class and requests a classwide response. Like individual responding, unison responding may have challenges. For example, some students may wait to see how their peers respond and then jump on the bandwagon, especially if students are expected to respond verbally or with gestures. Even if each student responds based on their own understanding (rather than matching peer responses), it may be difficult for a teacher to identify the types of errors being made or who is making the errors in unison responding. However, these challenges can be addressed by (1) using different modes of responding (described subsequently); (2) teaching students a signal for responding (e.g., respond when teacher claps, snaps, or raises hand); and (3) defining and teaching students a routine for responding that includes listening to the question, thinking about their responses, waiting for the signal, and responding in the requested format when signaled to do so. Research indicates that unison responding is generally more effective (i.e., results in better student outcomes) than individual responding (MacSuga-Gage & Simonsen, 2015) as it results in all students experiencing higher rates of OTRs.

MIXED RESPONDING

It is also possible to combine individual and unison responding in a mixed responding approach. With mixed responding, you intersperse individual OTRs among unison OTRs. Preliminary research suggests that a ratio of 70% unison to 30% individual responding may be more effective than either approach in isolation (Haydon et al., 2009). This finding further supports the general guideline of providing a variety of OTRs.

OTHER STRATEGIES FOR PROVIDING OTRS

In addition to the discrete teacher-directed OTRs presented using individual, unison, or mixed responding, consider other strategies to increase OTRs in your classrooms. For example, you can set the occasion for peer-to-peer OTRs by using partner or cooperative group work. Although these strategies expand the ways in which you can increase OTRs in your classroom, they require more preteaching of routines and a greater level of active supervision to ensure that all students are receiving and benefiting from OTRs in these instructional contexts.

Modes of Responding

In addition to planning a variety of strategies for providing OTRs, think about various ways that students may respond. You may provide OTRs that solicit a variety of *types of responses*, including yes or no, multiple choice, or production responses. In addition, each type of response can be produced in a variety of *response modes*. A common mode of responding is **verbal**, in which students produce a response using spoken or signed language. Verbal responses may be used in individual, unison, or mixed responding; unison verbal responding is also called **choral responding** or **call and response**. As an alternative to verbal responding, teachers may ask students to respond with **gestures** (e.g., thumbs up or down, hold up a number of fingers corresponding to a choice), which may also be used in individual, unison, or mixed responding.

Response cards are another efficient mode of responding. Response cards may be pre-printed cards containing a range of responses or may be blank cards or whiteboards on which students write their responses. With either strategy, students select or produce their response and then hold up their card or board when signaled to do so. **Student response systems** (clickers, apps, online quizzes, etc.) are a high-tech version of response cards in which students press buttons (or type) on an electronic device to select a response, and the device interfaces with a smartboard (or similar technology) to produce a graph or visual representation of student responses. Response cards and student response systems are typically used in unison responding and allow a teacher to detect the type and source of errors. Finally, **written or production responses** may be used in individual (e.g., illustrate how to solve a problem on the smartboard) or unison (e.g., write your response on your own paper, solve the problem on your individual whiteboard) responding.

To select an appropriate mode of responding, consider the various task dimensions (Darch & Kame'enui, 2004), including the OTR strategy, type of desired response, and the purpose of the OTR. For example, if you are using OTRs to assess students' understanding or application of a skill, it may be critical that you identify the type and source of errors. Thus, you may choose to have each student produce a response on a whiteboard so you can quickly review responses by scanning the whiteboards. If you are using OTRs during a rapid review session, you may prefer quick verbal or gestural responses.

Additional Empirically Supported Instructional Practices to Increase OTRs

In addition to designing your own instruction to incorporate high rates of various types of OTRs, consider empirically supported practices that facilitate effective student engagement. Simonsen et al. (2008) identified the following empirically supported practices: direct instruction, classwide peer tutoring, computer-assisted instruction, and guided notes. In the next paragraphs, we provide a brief overview of each strategy.

DIRECT INSTRUCTION

Direct instruction (DI) is an instructional approach often characterized by a scripted curriculum and highly structured activities. DI is supported by an extensive evidence base demonstrating positive outcomes for students, particularly in the area of improving basic skills (e.g.,

Becker & Gersten, 1982; Frampton et al., 2021; Mason & Otero, 2021; White, 1988). Although evidence-based DI curricula are scripted, it is also possible to apply the principles of effective instructional design (see Engleman & Carnine, 1982) exemplified in DI to other types of instruction or content areas in which DI curricula are not available. For example, in Chapter 6 we recommend using an explicit instructional approach (i.e., following a model–lead–test format) to teach social skills. We also recommend scripting responses to students' appropriate and inappropriate behavior and identifying strategies to prompt and monitor student behavior in response to instruction. Each of these principles is consistent with a DI approach. In fact, we use DI principles to design our undergraduate- and graduate-level university courses.

CLASSWIDE PEER TUTORING

With classwide peer tutoring (CWPT), all students participate as both tutors and tutees (e.g., Greenwood et al., 1989). In other words, this is *not* a situation in which teachers use more advanced students to support less advanced students. When using CWPT approaches, teachers explicitly teach students the routines of the activity, and all students then work in pairs to "tutor," or provide review of content or reading, each other using fast-paced activities. Research supports positive outcomes for students participating in CWPT (Greenwood et al., 1989), though additional high-quality studies are needed before considering it an evidence-based practice (Cook et al., 2017).

COMPUTER-ASSISTED INSTRUCTION

As the name suggests, computer-assisted instruction (CAI) is instruction facilitated by a computer program or online application. Obviously not all CAI is created equal; however, there are several empirically supported programs that result in positive outcomes for students (e.g., Ota & DuPaul, 2002). Especially during periods of remote instruction (e.g., during the COVID-19 pandemic), teachers have relied on online and technology-based approaches to deliver and support instruction (Johnson et al., 2023; Ran et al., 2022). Further, advances in artificial intelligence, virtual reality, and other emerging technologies may continue to influence how teachers design and deliver instruction and how students access and produce information (Van Mechelen et al., 2023). Although technology will (hopefully!) never replace teachers, effective programming may result in instructional activities that are specifically geared to a student's individual response patterns (advancing or reviewing content based on student responses) and opportunities for immediate individualized feedback, which is often difficult for a teacher to provide in a timely way to each student in a classroom context.

GUIDED NOTES

Finally, if you work with older students and use a lecture format, guided notes can be an effective strategy for maintaining active engagement among your students (Konrad et al., 2009; Lazarus, 1993). Guided notes may include (1) graphic organizers (e.g., timelines, content webs) that students complete during a lecture; (2) notes in which the main idea is provided and students identify supporting details; and (3) fill-in-the-blank notes, which require students to pay attention to the lecture to complete the relevant portions of their notes. Again, this is a strategy that we find effective in our undergraduate- and graduate-level courses.

SUMMARY

In this chapter, we discussed three critical principles of classwide PBIS: connecting and fostering positive relationships with and among your students; creating an inclusive, predictable, and safe classroom environment; and actively engaging your students in relevant instruction. To connect with members of your classroom community, we suggested creating opportunities to learn about your students, communicating positive updates with students and families regularly, and using simple strategies, like positively greeting students at the door, to establish and enhance connections. To create an effective environment, we recommended (1) collaboratively identifying, defining, teaching, prompting, practicing, and differentiating predictable routines and (2) arranging the physical environment to promote access and contextually appropriate behavior.

To actively engage students in instruction, we discussed designing relevant instruction and providing high rates of various OTRs, but we also noted that you should not sacrifice quality for quantity. In addition, we discussed a variety of strategies for providing OTRs (e.g., teacher-directed individual, unison, and mixed responding and peer- or group-based strategies) that can be used in conjunction with a variety of response types (e.g., yes or no, multiple choice, or production) and modes (e.g., verbal, gestural, response cards, written) to create endless OTR possibilities. We emphasized considering students' unique abilities and learning histories when designing and differentiating OTRs to ensure each student can access, engage in, and benefit from OTRs. We also suggested that you consider adopting and implementing a variety of other empirically supported practices to actively engage students in your instruction, including direct instruction, classwide peer tutoring, computer-assisted instruction, or guided notes as appropriate for your content and learners.

For each practice related to the three classwide PBIS principles covered in this chapter, we also suggested that you (1) select strategies that are likely to work, based on suggested guidelines and empirical evidence; (2) collect data to monitor and evaluate the effectiveness of each practice; and (3) adjust your practices as indicated by the data. (See Figure 5.1 for a checklist of classroom practices related to connecting, creating an effective environment, and actively engaging students.)

PHASES OF LEARNING ACTIVITIES: CHAPTER 5

Acquisition

1. Develop (or borrow) a survey to learn about your students' individual learning histories (e.g., experiences that influenced them and shaped how they engage in your classroom), needs, and preferences. Use the survey to gather information on one or more students, and consider how you would use that information to adjust instruction.

2. Design a classroom layout that addresses the suggested guidelines for physically arranging your classroom to create an inclusive, predictable, and safe environment.

3. Select a 15-minute segment of your instruction that you will focus on for increasing OTRs. For 3 days, collect data on your current rate of OTR use. Then identify strategies to increase the rate and variety of OTRs you include in your classroom.

Instructions: Complete this foundational practices checklist to assess the extent to which you have (1) connected and fostered positive relationships with and among your students; (2) created an inclusive, predictable, and safe classroom environment in your classroom; and (3) actively engaged students with your instruction. Mark "yes" for each item you have completed, scheduled, and/or reviewed, as necessary; mark "IP" (in process) for each item that you are in the process of completing; mark "no" if you have not started this item; and mark "?" if you need further information. For each item marked "no" or "?," consult with a behavioral expert (e.g., mentor teacher, special support staff, administrator) to request assistance or review content in this book and additional recommended resources for further information.

	Yes	IP	No	?
CONNECT AND FOSTER POSITIVE RELATIONSHIPS				
1. Have you taken time to **get to know your students** (i.e., understand each of your student's learning history, unique needs, and preferences)?				
2. Are you **positively and proactively communicating** with members of your classroom community on a regular basis (e.g., biweekly email)?				
3. Are you **positively greeting** each student at the door at least daily?				
CREATE AN INCLUSIVE, PREDICTABLE, AND SAFE CLASSROOM ENVIRONMENT				
Define, Teach, Prompt, and Practice Predictable Classroom Routines				
1. Have you **identified** and **described** typical classroom routines for your students and staff (including yourself)?				
2. Are key routines **posted and prompted?**				
3. Have you **taught** and **differentiated** routines to set each student up for success?				
Arrange Your Classroom Environment to Promote Access and Contextually Appropriate Behavior				
1. Does your classroom layout reflect student's **unique needs,** promote **accessibility and engagement,** and **minimize crowding and distraction?**				
2. Are you able to **adequately monitor and supervise** all areas?				
3. Have you planned and adjusted for transitions and **movement?**				
4. Have you created a **seating arrangement** that matches your instructional approach and allows all students to meaningfully participate in instruction?				
5. Have you used effective design to **prevent** predictable problems?				
ACTIVELY ENGAGE STUDENTS IN RELEVANT INSTRUCTION				
Present High Rates of Opportunities to Respond (OTRs)				
1. Have you considered students' unique **learning histories** (i.e., individual and cultural backgrounds) and needs when planning academic content?				
2. Do you present OTRs at a **rate** of three to five "simple" (short response) or one "complex" (production response) OTR(s) per minute during teacher-directed instruction?				
3. Do you **adjust** your rate of OTRs based on student academic and behavioral data?				
Present Varied OTRs				
1. Have you used **various strategies** for student responding (individual, unison, mixed, or peer-to-peer responding) during instruction?				
2. Have you included multiple **modes of responding** (verbal, gestural, response card, written, etc.) across OTRs during instruction?				
3. Have you incorporated appropriate **empirically supported strategies** to increase your OTRs (e.g., direct instruction, classwide peer tutoring, computer-assisted instruction, and guided notes)?				
4. Have you considered students' **unique needs** when planning the OTR strategies and modes of responding to ensure all students have the opportunity to engage in and benefit from OTRs?				

FIGURE 5.1. A checklist of classroom practices related to structure and active engagement.

Fluency

1. Positively greet students at the door each day for a week. Make notes about one detail you learned about each student (e.g., favorite sports team, after-school activity) in the quick interaction that you can use to connect with them again on a future day.

2. Collaborate with members of your classroom community (students, staff) to identify, describe, and teach at least three specific routines (e.g., beginning of class, cooperative group work, end of class).

3. Implement strategies you identified in Acquisition Activity 2 to increase OTRs and continue to monitor the rate with which you provide OTRs to students for the next 10 days.

Maintenance

1. Collect and review data on students' academic, social, emotional, and behavioral skills to determine whether the routines (including your positive greeting) and physical arrangement in your classroom are sufficient to promote access and contextually appropriate behavior.

2. Examine data you collected during Fluency Activity 2 and student data you collected to evaluate your use of OTRs. If data indicate that your OTR rate is consistent with guidelines discussed in this chapter and supporting positive student outcomes, fade your monitoring to weekly (and then biweekly) checks to maintain your current level of OTRs over time. (If your rate is not consistent or students are not benefiting, return to Acquisition Activity 1 and repeat this sequence.)

Generalization

1. Implement strategies to increase positive connections among your students and other members of your classroom community (e.g., insert peer communication opportunities in your OTRs; have students greet each other as they enter the classroom; designate a time to teach and practice social, emotional, and behavioral skills that support peer relationships).

2. Collaborate with members of your classroom community (students, staff) to identify, describe, and teach at least three additional routines (e.g., independent seatwork, teacher-directed instruction, safety drills) and use data to monitor student behavior for all taught routines.

3. Select a different instructional activity and repeat Acquisition Activity 2, Fluency Activity 2, and Maintenance Activity 2 for this instructional activity.

Other Skill-Building Exercises

1. Modify an aspect of the physical arrangement in your classroom and observe how student behavior changes (if it does) in response to your redesigned environment.

2. Increase the variety of OTRs you provide in your classroom by brainstorming a list of potential OTRs with members of your grade-level or discipline-specific team and your students.

CHAPTER 6

Establish and Teach Positively Stated Norms or Expectations

CHAPTER OBJECTIVES

By the end of this chapter, you should be able to . . .

1. Collaboratively select and define a few positively stated classroom norms or expectations.
2. Develop a plan to roll out classroom expectations (i.e., create a social skills unit).
3. Create individual lesson plans to explicitly teach each expectations in the context of each classroom routine.
4. Plan additional strategies to promote social skill generalization and maintenance.
5. Integrate academic, social, emotional, and behavioral skills instruction.

Imagine This: *You work in a school that is implementing schoolwide PBIS. Staff members have taught students how to follow expectations for all of the nonclassroom settings; all staff members are expected to implement a schoolwide token economy to recognize expected behaviors in the hallway, cafeteria, and other nonclassroom settings; and the principal mentioned that teachers should also teach students what is expected in their classroom. Schoolwide data indicate that ODRs are down (compared to the previous year) in every setting except the classroom, and you continue to hear teachers raise concerns about students' behavior in faculty meetings.*

As you are sitting and wondering what's going on in the classrooms in your building, the teacher next door, Ms. Hall, peeks her head into your classroom and asks if you have a couple of minutes to chat (i.e., complain and vent). She tells you that she has posted her classroom schedule and spends hours designing her academic lesson plans to actively engage her students by providing high rates of OTRs (as suggested in the previous chapter). However, she still finds herself struggling with students who "barely follow" her routines, often interrupt her instruction, and are otherwise "disrespectful" toward her, their peers, and her classroom environment.

"Shouldn't they just know better?" she says in an exasperated tone.

You reply, "Well, that would be nice. But have you and your students defined, explicitly taught, and practiced the schoolwide norms or expectations in your classroom routines?"

"Well, I have the expectations posted in my room, if that's what you mean," she replies.

You quickly realize that she has not implemented one of the most critical features of classwide PBIS: she has not defined or taught the schoolwide norms or expectations in her classroom. You also hear in the content and tone of her statements that she may not be fully engaging her students in defining, teaching, and practicing routines. You sit down to help her get started with engaging her students to define their shared classroom norms or expectations.

OVERVIEW OF POSITIVELY STATED NORMS OR EXPECTATIONS

In the previous chapter, we described strategies to connect with students and families; create an inclusive, predictable, and safe classroom environment; and actively engage students in relevant instruction. In this chapter, we turn to establishing and explicitly teaching positively stated classroom norms or expectations for all routines and instructional activities. In other words, this chapter is all about social, emotional, and behavioral skills instruction. In the past, teachers used to assume that students would walk into their classroom and know how to behave; teachers believed their job was to teach academics only. However, we now understand students benefit from support to develop necessary social, emotional, and behavioral skills to (1) engage in learning, (2) take care of themselves (e.g., engage in self-management, ask for help when needed), and (3) get along with peers, teachers, and staff. In short, students need to be taught social, emotional, and behavioral skills to succeed in school (e.g., Gresham et al., 2001).

Research supports the use of both evidence-based social skills curricula and teacher-created social skills lessons in improving desired outcomes (and decreasing undesired outcomes) for students (see Simonsen et al., 2008). Although social, emotional, and behavioral skills are ideally taught and emphasized schoolwide (e.g., Simonsen, Myers, et al., 2012) as we described in Chapter 3, it is also important to establish and teach classwide norms or expectations in addition to (or especially in the absence of) schoolwide instruction. Because our specific focus is on teaching expected classroom social, emotional, and behavioral skills, we describe how you can develop and teach your own social, emotional, and behavioral skills lessons; however, you may also want to consider adopting an evidence-based program or curriculum if data indicate there is a need. In the next sections, we describe how to (1) select and define positively stated classroom norms or expectations; (2) develop a plan for initial rollout of classroom expectations; (3) create individual lessons for explicitly teaching social, emotional, and behavioral skills connected to classroom expectations; and (4) plan for maintenance and generalization of skills throughout the school year.

SELECT AND DEFINE POSITIVELY STATED NORMS OR EXPECTATIONS FOR YOUR CLASSROOM

The first step in teaching classwide PBIS norms or expectations is selecting them! In this section, we present guidelines for selecting and defining classroom expectations in the context of classroom routines.

Select Classwide PBIS Norms or Expectations

Classroom norms or expectations should reflect shared values and learning histories of your classroom community (students and educators). In some districts, we've heard that the word *expectations* communicates an exclusively teacher-directed set of requirements for student behavior that may reflect the teachers' own preferences or learning history, and may not reflect the students and broader classroom community. In those districts, they moved away from selecting *expectations* and moved toward collectively defining shared *norms*. Whichever label you use, the process used to arrive at a shared understanding of contextually and culturally relevant norms or expectations is critical. We have used both words in the introduction to this chapter (and in the previous five chapters); we will use *expectations* going forward (as it's more consistent with other resources).

The following guidelines will assist you in selecting positively stated expectations with your students for your shared classroom community. First, select a *small number* of expectations. As we mentioned in Chapter 3, most students (and teachers) can remember three to five expectations. Therefore, selecting a small number of expectations increases the likelihood that the expectations will be remembered.

Second, state your expectations *positively*. In other words, focus on what *to* do (i.e., skills or behaviors to increase), as opposed to what *not* to do (i.e., behaviors to decrease). This is important, as it (1) is a step toward creating a positive classroom environment; (2) requires members of your classroom community to consider what you want to see in your classroom, which is sometimes harder than thinking about what you do not want to see in your classroom; (3) prompts students to engage in the desired behaviors instead of prompting the undesired behaviors; and (4) prevents students from finding the one thing you left off a "no, stop, and don't do" list of rules—skilled students can always find at least one thing you forgot to tell them not to do.

Third, choose expectations that are general enough to encompass the full range of expected or contextually appropriate behaviors and are applicable across all of your routines and settings. We sometimes refer to these as "umbrella" expectations, as many contextually appropriate behaviors and skills fall under the umbrella of the general expectations. Return to the concept of **general case programming** introduced in Chapter 2. Your goal should be to choose positively stated expectations that will prompt the general case of contextually appropriate behavior in your classroom. (We discuss the "programming" piece when we get to developing and teaching the expectations via explicit social, emotional, and behavioral skills instruction.)

Finally, if you are in a school that is implementing schoolwide PBIS or already has a small number of positively stated expectations, you should *adopt the same expectations* for your classroom. Consistency across all settings is important for all students, especially students who have elevated social, emotional, and behavioral needs. However, if you teach in a school with a 20-page student code of conduct that contains all of the consequences for breaking negatively stated rules, *please* create your own set of positively stated expectations for your classroom!

Within these guidelines (i.e., small number, positively stated, general, and consistent with positive schoolwide expectations), there are countless options for what your expectations may look like. As we stated, if your school has adopted positive schoolwide expectations (e.g., Take Care of Self, Others, and Environment), adopt these as your classroom expectations. Otherwise, some teachers and students choose a fun acronym based on their names, a classroom mascot or slogan, or another meaningful word that helps students recall each expectation. If your school does not have positive expectations, create your own list of expectations. Consider the following scenarios:

• Ms. Sammy works in a school that has three schoolwide expectations: Respect Others, Self, and Environment. Therefore, she and her students select "ROSE" as the acronym for their classroom expectations, and they begin to consider what ROSE looks like in their classroom.

• Mr. Perez teaches science in a school that does not have positively stated schoolwide expectations. His students are excited about an acronym based on astronomy—their favorite topic in his class. So, they begin with an acronym (STAR) and select expectations that are important to them for each letter: Safety, Teamwork, Achievement, and Respect. They realize this allows them to easily translate their expectations into slogans (Aim for the STARs!) and incorporate them into a classroom recognition system (STAR bucks).

Define Expectations within Classroom Routines Using a Matrix

Once you adopt or select classroom expectations, the next step is to operationally define what each expectation "looks and sounds like" in the context of all classroom routines. An easy way to start is to develop a classroom matrix, as we discussed for schoolwide expectations in Chapter 3 (see Figure 6.1 for a template of a classroom matrix). In the matrix, classroom expectations become row headings, and the classroom routines (discussed in Chapter 5) become column headings. Thus, the matrix defines what contextually appropriate behaviors look like in the classroom: it describes which behaviors—or social, emotional, and behavioral skills—are appropriate in the context of each routine. For example, raising one's hand to participate may be contextually appropriate during teacher-directed instruction and contextually inappropriate during small-group discussions (when students participate in a conversational style).

Because it is not possible to identify every example of contextually appropriate behavior in the matrix, we apply the concepts of general case programming (Chapter 2) in selecting examples that teach the range of contextually appropriate behaviors. At the intersection of each expectation with each routine (i.e., in the "boxes" in the middle), provide a few examples of social, emotional, and behavioral skills that are consistent with that expectation for that routine. That is, use a few general statements to illustrate what it looks like to demonstrate the expectation (row header) within the routine (column header). For example, for students to be safe (expectation) when transitioning (routine), they may (1) walk slowly; (2) keep their hands, feet, and materials to themselves; and (3) proceed directly to the next location. Consider the following examples for Ms. Sammy and Mr. Perez:

• In Ms. Sammy's classroom, students demonstrate respect for self (expectation) when completing independent seatwork (routine) by (1) trying their best, (2) helping a peer (if it's an OK time to do so), and (3) raising their hands to ask for help from the teacher when needed. Educators demonstrate respect for others (expectation) when supporting students during seatwork (routine) by (1) moving about the classroom, (2) answering questions or providing gentle redirections in a calm and quiet voice, and (3) recognizing students' efforts and social, emotional, and behavioral skills with specific praise.

		ROUTINES				
EXPECTATIONS		• • •	• • •	• • •	• • •	• • •
		• • •	• • •	• • •	• • •	• • •
		• • •	• • •	• • •	• • •	• • •

FIGURE 6.1. A classroom expectations-within-routines matrix. This matrix may be used to define your expectations for all classroom routines. The expectations, routines, and definitions should be designed to be contextually and culturally relevant for each setting and population.

- In Mr. Perez's classroom, students and educators show teamwork (expectation) during cooperative group work (routine) by (1) using active listening, (2) taking turns with participation, (3) responding kindly to others' comments and questions, and (4) contributing to the completion of the task.

We encourage you to engage students in developing your matrix. This will help ensure the language and examples are relevant for your students and considerate of their unique and collective learning histories. Also, they may be great at generating additional skills to prioritize and examples to include in the matrix. To help teachers think about how to engage students in this activity, McIntosh et al. (2023) created an example lesson plan for "co-creating classroom expectations with students." Although that resource focuses on students in elementary classrooms, teachers can use similar approaches to engage students in secondary classrooms.

As you develop your matrix with your students, try to ensure that there is minimal overlap among your expectations. In other words, examples of skills consistent with one expectation should not overlap with those of another expectation. You may find that creating your matrix results in revising or refining your expectations or routines. Thus, it's a good idea to complete this activity, at least as a draft, before finalizing classroom expectations (e.g., having students make posters). For example, if you selected "responsibility" and "achievement" as two of your expectations, you may find that it is hard to differentiate those two concepts, as many responsible behaviors will lead to achievement and vice versa. Therefore, you may choose to select only one of these and identify a different expectation that results in less overlap. Similarly, you may realize that you expect similar things across several routines, like entering the classroom, leaving the classroom, and moving among activities within the classroom. Thus, you may group these three routines into a general "transition" routine (see an example of a completed matrix presented in Figure 6.2). Once you have a draft of your expectations-within-routines matrix, you are ready to develop (1) a plan for initial rollout of classroom expectations and (2) individual lesson plans to explicitly teach each expectation within each routine (i.e., each box of your matrix; see Robbie et al., 2022, for further guidance and Center on PBIS, 2020, for a downloadable "Creating Effective Classroom Environments" plan template that includes a fillable matrix).

In the process of drafting the classroom matrix, ask students to complete a "personal matrix," either independently or with their families, to describe what expectations look like across one or more routines in their homes and community settings (see Leverson et al., 2021, pp. 47–51). As part of this activity, the classroom community can "validate and affirm" their unique and shared learning histories, adjust their classroom matrix to better incorporate students' learning histories, and "build" (i.e., explicitly identify where different behaviors are appropriate in school, home, and community contexts) and "bridge" (i.e., provide opportunities to practice with supportive feedback) contextually appropriate behaviors that are unique to classroom routines (see examples in Leverson et al., 2021, pp. 54–56). The personal matrix activity can facilitate a shared understanding of contextually appropriate behaviors, improve teachers' perceptions of students' contextually appropriate behaviors (Muldrew & Miller, 2021), and support improved equity in teachers' practice, when accompanied by additional supports (e.g., Gion et al., 2022). In addition, staff may engage in a similar activity to consider how their norms have changed over time and across contexts (Leverson et al., 2021, pp. 52–52). Consider the lessons learned from the personal matrix activity when developing a plan to roll out your classroom expectations.

ROUTINES				
Transitions	**Teacher-Directed Instruction**	**Cooperative Group Work**	**Independent Seatwork**	**Taking Care of Personal Needs**

EXPECTATIONS		Transitions	Teacher-Directed Instruction	Cooperative Group Work	Independent Seatwork	Taking Care of Personal Needs
	Kindness	• Use an "indoor" voice • Help others if needed/asked • Follow specific teacher directions	• Actively listen to the teacher • Quietly raise your hand to ask a question or contribute	• Actively listen to your peers • Use positive and constructive language	• Work quietly and maintain a distraction-free environment • Help a peer (when it's OK to do so)	• Quietly and discreetly take care of business • Raise your hand if you or a peer need teacher assistance
	Responsibility	• Bring needed materials • Turn in work, as appropriate • Move efficiently between locations	• Take notes on content • Ensure you have only appropriate materials out • Ask if you need clarification on content or instructions	• Actively contribute to the group discussion and task • Complete your share of the work • Note any follow-up work to be completed	• Label your work • Do your own best work • Ask for help if needed	• When possible, take care of needs during transitions • Take brief breaks when needed • Fill your water bottle during transitions; leave it on your desk when not in use
	Safety	• Walk slowly • Keep hands, feet, and materials to self • Proceed directly to next location	• Stay in your own learning space • Keep hands, feet, and materials to self	• Remain in your own learning space • Use materials as instructed • Use calm language if disagreements arise	• Stay in your own learning space • Use materials as instructed • Keep hands, feet, and materials to self	• Walk efficiently and directly between locations • Alert teacher to anything unsafe • Ask for support if you feel unsafe

FIGURE 6.2. This classroom expectations-within-routines matrix illustrates how expectations may be defined across classroom routines for a middle school content classroom.

DEVELOP A PLAN FOR AN INITIAL ROLLOUT OF CLASSWIDE PBIS EXPECTATIONS

Your matrix provides a great foundation for developing an initial plan for teaching, prompting, monitoring, and reinforcing (i.e., "rolling out") your expectations. The matrix is a map for establishing *stimulus control* (recall or review that term from Chapter 2) between the classroom routines (instructional stimuli) and a range of contextually appropriate behaviors that will be taught and reinforced within each routine. Therefore, you may think of your matrix as the start of a social, emotional, and behavioral skills "unit plan." When you develop any unit plan, you should determine the initial scope and sequence, plan for a desired level of student involvement, differentiate for students with unique needs, develop an evaluation or assessment plan for the unit, and identify strategies to promote and recognize skill use for the unit.

Determine Scope and Sequence

As you begin to plan your rollout, first consider how you will prioritize skills and when you will teach your initial social, emotional, and behavioral skills lessons. Some teachers (and schools) will prioritize social, emotional, and behavioral skills instruction during the first week of school and allocate the majority of instructional time to teaching students how to engage in contextually appropriate behaviors in all classroom routines (and school settings). Other teachers will introduce their expectations at the beginning of the first day of school but wait to systematically teach expectations within each routine as each new routine occurs within the typical instructional plan. For example, rather than teaching expectations in the context of cooperative learning groups during the first week of school, the teacher may wait until cooperative learning groups occur "naturally" in their classroom for the first time. Then, when introducing the new routine, the teacher may review expectations within that routine and focus on one expectation during the initial lesson. The next time cooperative learning groups occur, the teacher may review general expected behavior and focus on a second expectation, then repeat this process each time the routine occurs until all expectations are explicitly taught within that routine.

From research studies and expert recommendations, it is not clear that one approach is better than the other. Instead, it is clear that (1) social, emotional, and behavioral skills (i.e., contextually appropriate behavior consistent with classroom expectations) should be explicitly taught, (2) instruction should occur in context of the natural routine or setting, and (3) follow-up strategies are likely needed to promote skill use and generalization (e.g., Sugai & Lewis, 1996). Given these recommendations, it may be most effective to provide an initial introduction to your classroom expectations—that is, teach the general case of expected behavior in your classroom—and follow up with routine-specific lessons as each routine is introduced during the first weeks of school (and revisit throughout the year).

Plan for Student Involvement

Create opportunities to include students' ideas and voices in your unit plan. In addition to engaging students in developing the classroom matrix, get them involved in aspects of planning lessons (e.g., creating videos to illustrate expectation-following behaviors, developing games to review expectations) and ask for their input on strategies to promote and recognize social, emotional, and behavioral skills that are consistent with classroom expectations (i.e., skills in your classroom matrix). Even when students are involved in developing the matrix, unit, and lesson plans, it's critical to explicitly teach each expectation in each routine to set all students up for success. In other words, talking about what goes into the matrix or a lesson plan is very different from explicitly teaching and practicing (with feedback) how to use each of the skills in a contextually appropriate manner throughout classroom routines.

Develop an Evaluation Plan

As we describe in the next section, each individual lesson should include a plan to assess students' understanding and application of the targeted social skill (i.e., demonstrating social, emotional, and behavioral skills consistent with one expectation within one routine). In addition, you should consider general strategies to evaluate your overall unit plan. Typically, academic units end with a "unit test." However, a paper-and-pencil activity is less likely to capture the extent to which students appropriately use their social, emotional, and behavioral skills (i.e., contextually appropriate behaviors) in all classroom routines. Therefore, develop a plan to evaluate contextually appropriate behaviors for all classroom routines, either by (1) relying on the series of assessment plans included across individual lessons or (2) developing a general system to track students' behavior.

Recall (or quickly review) the measurement strategies discussed in Chapter 4 and apply those concepts to measuring contextually appropriate behavior in your matrix. For example, you may choose to randomly select one expectation and one routine each day and sample a 15-minute window within that routine to measure students' behavior. During that brief observation, you may tally the number of times students engage in social, emotional, and behavioral skills that are consistent with classroom expectations (e.g., demonstrate kindness during teacher-directed instruction by raising hand before speaking), use momentary time sampling to assess the percentage of students who are demonstrating contextually appropriate behavior (e.g., showing responsibility by quietly working during independent seatwork at the end of each 2-minute interval), or use additional measurement approaches to assess contextually appropriate behavior across classroom routines. As we said in Chapter 4, keep any measurement plan as simple as possible to meet the intended purpose (i.e., monitor expectation-following behavior for all routines and times).

Identify Strategies to Promote and Recognize Skill Use

Even with the best instruction, you will want to plan strategies to promote and recognize students' skill use to increase the likelihood that their social, emotional, and behavioral skills maintain and generalize. Again, skill-specific strategies are included in each lesson plan (as we describe in the next section), and you may want to consider general strategies that you implement for all expectations in all classroom routines. General visual and auditory prompts, like posters with your expectations and verbal reminders, are a great place to start. We also suggest greeting students as they enter the classroom and providing brief verbal reminders at the beginning of each classroom routine to prompt expected behaviors. (Remember, this is also a great strategy to connect with your students, as we described in Chapter 5.)

Use behavior-specific praise to recognize students demonstrating expected behavior during routines. You could also develop a recognition system in conjunction with your evaluation plan. For example, if you randomly select an expectation and routine each day and sample student behavior using an appropriate measurement system (as described previously), you could implement a classwide recognition system in which students earn points on days that they are "caught" engaging in contextually appropriate behaviors related to the "mystery" expectation during the "mystery" time; when they earn a specified number of points, they may earn access to a classroom privilege (e.g., listening to music during work, completing assignments with preferred materials, choosing a fun activity during recess, using electronic devices at the end of the class period) or other reward. (We will discuss additional strategies to acknowledge and increase contextually appropriate behavior in Chapter 7.)

DEVELOP AND DELIVER EXPLICIT
SOCIAL, EMOTIONAL, AND BEHAVIORAL SKILLS LESSONS

Once you have your overall plan for how you will roll out your social, emotional, and behavioral skills unit, it is time to develop individual lessons to explicitly teach each expectation within each routine. That is, develop a lesson plan to teach each "box" in your classroom matrix. A good social skills lesson plan contains clearly articulated foundational features (i.e., lesson focus, objective, materials, and teaching examples/nonexamples); explicit instructional activities to teach contextually appropriate behavior during the lesson (i.e., model, lead, and test); and follow-up activities to promote skill fluency, maintenance, and generalization following the lesson. Figure 6.3 presents a lesson plan template that includes all of these features (reprinted from Simonsen, Myers, et al., 2012). As you become more fluent in teaching social skills, you may be able to write a less detailed lesson plan. During the acquisition phase, however, you should script your lesson plan and provide sufficient detail to enable successful instruction.

Build a Strong Foundation for Each Lesson

Prior to considering how you will teach the lesson, clearly articulate the focus, objectives, and needed materials for your lesson. In addition, carefully plan your teaching examples and nonexamples to increase the likelihood of successfully teaching the "general case" of expectation following within the identified routine and decrease the likelihood of teaching misrules. In the following paragraphs, we provide additional suggestions for each of these components, including how to engage your students in collaboratively designing and implementing these lessons.

Identify the Lesson Focus

The lesson focus identifies the expectation you will teach and the routine on which you will focus. For example, your lesson may focus on being respectful during teacher-directed instruction. After your initial rollout of your social, emotional, and behavioral skills unit, you may want to include additional topics, like getting help, being a good friend, or interviewing for a job, based on identified areas of need for your students. Thus, this section will be helpful as you develop a more complete sequence of initial and follow-up lessons in your unit.

Write a Learning Objective

After you have described your lesson focus, write a clear instructional or learning objective for your lesson. Like the outcome statements presented in Chapter 4, effective learning objectives have four parts: the *conditions* in which the skill is expected, the *individuals* expected to demonstrate the contextually appropriate behavior, a clear description of the contextually appropriate *behavior*, and the *criteria* for success (i.e., meeting objective). An effective objective should also be aligned with your evaluation strategies (described in the section on follow-up activities for each lesson). For example, if Ms. Golden was teaching students to be responsible during transitions, her lesson objective might be: "Given transitions between classes and activities (*condition*), students (*individuals*) will demonstrate responsibility by cleaning up their space,

Social Skill Lesson Plan

Lesson Focus:

Demonstrating _____ (expectation) in _____ (setting).

Teaching Objective:

Following instruction, students will demonstrate _____ (expectation) in _____ (setting) by _____ _____ (describe behaviors) across _____ out of _____ sampled opportunities (criteria).

Teaching Examples:

Positive Examples	Negative Examples
•	•
•	•
•	•

Lesson Materials:

Lesson Activities:

Model:
Lead:
Test:

Follow-Up Activities:

Strategies to prompt:
Procedures to reinforce:
Procedures to correct behavioral errors:
Procedures to monitor/supervise:
Procedures to collect and evaluate student data:

FIGURE 6.3. Social skill lesson plan. This lesson plan includes the critical features described for teaching a classroom expectation within a classroom routine. From Simonsen et al. (2012b). Copyright © 2012 Sage Publications. Reprinted by permission.

bringing materials required for the next activity, and following directions to move to the next location or activity (*behaviors*) during 9 out of 10 transitions sampled after the lesson (*criteria*)." As implied by this objective, her evaluation plan would involve observing all students during the next 10 transitions and noting whether each student demonstrated responsibility during that transition. Once each student has demonstrated responsibility during 9 out of 10 transitions, they have met the learning objective. (Students who are not able to meet the objective may need further instruction or support.)

Plan for Needed Materials

To assist in effectively delivering your instruction, identify and create needed materials for your lesson. This is a great step to engage students in developing content for their own class or for your future classes. If you plan to use video clips, for example, ask students to record brief examples or to find existing example videos to model the skill, and include hyperlinks to those files within your lesson plan to save time trying to find them later. (If you use the same lesson over many years, be sure to check and update these links prior to teaching the lesson each time.) If you plan to use role plays during your activities, engage students in preparing scripts for those ahead of time and attach them to the lesson plan. If you need additional staff resources (e.g., a second adult to assist you with modeling a skill), note those resources as well to ensure that you are fully prepared to teach your lesson.

Select Appropriate Teaching Examples and Nonexamples

Perhaps the most important component of your lesson plan is selecting appropriate teaching examples and nonexamples. Your goal is to teach expected behavior that will maintain across time and generalize across similar activities (e.g., all types of teacher-directed instruction). Thus, you want to approach your selection of teaching examples and nonexamples with the goal of general case programming. (This would be a good time to briefly review content on choosing examples to teach the general case in Chapter 2.) When selecting examples and nonexamples, consider selecting (1) examples that highlight the range of contextually appropriate behaviors for each expectation (to promote response generalization or adaptation); (2) examples that also illustrate the variety of conditions in which the behaviors are expected (to promote generalization across the desired stimulus class); and (3) nonexamples that help your students clearly discriminate between contextually appropriate and contextually inappropriate behaviors.

Most students will understand the gross discriminations between contextually appropriate and contextually inappropriate behaviors. For example, most students understand that hitting is unsafe and standing with a 10-foot space bubble is safe. However, many students (and some adults!) struggle with the "gray areas" or identifying "the line" where contextually appropriate crosses into contextually inappropriate behavior for a given routine. For example, when do humor and sarcasm transition from funny and respectful to inappropriate and disrespectful? When does playful teasing become verbal aggression? By choosing examples that help students with those minimal discriminations, you can increase the likelihood that most students will be successful in identifying and using contextually appropriate behavior. Consider the following examples and nonexamples of kind behavior during cooperative group work:

Examples

- Tom actively listens (watches, nods in recognition, and takes notes) as his peers discuss their point of view, and he contributes his own point of view when it's his turn to participate.
- Joan works with her peers to identify components of the task that the group needs to complete for homework, and together they assign equal parts of the work to each member of the group.
- Hector politely states that he disagrees with a peer's point of view, asks the peer to clarify, and provides evidence to support his own point of view. When the peer still disagrees, they calmly agree to respect each other's point of view and move on.

Nonexamples

- Tom looks around the room when his peers are talking and interrupts to interject the "right" way to view something (i.e., his way).
- Joan grabs the list of remaining tasks, tells her peers who is doing what, and assigns the least amount of work to herself.
- Hector grumbles under his breath that his peer's point of view is stupid but refuses to comment audibly when asked. When Hector is asked to discuss his point of view, he stares out the window and ignores his peers.

As illustrated by the above examples and nonexamples, there are many facets to demonstrating contextually appropriate behavior and many ways students can make mistakes. (Imagine if you just told students to "be kind" and left it to your students to decide what that meant. You'd be at the mercy of each student's learning history with that expectation!) Therefore, it's always a good idea to put thought into your examples and nonexamples: consider possible misrules or mistakes related to that expectation, review common mistakes that have occurred within that routine, and select examples and nonexamples that minimize future errors and maximize students' likelihood of demonstrating expected behaviors.

Plan Explicit Instructional Activities for Each Lesson

After building a strong foundation for your lesson, choose instructional activities to engage students during the lesson. We emphasize an explicit approach to instruction and recommend using a model–lead–test format (i.e., "I do," "we do," then "you do") for your lesson. Although this sounds like an intense lesson plan, we believe an effective classroom social skills lesson plan can be delivered in as few as 10 minutes. Consider the following example:

If we were teaching a lesson on using considerate behavior during teacher-directed instruction, we would (1) *introduce* the lesson focus and objective; (2) *model* the expected behavior (e.g., demonstrate sitting with a calm body, actively listening to the teacher, and raising hand to participate); (3) *lead* students through a quick activity in which we read the examples and nonexamples in a random order and ask students to give a thumbs up or down for examples or nonexamples of considerate behavior, respectively (providing high rates of OTRs by using gestural unison response); and (4) *test* by noting (e.g., writing a "+"

or "–" next to students' names on a class roster) which students engaged in considerate behavior when we reviewed the definition of *considerate* at the end of the lesson. Following this brief lesson, we would also plan follow-up activities (described subsequently), but the actual lesson would be completed within 10 minutes (or fewer!).

Thus, social, emotional, and behavioral skills instruction can be both effective and efficient. In the next paragraphs, we provide more detail about the model, lead, and test components of lesson activities.

Model

As described in Chapter 2, modeling occurs when an "expert" fully demonstrates the desired social, emotional, and behavioral skill, or contextually appropriate behavior. This portion of the lesson is often called "I do," as the teacher (or identified expert) demonstrates the skill while other students watch. For social, emotional, and behavioral skills instruction, you may play the role of expert, enlist the help of older students, or preteach the skill to certain students in your classroom so that those students can model the behavior for their peers. Live modeling may also be supplemented by video modeling, which we suggested earlier as a way to involve students in helping you plan for social, emotional, and behavioral skills lessons.

Lead

During the "lead" portion of the lesson, engage students in an activity that you do together ("we do") to quickly check for understanding and application of the skill. In the brief example lesson above, the "we do" portion was a quick game (thumbs up and down) to check for understanding. In addition, role plays (involving all students in various roles), group practice with the skill with supportive feedback, and similar activities are also appropriate during the lead portion of the lesson. As we described in Chapter 5, be sure your instructional activities are accessible and differentiated to support all of your students' unique learning needs. Some students may benefit from additional examples, even more explicit instruction (e.g., task analysis of skill components), further practice opportunities with feedback, and other targeted or individualized approaches during the "lead" portion of the lesson.

One quick note: be careful about having students demonstrate nonexamples (i.e., contextually inappropriate behavior) during role plays or other activities; we want students to practice contextually appropriate behavior, and we generally want to avoid having students practice and get reinforced (e.g., get peer laughter) for contextually inappropriate behavior. Thus, it's better to have an adult demonstrate or role-play any nonexamples or contextually inappropriate behaviors.

Test

Before moving on from the lesson activities, it is important to collect data to ensure that each student acquired the skill during the lesson—this is the "you do" part of the format. (You will plan additional evaluation as a follow-up activity, but a brief "test" is needed before closing your lesson.) A simple way to test is to move into the identified routine and check for contextually appropriate behavior, as described in the brief social skills lesson example at the beginning of this section. Alternately, you may use a paper-and-pencil (or crayon) activity to test. For example, you could ask younger students to draw a picture of contextually appropriate behaviors for each classroom expectation and routine, and you could hang up a few of these pictures as visual prompts in your classroom. You could ask older students to write their own lists of contextually appropriate and inappropriate behavioral examples, which adds to your examples and nonexamples for future lessons. You could also give students time to make videos illustrating a range of contextually appropriate behaviors for that example, which would start a library of video footage you can use as part of your "model" in future lessons. As these examples illustrate, your goal is to provide an initial test of knowledge and skill acquisition.

Plan Follow-Up Activities for Each Lesson

Once you have designed the lesson activities (i.e., model–lead–test components delivered during the lesson), plan follow-up activities to build fluency and promote skill maintenance and generalization. In addition to providing differentiated instruction during the lesson, you can use follow-up activities to further differentiate social, emotional, and behavioral skills instructions to meet students' unique needs. Follow-up activities may occur in the days, weeks, or even months following the initial social skills instruction. We have already foreshadowed some of the follow-up strategies, and we provide additional details about each follow-up strategy in the next paragraphs.

Prompt Expected, Contextually Appropriate Behavior

To increase the likelihood that students will use contextually appropriate behavior during the targeted routine, consider various strategies to prompt. (This would be a great time to review the various types of prompts described in Chapter 2!) In particular, we have suggested using visual prompts, which may be created during the test portion of your lesson, and we recommend using verbal prompts (i.e., quick reminders about expected behavior) at the beginning of each activity. Simple verbal prompts about expectation-following behavior have been shown to reduce off-task behavior (Faul et al., 2012), and they only take 30 seconds (or less) of teacher time. Remember to consider students' unique needs when selecting prompts, to ensure they set all students up for success. You will eventually want to fade these prompts, as your goal is to ensure that students respond to the naturally occurring S^D associated with the routine (i.e., you would like them to demonstrate respectful behavior any time you are speaking at the front of class, rather than only after your reminder).

Actively Supervise Students

To determine whether students consistently follow expectations, it is critical to actively supervise students during the identified routine (and throughout other routines as well). **Active supervision** involves moving, scanning, and interacting with students (e.g., Colvin et al., 1997). Specifically, for all classroom routines, it is important to remember to *move*, in seemingly unpredictable (and, of course, supportive and nonthreatening) ways, so that students are never sure when or where you will appear. In addition, you should regularly *scan* your classroom to observe the behavior of all students. You want students to perceive that you have eyes on the back of your head and can see and hear everything in your classroom. Finally, you want to find opportunities to *interact* with all students. Interactions may include providing academic support, engaging in rapport-building conversations about personal interests or topics, and giving specific feedback about student behavior, as described in the next two sections.

Recognize Expectation-Following Behavior

You should look for opportunities to "catch" students engaging in contextually appropriate behavior and plan your recognition strategies in advance. At a minimum, you should use specific praise to let the students know what they did well (e.g., "Thank you for raising your hand. That is a thoughtful way to get my attention when I'm teaching."). Because providing specific praise can be difficult in the moment (you are more likely to say "good job"), you may want to script potential specific praise statements for a range of contextually appropriate behaviors in a specific routine. In addition, you may consider other recognition approaches, which may be specific to a given lesson or can be used as a general approach to recognizing all expectation-following behavior within your classroom (see Chapter 7).

Respond to Social, Emotional, or Behavioral Mistakes

Similarly, you should respond calmly and efficiently to contextually inappropriate behavior. Like any response to a mistake, your response should have an instructional focus. That is, rather than thinking of strategies to "punish" contextually inappropriate behavior, think about how you would respond to an academic error (as described in Chapters 2 and 3). To correct an academic error, you would likely provide a specific error correction in a calm and neutral tone, and you would help the student practice the academic skill correctly. Similarly, when a student makes a social, emotional, or behavioral mistake, you want to let the student know what her mistake was and what she should do differently next time, and give her a chance to practice the appropriate behavior. Again, this is not a "bad" behavior and definitely not a "bad" student, it's just a mistake of using a behavior in the inappropriate context. Remembering behaviors are appropriate (or inappropriate) based on the context can help guide us to an instructionally focused correction that sets the student up for practicing the contextually appropriate behavior (and identifying where the behavior they used would be appropriate). If the error persists, you may consider a more comprehensive response that may include reteaching, increasing prompts, increasing available reinforcers for contextually appropriate behavior, and implementing additional strategies to respond to undesired behavior (see Chapter 8).

Collect Data to Evaluate Students' Responses to Social Skills Instruction

To determine if your instruction was effective, plan to collect data (in accordance with your learning objective) following instruction. A reasonable plan for data collection involves sampling student behavior (e.g., collecting data for 10–15 minutes) during the next several times the routine occurs. The number of times you will sample behavior should be included in the criteria for your learning objective. Your measurement approach will depend on your operational definition for contextually appropriate behavior, and you should select the simplest strategy possible from the approaches introduced in Chapter 4. In addition, you may want to align your data collection approach with the broader plan you devised to evaluate general contextually appropriate behavior as part of your social, emotional, and behavioral skills unit (described in the previous section).

Adjust or Enhance Instruction and Supports Based on Data

As emphasized in Chapter 4, the goal of your data collection and evaluation plan is to effectively use data to make decisions. In the context of social, emotional, and behavioral skills instruction, your considerations (and decisions) include (1) whether all or most students have met the learning objective (decision: move on to next social skills lesson); (2) whether all or most students require additional instruction or support to meet the objective (decision: implement an additional Tier 1 strategy); (3) whether a small group of students require additional support (decision: implement Tier 2 support for students who require more support); or (4) whether an individual student is having chronic or significant challenges (i.e., demonstrating regular or significant contextually inappropriate behavior) and requires further support (decision: consider a Tier 3 intervention). Thus, you should adjust, enhance, or fade your instruction and supports based on data. See Figure 6.4 for a sample lesson plan that illustrates how all of these components may occur within one lesson.

PLAN FOR MAINTENANCE AND GENERALIZATION THROUGHOUT THE SCHOOL YEAR

Once you have completed the activities in the last two sections, you will have a complete social, emotional, and behavioral skills unit that includes an overall unit plan and a sequence of lesson plans to explicitly teach students appropriate social, emotional, and behavioral skills with respect to each expectation within each routine. This alone is an impressive amount of work and will go a long way to creating a positive, proactive, and effective classroom environment where contextually appropriate behavior is explicitly taught, prompted, monitored, and recognized. However, that unit will likely only get you through the beginning of the school year. In addition, you should develop a plan to promote skill maintenance and generalization throughout the school year (and beyond!). Among the available strategies, we highlight three main approaches: plan periodic reviews, systematically fade prompts and feedback over time, and provide additional instruction and support to promote generalization across new contexts.

Plan Periodic Reviews

Following your initial rollout of your social skills unit plan, you should plan to review previously taught social, emotional, and behavioral skills (and contextually appropriate behavior) periodically. In particular, consider providing a review prior to any times of year that have been problematic in the past. (For most classrooms, reviews are important in October or November as you head into seasonal breaks, in February or March as you head into spring, and in April or May as

Social Skill Lesson Plan

Lesson Focus:

| Demonstrating | _kindness_ | (expectation) in | _group discussion_ | (setting). |

Teaching Objective:

Following instruction, students will demonstrate _kindness_ (expectation) in _group discussion_ (setting)

by _asking questions or sharing relevant comments, allowing others time to speak, and communicating_

thoughtfully (describe behaviors) across _4_ out of _5_ sampled opportunities (criteria).

Teaching Examples:

Positive Examples	Negative Examples
• Asking questions or sharing comments in a nice tone that are relevant to the topic	• Speaking out of turn
• Waiting for others to complete thoughts	• Cutting other students off
• Communicating thoughtfully or using kind words	• Using unkind or inappropriate language

Lesson Materials:

Time from school psychologist and building paraprofessional
Chart paper and markers
An article on an important science topic

Lesson Activities:

Model:

Let students know that the school psychologist and building paraprofessional are coming in to have a discussion with teacher about being respectful during group discussion.

School psychologist will lead discussion and ask questions: What are the benefits to discussing ideas as a group? Why is it important to be kind to one another during group discussion? What does it look like to be kind during discussions?

Paraprofessional will display negative examples: cut teacher off when speaking, use unkind words, and speak out of turn.

Teacher will display positive examples: wait for paraprofessional to finish thoughts/ideas and use kind language.

Lead:

Ask students to begin by identifying who was being kind, the teacher or the paraprofessional, and why. Ask students why it's important to be kind during group discussion. Then, on chart paper, have students generate a list of ways they would be kind to themselves and others during group discussion.

Test:

Let students know that we're going to practice the skills we've just learned. Have students read an article about a "hot topic" in science and then generate a group discussion. Reinforce kind behavior with verbal praise and redirect unkind behavior as needed.

Follow-Up Activities:

Strategies to prompt:
Initially, begin each group discussion by saying "Let's remember to be kind by . . ." and have class answer "Raise our hand, wait our turn, use kind words." Then move to "Let's remember to be kind" or point to the list the students made of how to be kind during group discussion.

(continued)

FIGURE 6.4. This lesson plan illustrates how one of our former students (Thanks, Sarah-Anne Nicholas!) designed a lesson to teach one classroom expectation (kindness) within one classroom routine (group discussion) in a science class.

Procedures to reinforce:

Specific and contingent verbal praise coupled with a schoolwide reinforcer (i.e., positive ticket) for individual students; if the entire class is kind during group discussion, the class will get a nucleotide base (A, C, T, or G) to put on a blank DNA double helix. Once the class receives 12 bases, they can choose from a preapproved list of musicians to listen to during the next lab class or choose to have 5 minutes of free time at the end of that period.

Procedures to correct behavioral errors:

Quick redirect: e.g., "saying . . . wasn't kind. Please use kind words" and then move on.

Differential reinforcement for lower rates of unkind behaviors if student has chronic issue.

For more significant or chronic behavioral errors, join that student during the next few discussions to model and support kind behavior.

Procedures to monitor/supervise:

Moving around class, sitting down with students every so often, interacting/facilitating discussion, correcting/reinforcing.

Procedures to collect and evaluate student data:

Have student list available and note "+" (or "–") next to student's name for kind (or unkind) behaviors. At the end of each week, review data to determine need for reteaching/review, and so forth.

FIGURE 6.4. *(continued)*

you approach the end of the year.) In addition, you should consider reviewing expected behavior after any extended break or schedule disruption (e.g., winter break, spring break, extended weather-related school closure). Finally, you should plan review lessons when your data indicate that a review is necessary. When you start to see a decrease in contextually appropriate and an increase in contextually inappropriate behavior, it's time to go "back to basics" and review expected behaviors for all routines. (It may also be a time to consider increasing available reinforcement for contextually appropriate behavior, using strategies discussed in Chapter 7.)

Fade Prompts and Feedback to Promote Maintenance

Although we recommend planning for periodic reviews of expectation-following behavior throughout the year, we also suggest that you fade "added" prompts and feedback throughout the school year once data indicate that most students are meeting learning objectives. You may want to purposefully increase prompts, feedback, and additional recognition strategies so they are on a similar schedule to periodic reviews, or when data indicate that an increase is needed. However, to ensure that contextually appropriate behavior is occasioned and maintained by the natural classroom environment and routines, your overall goal is to fade supports to those present in your typical environment.

That is, once most or all students have met your learning objectives for contextually appropriate behavior and your data indicate that students are consistently displaying contextually appropriate behavior in classroom routines, you may want to systematically decrease the number of prompts you provide across routines or use one of the other prompt-fading strategies described in Chapter 2 (e.g., decreasing information) so that the S^Ds present in the routine occasion the desired behavior in the absence of prompting. Similarly, you may want to gradually fade the amount and intensity of feedback you provide so that natural reinforcers in the environment (e.g., positive peer and teacher attention at natural intervals, learning and receiving good grades, moving to the next fun activity) become sufficient to maintain the students' contextually appropriate behavior in the absence of added rewards.

Provide Additional Instruction and Support to Promote Generalization to New Contexts

Your initial social, emotional, and behavioral skills unit and periodic reviews, in combination with other classwide PBIS practices, should be sufficient to maintain most contextually appropriate behavior across the majority of the school year. However, students will likely need specific instruction and supports to engage in contextually appropriate behavior across novel routines and activities (e.g., class field trip, indoor recess, class party, change in physical location of the class, snow on the playground or walkways). In these instances, plan to teach contextually appropriate behavior in advance and use similar strategies to follow up during the new routine or context.

INTEGRATE ACADEMIC, SOCIAL, EMOTIONAL, AND BEHAVIORAL SKILLS INSTRUCTION

To maximize efficiency and further promote maintenance and generalization, consider strategies to integrate your social, emotional, and behavioral skills instruction within your academic instruction or other school-based programs and practices. For example, embed a brief skill review and prompt for classroom expectations in the start of each lesson plan, and add reminders (potentially with scripted examples) of how to praise contextually appropriate behaviors and correct behavioral mistakes in the context of other scripted instruction. We have seen teachers (1) modify the slides they're using to deliver instruction to include social, emotional, and behavioral skills instruction; (2) modify electronic versions of their lesson plans to include scripted reminders to prompt, praise, and correct social, emotional, and behavioral skills; and even (3) add sticky notes to curricular resources to remind themselves to prompt and praise key contextually appropriate behaviors. For more information about how to integrate academic, social, emotional, and behavioral instruction, check out resources and research posted by the Integrated Multi-Tiered Systems of Support Research Network (*www.mtss.org*).

SUMMARY

In this chapter, we described strategies to (1) select a few positively stated classroom expectations and operationally define them in the context of classroom routines using a classroom matrix, (2) develop an overall (i.e., unit) plan to roll out initial social, emotional, and behavioral skills instruction, (3) create lesson plans for explicitly teaching each expectation within each routine, and (4) develop a broader plan to promote skill maintenance and generalization throughout the school year. For each strategy, we emphasized engaging students, planning, and delivering explicit instruction. We also shared how efficient (e.g., 10-minute lesson) and effective this approach can be, and how you can (1) plan for maintenance and generalization and (2) integrate academic, social, emotional, and behavioral skills instruction. With all of that content, you should now be prepared to engage your students in creating and implementing an effective plan to establish and teach contextually appropriate behavior in your classroom.

PHASES OF LEARNING ACTIVITIES: CHAPTER 6

Acquisition

1. Collaboratively with your students, identify a few positively stated expectations in your classroom and create a matrix to define those expectations within your routines.

2. Select one expectation and one routine, develop an explicit social skills lesson plan (using the template provided in Figure 6.3), and deliver the lesson to your class. Collect data, using the specified evaluation plan, to determine if students respond to the instruction.

Fluency

1. Design a unit plan to roll out social skills instruction in your classroom.

2. Design and implement additional lesson plans for the remaining "boxes" in your matrix (i.e., remaining expectations across all remaining routines). Again, use your data plan to evaluate the effects of your instruction.

Maintenance

1. Review data from your social skills unit data plan and determine whether students are continuing to display contextually appropriate behavior.

2. After you have taught all of the lesson plans from Fluency Activity 2, revisit previously taught lessons during planned (or data-indicated) periodic reviews in your classroom. Plan review lessons and see if you can develop and implement the lessons with less external support (i.e., referring to this chapter less often, asking for less help from peers).

Generalization

1. Consider additional social, emotional, and behavioral skills that you and other members of your classroom community would use regularly in your classroom. Develop lesson plans to explicitly teach these new social, emotional, and behavioral skills.

2. Develop a plan to promote your students' skill maintenance and generalization through the school year. (This will also require you to generalize the strategies you used when developing your unit plan and specific lesson plans.)

Other Skill-Building Exercises

1. Script a variety of statements to provide specific feedback to students who engage in contextually appropriate behavior (i.e., specific praise statements that are relevant for your students) and contextually inappropriate behavior (i.e., specific error corrections that are neutral, relevant, and instructionally focused).

2. Look for opportunities to "catch" students engaging in contextually appropriate behaviors and practice providing specific feedback (i.e., praise) to recognize students' efforts.

CHAPTER 7

Implement a Continuum of Strategies to Increase Contextually Appropriate Behavior

---

CHAPTER OBJECTIVES

By the end of this chapter, you should be able to . . .

1. Identify how the behavioral mechanism of reinforcement applies to your classroom.
2. Design a culturally responsive, inclusive, and effective reinforcement system for your classroom.
3. Implement and evaluate your classroom reinforcement system.

Imagine This: *Miss Bernard had established and taught her classwide expectations, just as she'd learned in her classroom behavioral support course. She also set up a classwide token economy, where students were given "Bernard Bucks" for engaging in expected behavior. Students could trade in their Bernard Bucks at her class store, where Miss Bernard had stocked items like pens, pencils, and coupons for classroom activities (e.g., computer time, lunch with teacher). One day, another teacher asks Miss Bernard, "Why are you rewarding students for what they should be doing anyway?"*

Miss Bernard smiles and replies, "Well, we always respond to behaviors that don't meet the expectations. Why not respond when behaviors do meet the expectations?"

The other teacher replies, "Well, students should be meeting the expectations."

Miss Bernard replies, "Don't you like it when someone tells you that you did a good job?"

The other teacher thinks about this a moment and then says, "Yes, I do. Just last week the principal said she liked how I had organized my lesson plans, and I felt great about that. I even mentioned it to my wife."

Miss Bernard smiles and says, "I like to think our students appreciate the recognition, too."

ESTABLISHING A CONTINUUM OF STRATEGIES TO INCREASE CONTEXTUALLY APPROPRIATE BEHAVIOR

When we teach students an academic skill, we provide ample feedback about their performance of that skill. For instance, if we taught students the formula for finding the area of a rectangle (i.e., width times height—just in case you needed a refresher!), we may show students various rectangles with side measurements and ask students to find the area. If students gave us the correct answer, we'd likely respond with "That's right!" or "You got it!" It's unlikely that we would remain silent; picture that, and you'll agree it feels awkward. Similarly, if a student gave an incorrect response, we'd likely respond with "Not quite, do you want to try again?" or "Why don't you take another look and use the formula?" Either way, we provide the student with feedback on their response. If the student provides an incorrect response, then subsequently corrects it after our feedback, we tell the student, "Yes, that's right," and maybe even include a "Nicely done!"

When we teach students the expected contextually appropriate behaviors in our classroom, we should also be providing feedback on the performance of the skills taught. Traditionally, in our schools, contextually inappropriate behaviors garner more attention than their contextually appropriate counterparts. In many schools, students can recite the "rules" (e.g., "No running," "No swearing," "Late homework equals shorter recess"), but the students do not know which behaviors *are* expected of them. Since we are actively teaching our students the expected, contextually appropriate behaviors (i.e., social, emotional, and behavioral skills) for our schools and classrooms (see Chapter 6), we need to make sure we are providing feedback as students acquire and build fluency with these skills. Unfortunately, when students demonstrate the expected behaviors, we often fail to provide feedback. Why not tell them they are meeting or exceeding our behavioral expectations, just like we do when they demonstrate an expected academic response? Think about the following scenarios:

- Justine's teacher asks for a volunteer to identify the capital of Vermont. Justine raises her hand and says, "Montpelier." The teacher responds, "That's correct, Justine. Well done!"
- Justine's teacher asks the class to quiet down. The class quiets down, and the teacher begins her lesson.

In the second scenario, Justine's teacher misses an opportunity to give feedback on her students' demonstration of the expected behavior (which she just requested!). We challenge you to think about providing positive feedback (i.e., praise) for expected behaviors the same way that you respond to correct academic responses: quickly, overtly, and consistently. Were Justine's teacher to read this book, we hope the second scenario would look more like this:

- Justine's teacher asks the class to quiet down. The class quiets down, and Justine's teacher says, "Thank you for showing that you're ready to learn! That's exactly what being engaged looks like." Then she begins her lesson.

The teacher's praise is specific, efficient, and reminds the class of their established expectation of "being engaged." Those two sentences create the opportunity for a positive interaction between her and her students, they start the lesson off on a positive note, and they let the students know that the teacher has noticed and appreciated their efforts. Her praise may increase the likelihood (remember our definition of reinforcement?) that the behavior of quieting down will occur in the future, especially when asked (establishing stimulus control). Certainly, if the class hadn't quieted down, the teacher would've reminded the students again and perhaps even issued an aversive consequence. Why not provide attention contingent on the expected behavior as well? If we want a behavior to occur again in the future, a contingent pleasant (to the learner) consequence needs to be delivered immediately after the behavior occurs.

A quick specific praise statement is one option for responding to contextually appropriate behavior. In this chapter, we explore a continuum of evidence-based strategies for encouraging contextually appropriate behavior. Remember, we all learn through reinforcement. If we want students to gain fluency with the social, emotional, behavioral, or academic skills we've taught, we need to provide contingent reinforcement when students demonstrate those skills, which will increase the likelihood that expected behaviors occur again in the future. (We will also discuss ways students can get involved with reinforcing their peers and themselves—it doesn't always have to be on us!) As students gain fluency with contextually appropriate behaviors and move into the maintenance phase of learning, we can think about fading reinforcement and moving toward more natural consequences for contextually appropriate behaviors (e.g., simple praise, good grades, avoiding unpleasant consequences, satisfaction from helping others). First things first, though: let's look at our continuum of responses to contextually appropriate behaviors.

BEHAVIOR-SPECIFIC FEEDBACK: PRAISE

The first and simplest strategy on our continuum of responses is providing a behavior-specific praise statement contingent on contextually appropriate behavior. Praise is the most common social reinforcer. A **behavior-specific** praise statement includes the behavior being praised and is directed toward a certain learner or learners. A behavior-specific, **contingent** praise statement is delivered immediately after (i.e., as a result of) the behavior targeted for increase. Specific, contingent praise has long been associated with an increase in contextually appropriate student behavior (e.g., Chalk & Bizo, 2004; Ferguson & Houghton, 1992; Sutherland et al., 2000; Royer et al., 2019; Whitney & Ackerman, 2020).

The following are some examples of behavior-specific praise statements.

- "Madi, that's exactly what we mean when we talk about being on task. Thanks for being so responsible today!"
- "Jordan, it was very kind of you to help Lisa pick up her belongings. Great example of how to be considerate to others."
- "Aimée, your desk is really organized. Thank you for contributing to a clean classroom environment."
- "Class, you're doing a terrific job walking quietly in the hallway, just like we practiced. I only hear whispers and hands are at sides. Keep it up!"

In all of these examples, the behavior being praised is stated explicitly. Explicitly stating the expected behavior serves several purposes. First, it helps students make the connection between the social reinforcer and the behavior being reinforced (i.e., they know exactly why the praise statement is being delivered). Second, it serves as a verbal prompt to any students who may not yet be engaging in the expected behavior (e.g., when the student next to Aimée hears her being praised for her neat desk, that student may straighten up their desk). Last, explicitly stating the expected behavior lets students know that you are paying attention to what they're doing, much more so than a nondescript "Good job" or "Nice going." For many students, adult attention is reinforcing; this kind of specific, positive attention from a teacher can have a marked effect on the likelihood of a behavior occurring in the future.

In addition to keeping your praise statements behavior-specific and contingent, you should also ensure that your praise sounds sincere and incorporates culturally relevant, inclusive language. Remember, "sincerity" is not something that is observable and measurable, so let's consider some behaviors associated with "being sincere" when delivering praise. The way that you deliver your praise statements should be consistent with your natural demeanor when you teach and interact with your students. For instance, if you are normally cheerful and perky, your praise will probably sound cheerful and perky as well. If you tend to be more low-key and your humor is subtle, cheerful and perky praise will sound inauthentic and maybe even make your students suspicious or uncomfortable. If you tend to be matter-of-fact, deliver your praise that way, too. Be mindful of the language you use when providing praise; it should be culturally relevant and respectful of individual and collective learning histories. Talk with students and their families about how they like (or don't like) to be recognized for doing well and be sensitive to students who are uncomfortable receiving adult attention or public praise. (You can even survey students about their praise preferences; Fefer et al., 2016.) Remember to vary the language that you use when acknowledging expected behaviors, too. Students can satiate on certain phrases, so you shouldn't begin every praise statement with "Thank you for . . ." or "That's exactly how you . . ." Practice different variations to build fluency. Finally, when delivering praise statements, be mindful of your body language and associated behaviors that impact how your praise statements are received, depending on students' learning histories and personal preference (e.g., orienting toward the student, eye contact, proximity, smiling, nodding).

In Chapter 2, we discussed function (which we will revisit in Chapter 10). If students find teacher attention reinforcing (i.e., they engage in certain behaviors associated with a high likelihood of being followed by teacher attention), then contingent praise may increase the likelihood of the behavior being praised. What about those students who are less interested in obtaining teacher attention—or those students who prefer to avoid it altogether and behave accordingly? If you have students who find adult attention aversive and you provide public praise when they demonstrate expected behavior, you may inadvertently punish the behavior you praised—that is, the student learned that the expected behavior resulted in something they prefer to avoid, so in turn, they avoid the behavior! If you know that some of your students are uncomfortable with or try to avoid public attention, find other ways to provide behavior-specific positive feedback. For example, you could put a sticky note on the student's desk or write some specific feedback related to social behavior on a paper that you're returning (e.g., "Strong effort on this spelling test, and your thoughtful contributions during our class on gerunds really helped your peers understand the content better."). This feedback may not be immediate, but distance between the expected behavior and the positive feedback is preferred to embarrassing our students or discouraging future demonstrations of the expected behavior. In addition, meeting privately with a student after class is another way you could deliver praise unobtrusively.

We consider behavior-specific praise a "nonnegotiable" practice; it should be part of every teacher's continuum of acknowledgments. That said, behavior-specific praise may be highly effective, but is not sufficient on its own to sustain continued demonstration of contextually appropriate behaviors. While behavior-specific praise may be an effective reinforcer for some behaviors and some students, praise will not function as a reinforcer for some students and praise, even when highly specific and delivered often, and may not be intense or frequent enough to maintain desired levels of the expected behavior—especially for students with elevated social, emotional, and behavioral needs. Luckily, teachers can choose from several evidence-based strategies that provide a more overt contingency between contextually appropriate behaviors and a pleasant (for the learner!) consequence, including tangible or activity-based incentives. We describe some of these other strategies next.

GROUP CONTINGENCIES

In a classroom, it is neither possible nor desirable to reinforce each discrete instance of contextually appropriate behavior—imagine your day being one continuous loop of behavior-specific praise statements: "Gavin, thank you for arriving on time," "Great job hanging up your jacket, Tommy," "I want to recognize the group who just sat down quietly before the bell rang," and "Ty, you remembered to put your homework on my desk, great!" could all be uttered in the first 15 seconds of your day, and sustaining that pace would eliminate any time for instruction (and likely any desire to keep being a teacher!). Luckily, most students don't need a continuous schedule of reinforcement to sustain their contextually appropriate behaviors. Many other options exist. Perhaps you want to have one reward that the whole class can earn (e.g., a class party or movie day, a chance to decorate the classroom however they choose—with some guardrails agreed upon by the classroom community); if so, you may opt to implement a group contingency in which all students earn the same reinforcer. There are three types of group contingencies, which we discuss below. (See Alberto et al., 2021, for a more complete discussion of group contingencies, and Beaver et al., 2023, for a review of supporting evidence.)

Dependent Group Contingencies

In a *dependent* group contingency, the delivery of the group's reinforcement is contingent on one or a few individuals in the group demonstrating the expected behavior. In other words, one or a few of your students need to perform a specific, contextually appropriate behavior in order for all group members to receive the reward. For example:

• Javier and Bernie are third-grade students who have a high rate of contextually inappropriate behavior (i.e., play fighting and yelling while entering the classroom, then taking extended time to settle into their seats) at the start of the day. When talking with them, the teacher learns that they both enjoy movies and express a desire to do things with their class. The teacher sets up this dependent group contingency: Every morning that Javier and Bernie both come in and sit down quietly within 1 minute, the class gets a point. When the class has 10 points, the teacher will arrange an afternoon movie party for the class.

- Tay, a high school student who is highly reinforced by peer attention, needs additional supports (including a point sheet) to stay on task in the classroom. Tay's teacher sets up this dependent group contingency: Whenever Tay earns all of her points for being on task, she gets to announce to everyone that they have the last 5 minutes of the class to talk or listen to music.

- One of Mr. Kim's reading groups, the Tater Tots (groups select their own names!), have been inconsistent in completing their computer-assisted instruction. Mr. Kim sets up this group contingency: When the Tater Tots reading group reaches a cumulative 250 minutes of computer-assisted instruction, the whole class will participate in a special picnic lunch and activity.

Now, you may be asking yourself, "That sounds nice, but what happens if Javier and Bernie, Tay, or the Tater Tots do not demonstrate the expected behavior or do not meet the criteria set by the teacher? Won't the other students be unhappy that these individuals 'cost' them an incentive?" And, if you haven't set up your dependent group contingency thoughtfully and carefully, the answer to that second question could very well be "yes." Peer pressure is a powerful tool and should be used judiciously—or not at all. If you can set up your dependent group contingency so it is "no-fail" for the learner or learners on whom the contingent reward depends, it may be an effective way to get those learners to engage in the desired behavior(s).

How do you make your dependent group contingency no-fail? First, you must make sure that the students on whom the contingency depends can actually perform the target behavior. They should be fluent with the target behavior; perhaps it's a behavior they have demonstrated but are not performing reliably or in the appropriate context. In our examples above, Javier and Bernie will need explicit instruction and practice on how to enter the room quietly and sit down quickly to ensure that they can engage in the target behavior fluently and consistently. The teacher should also provide clear verbal (e.g., "Good morning, Javier and Bernie! Remember to come in quietly and go directly to your seats") and visual (e.g., a 1-minute timer) prompts. The teacher should also engage the involved students (in this example, Javier and Bernie) in developing the contingency to ensure they understand it and find it acceptable. The teacher should also enjoin the other students in the class in encouragement efforts; after all, encouraging others is a social skill that we can teach, prompt, and reinforce just like any other. Other students can support Javier and Bernie by checking in with them in the morning, offering prompts, praising effort, and modeling with their own behavior (i.e., entering the room quietly and sitting down quickly).

Imagine a classroom where all students were cheering on a few learners who were working to master an expected behavior—this could improve connections and relationships between students and build community. Also, in a dependent group contingency, students should only earn (and never lose) privileges for the class. It should always be just a matter of time before the reward is earned, which is the case in each of our three examples. Finally, and most importantly, the student(s) on whom the reward depends must choose to participate and be excited about the possibility of contributing to earning a reward for the class; no student should be put in this position unless they are fully on board and able to understand the contingency (and their role in it). Unless a dependent group contingency is designed with careful attention to the considerations we've mentioned, you run the risk of embarrassing or shaming individual learners and causing harm to the classroom community. And, unless you are 100% certain that the target desired behavioral goal will be achieved as a no-fail for the individual learner(s) and you are committed to teach the required skills for all students in the class (including how to encourage each other), select another option for group reinforcement.

Potential Pros of the Dependent Group Contingency

- Potential to enhance an already supportive classroom community that values all members.
- Helping individual learners get recognition from and feel valued by other members of the classroom community.
- Getting individual learners excited about earning a reward for the class and getting the rest of the class to "cheer on" individuals.
- Helping individual learners recognize potential value in working toward something that benefits others as well as themselves.

Cons of the Dependent Group Contingency

- The possibility that individual learners won't meet the criteria or goal for earning the incentive and will be embarrassed (and potentially punished by disappointing their peers, damaging classroom community and decreasing future rates of attempting the expected behavior).
- The possibility that individual learners are not interested in a shared incentive, decreasing the likelihood that they engage in the expected behaviors.
- The possibility of peers making unkind comments or otherwise demonstrating unhappiness directed at individual learners.
- Other students in the class who engaged in contextually inappropriate behaviors may still experience the reward.

Interdependent Group Contingencies

Another possibility for delivering group reinforcement is the *interdependent* group contingency. In an interdependent group contingency, delivery of the reward depends on every student in the group meeting the criteria for earning the reward. In other words, everyone in the group must engage in the expected behavior in order for everyone to receive the reward. For example:

- At the beginning of a class where socializing is interfering with learning: "If everyone can be seated and quiet within 1 minute, everyone will have 5 minutes at the end of class to socialize."
- After a lesson on what considerate cafeteria behavior looks like: "On the first day everyone demonstrates considerate cafeteria behavior, we'll celebrate with a popsicle party. Let's try to make that happen today!"

The pros and cons of the interdependent group contingency are similar to those for the dependent group contingency. Peers may be unhappy with those group members who do not (or cannot) engage in the expected behavior or meet the criteria. Some members of the group may not be motivated by the reward (or their peers) enough to change their likelihood of engaging in the expected behavior. Extensive teaching of the expected behavior, how to encourage each other, how to opt out, and how to cope with any potential disappointment must occur before the contingency is announced. On the other hand, if you've carefully set up your interdependent group contingency as a no-fail for *all* learners in your classroom, imagine what it would look and sound like to have all students encouraging one another to meet a common goal! Students would be prompting and praising one another, and your classroom would feel like a positive and supportive community for all learners.

Setting up an interdependent group contingency requires careful and thorough teaching of the expected behaviors (e.g., contextually appropriate responses when the goal is not achieved, what encouraging each other looks like, how to self-advocate if you're uncomfortable participating), as well as frequent prompting and modeling from you: encourage all learners, report frequently on progress, and ensure that everyone believes that achieving the group reward is possible and, indeed, highly likely. Again, if you cannot ensure that your desired behavior is a no-fail for all learners in your group, select another option for group reinforcement.

Potential Pros of the Interdependent Group Contingency

- Potential to enhance an already supportive classroom community that values all members.
- Helping all learners feel valuable to and valued by other members of the classroom community.
- Getting individual learners excited about earning a reward for the class and getting the rest of the class to "cheer on" individuals.
- Helping individual learners recognize potential value in working toward something that benefits others as well as themselves.
- All students must demonstrate the expected behavior—although there should be a way that students who are uncomfortable participating can opt out.

Cons of the Interdependent Group Contingency

- The possibility that individual learners won't meet the criteria or goal for earning the incentive and will be embarrassed (and potentially punished by disappointing their peers, damaging classroom community and decreasing future rates of attempting the expected behavior).
- The possibility that individual learners are not interested in a shared incentive, decreasing the likelihood that they engage in the expected behaviors.
- The possibility of peers making unkind comments or otherwise demonstrating unhappiness directed at individual learners who do not demonstrate the expected behavior.

Independent Group Contingencies

In an *independent* group contingency, each individual member of the group receives the reward when they demonstrate the expected behavior. That is, any student who demonstrates the expected behavior receives the reward; those students who do not demonstrate the expected behavior do not receive the reward. For example:

- "Everyone who demonstrates considerate cafeteria behavior will receive a popsicle."
- "Everyone who encourages a peer will receive a ROCK ticket."
- "Everyone who arrives on time to class all week earns a 'turn in homework late' pass."

In an independent group contingency, everyone is responsible for earning their own reward, which eliminates some of the concerns with the dependent and interdependent group contingencies. On the other hand, you lose the opportunity for building community that can be part of thoughtfully developed and carefully implemented dependent and interdependent group contingencies. In the independent group contingency, students who are not particularly interested in the reward simply may not engage in the desired behavior. Also, students who routinely are unable to earn the reward may find the independent group contingency frustrating and demoralizing. As with the other two group contingencies, development of the independent group contingency must include careful attention to your students and their unique and shared learning histories. If you believe that implementing any group contingency (or, for that matter, any behavioral support practice) in your classroom has the potential to cause shame, humiliation, or damage to relationships, use a different strategy.

Potential Pros of the Independent Group Contingency
- Each learner is responsible for earning their own reward (unlike the other two group contingency types). If an individual does not earn a reward, other learners are not affected.

Cons of the Independent Group Contingency
- Learners who are not motivated by the reward may not engage in the behavior.
- Students who are routinely unable to earn the reward may become frustrated.
- The "every person for themselves" aspect of this contingency does not have the potential to foster classroom community and support as much as the other two group contingencies do.

If group contingencies aren't a good fit for your classroom, don't despair! There are other options for reinforcing appropriate behavior, discussed below—and hopefully you learned more about some of the important considerations when selecting culturally responsive, thoughtfully designed behavioral support strategies. You may also consider using a group contingency in conjunction with other strategies—it's all about what is contextually appropriate for your classroom and your students.

The Student/Teacher Game

The Student/Teacher Game (Center on PBIS, 2020) is based on a widely researched, evidence-based practice based on an interdependent group contingency called the Good Behavior Game (GBG; Embry, 2002; Tingstrom et al., 2006). Since its development in 1969, the GBG has been shown to reduce many types of contextually inappropriate behavior for a variety of student populations (e.g., Kleinman & Saigh, 2011; Nolan et al., 2014; Tanol et al., 2010) with some differences in outcomes by student subgroup (cf. Smith et al., 2021). The Student/Teacher Game can be modified to encourage specific contextually appropriate behaviors. Our favorite version of implementation is as follows: divide your classroom into two (or more) teams and select a specific expected behavior (e.g., listening to others carefully and quietly during a group discussion). Whenever you observe a student demonstrating the behavior, their team gets a point. The team with the most points at the end of the lesson (or day, or time period—game length should reflect context and preferences of students and staff) earns an incentive. If both teams earn many or the same number of points (or exceed a point goal your classroom establishes), you may choose to reward both groups (Tingstrom et al., 2006). The Student/Teacher Game is an efficient and practical way to increase the likelihood of appropriate behavior, and it can be adapted for cultural and contextual fit (Nolan et al., 2014).

BEHAVIORAL CONTRACTING

Behavioral contracting is another option on our continuum of supports for encouraging contextually appropriate behavior. Although behavioral contracting is traditionally used as a support for individual students, we can also use behavioral contracts to increase expected behaviors at the classwide level. Behavioral contracts are often used in conjunction with other reinforcement strategies, like group contingencies or token economies. You are likely familiar with how contracts operate in the "real world"; they are often part of employment agreements or ways for two or more entities to formalize and put official contingencies in place around a partnership. You may also know that contracts are written, that they often involve negotiation between the interested parties, and that all involved parties sign the document to make it a legally binding agreement. While classroom behavioral contracts aren't legally binding, they do contain explicit "if . . . then" statements to which all parties agree. At the classroom level, we have seen these called "classroom constitutions" or "agreements," and they are developed and signed by all members of the classroom community (i.e., all students and educators).

Behavioral contracts can also be developed with individual students (either all students in class, a targeted group, or a few students who need additional support as part of a Tier 3 plan). For example, a behavioral contract for individual students might contain statements like these:

- "If Luke can complete 80% of his homework for 2 weeks, earning an 80 or above on each assignment, he will be able to host a class party with games and activities of his choice."
- "If Britni can meet the hallway behavioral expectations for 9 out of 10 transitions, she will earn lunch with the teacher on a day of her choosing."
- "If Syd and Jack can complete all assigned work and follow all teacher directions for a period of 1 week, they will be allowed to sit next to each other during class."

A behavioral contract should explicitly state what supports the teacher or other staff members will provide, a detailed explanation of what happens when the specified criterion is met, and a detailed explanation of the outcome—including next steps or options for trying again—if the criterion is not met. Each person mentioned in the contract signs it, including the teacher; after all, the teacher has an obligation under the contract, too (i.e., to deliver the reward when the student completes the task successfully). The contract is a visual prompt for both teacher and student that clearly states the expected behavior and the outcome for engaging in that behavior. Here are a few things to remember if you decide to use a behavioral contract with a student or with your class (see Alberto et al., 2021, for a more detailed explanation of behavioral contracting):

- The contract must be fair: can the learner complete the behavior asked of them?
- The reward must be delivered *after* the behavior occurs; delivering a reward before a behavior does not count as reinforcement. Technically, it's bribery!
- The contract should be positively stated; that is, it should state the expected behavior (e.g., "Arabella will use her break card to signal she needs to take space") rather than the absence of inappropriate behavior (e.g., "Arabella will not leave her seat without permission").
- The contract should stress specific behaviors, rather than obedience; avoid statements about "respecting all teachers" and "following rules." Keep the expected behaviors observable and measurable so it's clear if the student meets the expectations or not.
- Contracts should also state what—if anything—happens if the student does not meet the expectations stated in the contract. Is there a contingent consequence?
- Remember, if you sign a contract, you need to deliver on what you've promised.
- Contracts should reflect student (and family) voice; the student and their family should provide input about the terms and have a chance to read and provide feedback before everyone signs. This is a great opportunity for a student to practice self-advocacy skills, which you should teach in advance if students do not already have those skills in their behavioral repertoire.

As we mentioned, contracts can be used for individual students or for a group of students. Some teachers use a class contract when they develop group contingencies. Using behavioral contracts with individual students who have elevated social, emotional, or behavioral needs and can benefit from more targeted or more intensive supports can provide a helpful framework for tracking progress toward goals developed as part of a behavior support plan or other specialized services (see Chapters 9 and 10 for a discussion of targeted group and individualized behavioral support options, respectively). Contracts hold both staff and students accountable for meeting the documented expected behaviors and can be an effective strategy on your continuum of classroom supports for encouraging contextually appropriate behavior.

TOKEN ECONOMIES

Token economies are one of the most widely used and well-researched behavioral support strategies. Token economies have been successful at improving academic outcomes and increasing contextually appropriate behaviors across all kinds of students in all kinds of settings, including residential settings for adjudicated adolescents, stand-alone special education classrooms, and general education classrooms (e.g., Alberto et al., 2021; Kim et al., 2022; Soares et al., 2016).

Because of their flexibility, adaptability, and long history of effectiveness, we encourage you to consider using a token economy as one the ways to acknowledge (and hopefully increase) contextually appropriate behavior in your classroom. If your school is already implementing a token economy as part of their schoolwide PBIS recognition system (recall Chapter 3), consider ways to leverage that to support student behavior in your classroom. If there is not a schoolwide token economy or if your students do not find it reinforcing, you can create your own token economy in your classroom.

Creating a classroom token economy provides multiple opportunities to collaborate with your students and their families and reflect their voices and identity: solicit input about the tokens themselves (What should they be called? What can they look like?), the incentives and rewards offered (What are students' preferences? What rewards are culturally responsive and reflective of learning histories?), and structural components of the token economy (How often should exchanges occur? What is the exchange rate? When should we reevaluate?).

Token economies are less subject to satiation than other types of reinforcement systems—there are usually multiple backup reinforcers to select from and they are dynamic: the system can be easily adjusted as warranted by data (e.g., data indicate expected behaviors are not increasing), shifts in priority (e.g., there has been a surge in contextually inappropriate cell phone use that your school wants to address), or changes in the environment (e.g., a newly hired assistant teacher offers a crafting activity once a week that students can "buy" into with their tokens). Token delivery should be paired with behavior-specific praise so students are aware of exactly why they are receiving the token. We describe the components of the system below and include an example of a token economy in Box 7.1.

Creating a Token Economy

To create a token economy, you will need the following:

Tokens

Tokens are generalized conditioned reinforcers delivered contingent on an expected behavior that have no inherent value; their value comes from their ability to be exchanged for something of value (i.e., backup reinforcer). Effective tokens are portable, durable, and easily handled (Alberto et al., 2021). Examples of tokens include tickets, poker chips, laminated "money" with the teacher's face on them (yes, some teachers do that!), pompom balls, stickers, points, and tally marks. If your tokens are tangible items that your students collect (e.g., "money," tickets), then you will need to have a receptacle for their tokens. These could be individual "banks" (e.g., bags or containers on the desk), or the tokens could be stored at a central location in the classroom (e.g., pocket charts where each student stores their tokens, a manila folder for each student stored in a classroom file cabinet). Stickers can be placed on individual student charts (that may be kept at each student's desk) or on a master chart accessed by the teacher. Some tokens aren't tangible, such as points or tally marks. For these kinds of tokens, teachers usually keep a master chart at their desk or on a clipboard where they can easily update students' earnings. Some teachers opt for hole punches (i.e., each appropriate behavior earns a hole punch on a card carried by the student), connect-the-dots (i.e., where students can connect two dots each time they engage in appropriate behavior), or puzzle pieces; when students punch all the

BOX 7.1. APPLIED EXAMPLE OF A TOKEN ECONOMY

Ms. Franklin's Token Economy

In Ms. Franklin's seventh-grade class, students can earn overt acknowledgment (in addition to behavior-specific praise) when they demonstrate the expected behaviors defined in their classroom norms ("Safe," "Engaged," "Thoughtful"). Ms. Franklin applies what she's learned in this book to ensure her token economy is efficient and effective; we explore the components of her token economy below.

Tokens

Ms. Franklin uses "SET Bucks" as her token; these are slips of paper with the classroom norms (i.e., "Safe," "Engaged," "Thoughtful") on them, a space for the student's name, and a space for the date and time given. When she distributes SET Bucks, Ms. Franklin lets the student know what they're for (e.g., "Thanks for being thoughtful and listening during the group discussion") and circles the relevant norm (i.e., "Thoughtful"). Rather than reward all expected behaviors all the time, Ms. Franklin often focuses on one expectation ("Today, we're focused on being thoughtful to each other") or one routine ("During morning meeting this week, let's all practice being engaged"). Ms. Franklin also gives each student five SET Bucks each week that they distribute to one another when they see peers demonstrating expected behaviors.

Backup Reinforcers

Ms. Franklin frequently asks students what they'd like to earn and revises her menu of rewards based on their feedback. Students never need to "buy" anything Ms. Franklin considers a necessity for a comfortable, safe, and productive environment (e.g., writing utensil, paper, comfortable seating, healthy snacks); she makes sure those items are always available. See Figure 7.1 for an example of a typical reinforcer menu in her class.

Exchange System

Ms. Franklin teaches students how and when (e.g., during breaks, at the beginning and end of class) they can ask for and access the backup reinforcers, most of which are continuously available. If a student wishes to redeem SET Bucks for something with logistical considerations (e.g., special lunch with a friend), she teaches that they ask 1 week in advance. Each quarter, she has a "spend down raffle," where any unused SET Bucks go into a raffle and a bigger-ticket item (e.g., gift card) is awarded before balances reset to zero.

Monitoring

If her weekly review of ODRs and her notes show an increase in a specific contextually inappropriate behavior, Ms. Franklin teaches (or reteaches) a contextually appropriate replacement behavior and increases distribution of SET Bucks for that replacement behavior. She keeps track of each student's SET Buck earning and spending in a Google form she accesses from her tablet; she reviews these data weekly to review if (1) she's consistent in delivery and (2) if any students have lower rates of earning and may need more intensive reinforcement. She also monitors which items student access, which helps her identify preferences (in addition to checking in with students and families monthly to solicit ideas for backup reinforcers).

holes on the card, connect all the dots to create a picture, or receive all pieces to complete a puzzle, they earn the backup reinforcer. You and your students may be interested in exploring some digital options, too; there are apps and programs available to track earned points (we like Be+ [Be Positive], a free app from the Center on PBIS you can use from your smart device). There are multiple options for tokens; partner with your students and their families to get their feedback and help with selecting a culturally and contextually appropriate token for your classroom.

In addition to selecting tokens, you'll need to determine how and when they'll be distributed. Which contextually appropriate behaviors will you reward—all, or a specific few, or those associated with a specific routine? Will you distribute tokens after every instance of the expected behavior, or will you distribute tokens more intermittently? Will all expected behaviors earn the same number of tokens? Will students have the option to give each other tokens paired with a compliment (i.e., specific praise) about a peer's kindness (or other expected behavior)? One advantage of generalized conditioned reinforcers (like tokens) is that they can bear a quantitative relationship to the effort required to demonstrate the behavior. For instance, for many students, helping someone who has dropped all of their belongings will require more effort than walking quietly in the hallway and, thus, might be rewarded with a greater number of tokens.

Backup Reinforcers

Once you've established what you will use for tokens, partner with your students to develop a menu of what they can earn with their tokens. Figure 7.1 shows an example of a reinforcer menu. Offering a variety of reinforcers that reflect student voice increases the likelihood of students engaging with your system and being motivated to earn available rewards. Consider having reinforcers from different categories (i.e., social, tangible, activity) and that address different functions (e.g., brief break, activity with a peer, time with a preferred educator, access to sensory activities), and maintain an up-to-date menu of what's available for exchange. The logistics around activity reinforcers like being the office helper or having lunch with a preferred

Available Item	Cost (in SET Bucks)
Sticker	$1
Choice of drink from classroom fridge	$3
Listening to music during independent work	$3
Assistant to Ms. Franklin for 1 day	$5
"Turn it in late" homework pass	$5
Work with a friend	$5
Choose activity for community-building time	$8
Item from Franklin's Tower*	$15
Special lunch with a friend and staff member	$25
*shelving unit with books, small stuffed animals, trinkets, etc.	

FIGURE 7.1. An example of a backup reinforcer menu.

adult should be worked out *before* they are available as selections for students. Examples of backup reinforcers include:

Social

- Watercolor painting with a friend
- Helping the teacher or a preferred staff with classroom chores or errands
- Visiting another classroom

Tangible

- Stickers
- Selecting items from a "treasure chest" or "gift bag" (which can be stocked by the teacher and/or student and family donations of toys or items they no longer use)
- Pens, pencils, erasers, notebooks

Activity

- Game or other activity in class
- Using the computer
- Listening to music

We intentionally left food out of our examples. While food items can be highly desired backup reinforcers, we opted to omit them from our list of suggested backup reinforcers due to potential allergies, cultural considerations, and our discomfort with using a biological necessity (i.e., primary reinforcer) as a reward. We believe tokens should be exchanged for privileges and "wants," rather than items that meet potential needs. If you do plan to include food items on your backup reinforcer menu, please partner with your students, families, and colleagues to ensure your selections are contextually and culturally appropriate and there is no restriction on regular food availability outside of the token economy. For example, if snacks are part of the school day for all students, students in your class should not have to "purchase" snacks as part of the token economy. (Also, be sure you've checked your school's and district's wellness policy, as more districts are moving away from food-based activities and rewards.)

Again, if you're wondering, "How do I know what my students would like to earn?" the simplest answer is, "Ask them (and their families)!" Consider distributing a survey to your students and their families asking about their interests and what they might like to earn; you can also provide them with options and ask them to rank order the options in order of preference. If you want to have your system up and running on the first day of school, select a variety of rewards and solicit student feedback as soon as you have the chance. Also, if students have free time before class begins or at other times during the day, observe how they spend that time: Do they like to talk to one another? Go outside? Use the computer? Listen to music? Use your observations to shape your selection of backup reinforcers.

Sometimes teachers have a classwide reward available where any earned tokens go toward the designated reward (a combination of a token economy and group contingency). For instance, every time a student or the class engages in an expected behavior, the teacher puts a marble (i.e., token) in a glass jar. When the jar is full, the class receives a predetermined reward (e.g., movie, extra recess). While this may be an efficient version of a token economy, it may be less effective at reinforcing expected behaviors. In this kind of system, not all students have to engage in appropriate behavior to earn the reward—a student might never earn a marble, but when the jar is full, she watches the movie with the rest of the class. Also, not all students may be interested in earning the reward, and may not be motivated to earn it. Some students may benefit from the more obvious contingency that individualized, tangible tokens provide: you engaged in the expected behavior, and you earned this token, which can be exchanged for something *you* value. While we agree that the "marble jar" and other classwide contingencies can be fun and may motivate many of your students, more systematic token economies may work better at shaping student behavior. You can also consider having "donations" to a classwide reward as an option for students; for instance, a student with 25 tokens may exchange 20 for a pass to the courtyard and donate 5 to the classwide board game fund (when there are 250 tokens collected, the class gets an afternoon board game break).

The Exchange System

With your tokens and backup reinforcers determined, you're ready to develop the exchange system. The system includes the exchange rate (i.e., what does each backup reinforcer "cost" in tokens?) and the actual logistics of the exchange itself (e.g., When will the exchange take place? How often? Where?). Teach students about the token economy and the exchange system just like you'd teach any other skill or expected behaviors. Often, teachers use a "school store" kind of system for their classroom token economy: at a designated time, students can exchange earned tokens for available backup reinforcers. We recommend doing this at the end of the day or the end of the week to avoid disrupting class time and to avoid the potential distraction of having a cool backup reinforcer in hand or questions about when an activity voucher for lunch with a friend can be redeemed. Some teachers use a raffle as part of their exchange system, wherein tokens (with students' names on them) are put into a container and then a winner is drawn; the winner gets the reward. If you want to have a raffle, we recommend doing that *in addition* to allowing students to exchange their tokens for individual backup reinforcers first. Then, all exchanged tokens can be placed into the raffle. This ensures that all students receive rewards for demonstrating the expected behaviors, and a few will receive something extra special. If you only have a raffle, most of your students will not receive a reward, only the chance of winning, which may not be motivating (especially for those students who earn the fewest tokens and thereby have the lowest odds—who also tend to be the students who have more intensive behavioral needs and would benefit the most from contingent reinforcement for contextually appropriate behaviors!).

Monitoring Your System

A critical part of managing a successful token economy is collecting data on its effectiveness. If possible, establish a baseline measure of the targeted student behavior (i.e., those behaviors on which your token economy will focus) *before* you implement your token economy (of course, this will not be possible if you implement at the beginning of the year, as we've suggested). Continue to collect data on your students' behavior as you implement the token economy; hopefully, you will see a decrease in contextually inappropriate behavior and an increase in contextually appropriate behavior. In addition, keep data on your distribution of tokens and backup reinforcers; ideally, you should track the number of tokens you distribute to each student, perhaps on a clipboard or in an app that creates a spreadsheet, graph, or other easily interpretable way to look at your data. Assess which students are earning the fewest tokens, and reflect on possible reasons: Are they not fluent with the expected behavior? Might they prefer different reinforcers? Do they fully understand the system? Are you prompting for the expected behavior and reminding students what they can earn? Look for general patterns, too: if there is a lull in token earning, think about the possible reasons. Have you stopped giving them out as often? Have students stopped engaging in the expected behavior as often? Has the system become stagnant? Use the data you've collected to make decisions and tweak your token economy accordingly.

Other Considerations

In addition to selecting tokens, choosing backup reinforcers, establishing an exchange system, and teaching your system to students, there are other aspects of token economies that teachers should consider. First, your tokens should be unique so they are not easily replicated. Consider using tokens that require a staff member's signature rather than common items like paper clips. Second, be mindful of students who collect but don't spend tokens. While generalized conditioned reinforcers should not be reinforcing by themselves, sometimes students will just want to collect as many as possible. (Consider that money, the most well-known generalized conditioned reinforcer, is not designed to be reinforcing; rather, it's the backup reinforcers we can purchase with our money that give this "token" its value. This does not, however, stop some people from accumulating as much money as they can, without ever exchanging it for goods and services beyond the necessities!)

To prevent students from accumulating too many tokens, schedule more frequent exchange opportunities. Consider adding expiration dates to your tokens; if they have a "use by" date (after which they become invalid), students will be more likely to use them. If possible, change your token to indicate that old ones have expired (e.g., change the color of your tickets). Another way to prevent accumulation of tokens is to have "pay-to-play" events on a monthly or quarterly basis. For example, a staff–student basketball game could "cost" 10 tokens to watch (and the staff ensure that all students who have enough tokens "pay" for the event). Or, 10 tokens could buy a student an extra-credit question on a quiz or test. Last, you can consider collecting all unused tokens at the end of the week, month, or quarter and putting them in a drawing for a bigger reward. Remember, if students accumulate enough tokens to "buy" whatever they want at any time, they may be less inclined to engage in the expected behavior. If you are keeping accurate data on your token distribution (as discussed above), you will be able to tell which students have too many tokens (as well as which students are earning too few).

Often, when we suggest token economies for older (e.g., high school) students, teachers balk at the idea of such a system, fearing that students will not "buy in" to the system, and that they'll think it's silly and insulting. In our experience, this is not true; token economies have been used successfully at all grade levels, and even in settings like juvenile justice and other residential centers that support students with significant social, emotional, and behavioral needs. To make the token economy work with older (and really, with any) students, you must be sure to (1) buy into the system yourself and (2) partner with students and their families to identify preferred rewards. Think about it: if you present the system to your students as "Hey, everyone—I know you're going to think this is corny, but I read it in a book," they may not be too enthusiastic. If, on the other hand, you present it as "Hey, everyone—I'm going to try this really cool system where you can earn different things you like just for engaging in the expected behaviors; tell me some things you'd like to earn!" you have a much better chance of the system being a success. As we said before, observe your students (in addition to soliciting and incorporating feedback from them and their families). Do they arrive at school with beverages from the local coffee shop? Have a raffle for a gift card from that shop. Do they all have a certain pen or notebook? Consider stocking those items in your classroom store.

In addition, consider academically based rewards for students, particularly if your token economy focuses on academically based behaviors. For example, for every completed homework assignment handed in, a student earns one point. At 20 points, the student earns a "Turn in Homework Late" pass redeemable on a future assignment. Or students could earn a token for every relevant question asked during a series of class discussions. If students earn five tokens, they can exchange the tokens for an extra point on the upcoming quiz or test. Academically based rewards are likely to be most effective in classrooms where students are already fluent with contextually appropriate social behaviors and where students are highly motivated by grades and academic success.

FADING SUPPORT: DECISION RULES

So, you've established and taught your expected behaviors. You prompt for them regularly, and you reward those behaviors with behavior-specific praise and a systematic, contextually appropriate token economy. For several months, all runs smoothly, and then you hit a plateau. Your data show that the students' contextually appropriate behavior is no longer improving (or perhaps it can't be improved further). Students are not as excited as they once were when you announce that it's exchange day and they can visit the classroom store. What's going on?

As educators, our goal is to help students develop the academic, social, emotional, and behavioral skills that will increase the likelihood of them meeting whatever life goals they may have (e.g., obtaining and maintaining employment, higher education or learning a trade, establishing and maintaining meaningful relationships). When we first teach students an academic concept, like reading, we provide a lot of support: we coach, we help students sound out words, we introduce them to strategies to help with decoding, and we cheer them on with positive feedback and praise for correct academic behavior. As students move from acquisition to fluency with their reading skills, we begin to fade supports. When they stumble, we may remind students of a particular strategy they can try, but we generally let students execute their new skills independently, and we cheer and praise those skills less (and usually shift focus to the next set of skills or concept targeted for learning). We need to follow the same model with the contextually appropriate behaviors we have determined are valuable in partnership with students and their families: as students gain fluency with these behaviors and move toward maintenance and generalization, we systematically fade our behavioral supports (including thinning our schedule of reinforcement) and allow students to execute the skills independently. Hopefully, the contextually appropriate behaviors our students have learned will be reinforced and maintained by natural consequences (probably the reason those behaviors were selected as goals in the first place!). For example, saying "good morning" and "thank you" will likely result in smiles, "you're welcome," and positive responses from others, which may maintain the student's use of those phrases. Participating in class discussions may result in better grades and increased comprehension of the material, consequences that may maintain class participation.

There are several options when data indicate it's time to fade our behavioral supports (i.e., students can perform the expected behavior independently with minimal guidance or direction). We can collaborate with students and families to determine if there's a "next level" of the behavior that we'd like to target for improvement; we can reward more complex levels of behavior that build on contextually appropriate behaviors with which students are already fluent. For instance, if students are reliably able to demonstrate active-listening skills during class discussions, we might want to reinforce instances of making cogent, relevant contributions to the discussion (if all partners agree that this is a meaningful goal for the students). Another example would be to move from providing reinforcement for the expected behavior of lining up quietly and on the right to providing reinforcement only when students line up quietly on the right *and* move to their next class quickly and with their hands to themselves. By the end of the school year, we may only be reinforcing contextually appropriate behaviors that are "above and beyond" our established classroom expectations, such as offering to show a new student around the school or offering to help a substitute teacher who is lost.

You can also fade support by increasing the "amount" of the expected behavior required to earn a reward. For example, if we were previously reinforcing every instance of hand raising, we can move to reinforcing every third hand raise (i.e., a fixed-ratio intermittent schedule of reinforcement) or to an average of every third hand raise (i.e., a variable-ratio intermittent schedule of reinforcement; see Alberto et al., 2021, for a discussion of schedules of reinforcement). If we were rewarding students for 30 minutes of on-task behavior, we can lengthen the duration of expected behavior to 45 minutes. If we slowly increase our expectations, we promote maintenance and generalization of the behaviors and increase the likelihood that they will be maintained by a more natural community of reinforcers.

We can also fade support by decreasing the frequency and intensity of our reinforcers. If 45 minutes of on-task behavior earned 10 minutes of computer time, we can amend our exchange rate so that 45 minutes of on-task behavior earns 5 minutes of computer time. Usually, students respond better to increasing the level or "amount" of behavior (as described above) than decreasing the "amount" of reinforcement; some teachers employ a combination of all methods of fading. One caveat, though: don't fade your reinforcement too quickly. If you remember our definition of extinction, when we withhold reinforcement from a behavior that was previously reinforced, the behavior usually goes away (i.e., is extinguished). If we decrease our reinforcement for expected behavior too quickly or too drastically, our students' expectation-following behavior may be extinguished—this phenomenon is called "ratio strain" (i.e., when reinforcement is faded too quickly to maintain the new behavior).

Deciding when to fade support should not be arbitrary; the decision should be based on data. When developing your reinforcement system, think about your *decision rules*. Decision rules are established to determine when and how the system should be changed. For example, when you take baseline data on your students' rate of verbal contributions to class discussions, you observe that your students participate an average of 10 times an hour during class discussions. You and other stakeholders (i.e., students, families, administrator) agree that this rate should be higher—after all, classrooms with more student participation tend to have better outcomes!—so the next step is to determine your goal for participation. If you set a goal of, say, 40 participations per hour-long class discussion, you will change your reinforcement system after students are reliably meeting that goal. They should achieve the goal at least three times before you change your system, though; any group of students can have one overabundant day of participation. We are looking to establish a pattern; three data points (i.e., three consecutive hour-long discussions with 40 or more instances of participation) would be the bare minimum, but five data points would be ideal. So, your decision rule might look like this: "When students achieve the goal of 40 instances of participation during an hour-long class discussion across five consecutive opportunities, I will begin to fade reinforcement by reinforcing participation using an intermittent, variable ratio of three." Then, you would reinforce after an average of three instances of participation. For example, you reinforce after two, then four, then five, then one, and so on. Collect data to ensure that students are maintaining their current level of participation; if so, you can likely increase the ratio to an average of every five instances of participation. You could also add a second decision rule that focuses on increasing the sophistication of the expected behavior: "When students are maintaining (i.e., for 10 consecutive discussions) an average of 40 instances of participation during an hour-long class discussion on an intermittent variable ratio of five, I will begin reinforcing comments that include specific references to previous course content."

In addition to having decision rules for fading supports, you should also have decision rules about what to do if desired behaviors do not increase as expected. For instance, another decision rule for the above example might be the following: "If students' rate of participation does not exceed 10 instances per hour-long class discussion after 10 class discussions, I will reteach participation expectations and ask students about their preferences for backup reinforcers." It's important to have a plan, and to use data to make decisions according to that plan. It's better to be prepared for something not working and to have a Plan B than to just say, "Well, that system didn't work. I'll scrap it."

SUMMARY

In this chapter, we introduced you to a continuum of strategies for encouraging expected, contextually appropriate behavior in your classroom. At a minimum, you should use behavior-specific praise statements to reinforce contextually appropriate behaviors. Group contingencies are another way to increase the likelihood of appropriate behavior; be careful and thoughtful with group contingencies and stay mindful of the potential issues we discussed. You could use behavioral contracting to hold staff and students accountable for a stated contingency between the expected behavior and reinforcement. We discussed token economies in detail; this evidence-based practice can be designed to be contextually appropriate for any setting and has been effective at increasing all types of contextually appropriate behavior with all types of students. Finally, we talked about the necessity of fading reinforcement in order to increase the likelihood that students will maintain and generalize the behaviors you've taught. Remember, reinforcement increases the likelihood that a behavior will continue in the future—and we want our students' contextually appropriate behaviors to do just that.

PHASES OF LEARNING ACTIVITIES: CHAPTER 7

Acquisition

1. What makes praise specific and contingent? Give an example of behavior-specific praise and describe why behavior-specific praise is more likely to increase behavior in the future than "Good job."

2. Identify the basic components of a token economy. Describe, with specific details, how you would set up a token economy in your classroom.

Fluency

1. What does having a "continuum of responses" to encourage contextually appropriate behavior mean? Why should you have more than one ready response?

2. Give an example of a (a) dependent group contingency, (b) interdependent group contingency, and (c) independent group contingency. Also, list a pro and a con for each type of group contingency.

Maintenance

1. Describe the principles of positive and negative reinforcement (as you learned in Chapter 2) and how they relate to encouraging contextually appropriate behaviors.

2. How can you fade reinforcement in your classroom? Describe your decision rules and how you will fade support while maintaining and increasing contextually appropriate behaviors.

Generalization

1. How can you involve students and families in the development of your classwide reinforcement system? What are some reasons for involving others in the process?

2. How can you ensure that your classwide reinforcement system is culturally and contextually appropriate for your students? What aspects of the classroom, your students, their families, and the larger community should you consider?

Other Skill-Building Exercises

1. You want to design a behavioral contract for your class. Describe (a) the behaviors your contract will target and the rationale for selecting those behaviors and (b) how you will design and implement the contract. Include an example of the contract.

2. Describe how reinforcing contextually appropriate behavior fits in with the other classroom behavioral support strategies we've already discussed (i.e., maximizing structure and establishing and teaching your expectations). Why do you need all three components in place? What would happen if you didn't have a system for reinforcing contextually appropriate behavior?

Implement a Continuum of Strategies to Decrease Contextually Inappropriate Behavior

---

CHAPTER OBJECTIVES

By the end of this chapter, you should be able to . . .

1. Identify different types of strategies to decrease contextually inappropriate behavior.
2. Design a culturally responsive, supportive, and instructionally focused system of responses to contextually inappropriate behavior.
3. Implement and evaluate your strategies for preventing and reducing occurrences of contextually inappropriate behavior.

Imagine This: At the beginning of the school year, Mr. Stone partnered with his students to establish classroom norms ("The Stone Standards"), which he taught explicitly across all classroom routines. He implemented a token economy (students earn "Stone Stars") to reinforce expected behavior. For the first month or so, his students earned many Stone Stars for frequently demonstrating the expected behaviors; however, as the second quarter of the year began, he observed an increase in common contextually inappropriate behaviors. Students were off task more frequently; they responded more slowly to directions and a few began saying unkind things about Mr. Stone ("Stone stinks!" they'd whisper as he walked by their desks).

Mr. Stone, who had limited training in classroom behavioral support, thought that his school's commitment to a PBIS framework just meant rewarding contextually appropriate behavior. He was unsure of how to respond to behaviors that didn't align with the norms he and his students had established. He tried ignoring the behaviors, but would quickly get frustrated and say loudly, "Stop talking!" or "I do **not** stink!" These responses only seemed to increase the students' contextually inappropriate behavior. He gave detentions, sent students to the office, and finally just resorted to teaching to whichever students were listening, while the others listened to music or talked with one another.

One day, Ms. Bernard came into Mr. Stone's room to borrow a stapler. Many students were out of their seats, she overheard some loud student-to-student conversations about last night's game, and a few students had their heads down and earbuds in. Mr. Stone was working with a few students at his desk.

Later, in the teachers' lounge, Miss Bernard approached Mr. Stone. "Tom," she said, "What's going on in your classroom?"

"Well, I did all of the positive things I was supposed to do, but they didn't work. I know you have your Bernard Bucks and everything is great in your classroom, but the Stone Stars just didn't have the same effect. I don't know what else to do," said Mr. Stone.

"Well, you can't just implement your system and leave it alone," said Miss Bernard. "You have to evaluate it regularly and revise according to your data and any feedback you get from students and families. And you have to have some response strategies in place for when things don't go according to plan."

"But I'm not into punishment," said Mr. Stone. "It's not my thing."

"We're talking about strategies to decrease behaviors that don't align with classroom norms. It's about having a consistent system, about reteaching when needed, using restorative processes to repair harm, and ensuring that your responses actually decrease contextually inappropriate behavior," Miss Bernard said.

"I'm listening," said Mr. Stone.

After talking to Miss Bernard and following her suggestions, Mr. Stone reevaluated his token economy and established a clear and consistent continuum of strategies to discourage contextually inappropriate behavior. He and the students collaborated on lessons and role plays to reteach and practice behaviors that aligned with their established classroom norms. Shortly thereafter, while reviewing behavioral data, he saw an increase in the expected behaviors and a reduction in contextually in appropriate behaviors. "Stone rocks," he thought proudly.

ESTABLISHING A CONTINUUM OF STRATEGIES TO DECREASE CONTEXTUALLY INAPPROPRIATE BEHAVIOR

So far, we have provided you with evidence-based practices to increase the likelihood of contextually appropriate behavior in your classroom. You've learned about creating a positive, welcoming, and collaborative classroom climate; actively engaging all learners in your instruction; and establishing, teaching, prompting, and reinforcing contextually relevant behavioral expectations. You've learned how to be proactive, how to precorrect to increase the likelihood of expected behaviors, and how to apply foundational behavioral principles in your classroom. Perfect! Now you can sit back and relax . . . Right?

As Mr. Stone could tell you, not quite. Even with the most effective, data-driven, and proactive classroom management plan, your students will still engage in contextually inappropriate behaviors for a variety of reasons. Remember, your students are exposed to a variety of setting events—many of which will remain unknown to you—that may alter the value of typically available consequences. For example, if a student has a fight on the bus (setting event) and arrives at school feeling angry or unsettled, the typically available consequences for coming in and sitting quietly (e.g., a smile and praise from the teacher, avoiding a reprimand) are less valuable. In fact, potential consequences for not doing work and swearing at the teacher (e.g., being sent to the office or in-school suspension; avoiding the classroom environment and peer with whom they fought) may be much more valuable because of the setting event.

Besides setting events, there are many other factors that can result in a decrease in students' contextually appropriate behavior. Students may be satiated with the available reinforcers, there may be a schedule change that alters the normal routine (and displaces an S^D for contextually appropriate behavior), or they may be engaging in more efficient, effective behaviors to meet their needs. For example, students may be able to earn time to socialize with peers at the end of class, but they *could* socialize immediately. If students do not perceive a valuable reason to wait (e.g., there is not a competing, compelling reinforcer—they aren't more interested in what the teacher is saying or they aren't concerned about potential responses to chatting when the expectation is to be listening, for example), they may not. We need to be prepared to effectively respond to contextually inappropriate behaviors; a continuum of strategies to decrease contextually inappropriate behaviors is a critical feature of a comprehensive classroom behavior support system. Below, we discuss several strategies for preventing and decreasing the likelihood of contextually inappropriate behaviors and increasing the likelihood of contextually appropriate behaviors that align with our classroom expectations.

PREVENTING CONTEXTUALLY INAPPROPRIATE BEHAVIOR BEFORE IT OCCURS: FOCUS ON ANTECEDENTS

In previous chapters, we have focused on setting up your instructional environment to increase the likelihood of contextually appropriate behaviors (e.g., creating an inclusive, predictable, safe, and engaging classroom [Chapter 5]; establishing and teaching positively stated norms or expectations [Chapter 6]; and implementing a continuum of strategies to reinforce contextually appropriate behaviors [Chapter 7]). Another efficient way to increase the likelihood of contextually appropriate behaviors is to *prevent* the likelihood of contextually inappropriate behaviors. In addition to the proactive strategies we've already covered, we can enhance our focus on prevention by observing and reflecting on elements of the environment that are likely to occasion both contextually appropriate and contextually inappropriate behaviors and then modify the environment accordingly. This is called "antecedent manipulation" (flip back to Chapter 2 if you'd like to refresh your fluency with antecedents!). Antecedent manipulation can be done at the individual-student (as discussed in Chapter 10) or whole-class level, and it is an effective way to prevent many contextually inappropriate behaviors. Remember, "what can be predicted can be prevented" (Scott & Eber, 2003, p. 134). If a student has engaged in contextually inappropriate behavior in the past, it's reasonable to assume that the behavior will occur again unless we intentionally make a change to the environment to decrease its likelihood.

For example, several of Mr. Chord's fourth graders engage in behaviors disruptive to their learning (e.g., walking around, loudly continuing conversations from the playground) when they return from recess; Mr. Chord provides frequent error corrections ("Please sit down") and praises the students who are sitting quietly, but the disruptive behaviors continue. After some reflection (and after a quick peek at this book), Mr. Chord decides to introduce a moderately preferred activity to transition students from recess (a highly preferred activity) to academic work (a less preferred activity). When his students come in from recess, Mr. Chord asks them to find a comfortable spot in the classroom and listen as he reads the class book for 10 minutes. Because the class books are selected by the students, most are invested in this activity; there are limited demands placed on the students; and this reading time provides a chance for them to transition physically and mentally from the social, emotional, and behavioral aspects of recess to engaging actively with instruction.

When we think about antecedent modification, we need to think *functionally*. If our observations of students' contextually inappropriate behaviors lead us to infer that those behaviors are functioning to gain our attention, we should intentionally and frequently provide students with direct attention that is not contingent on any specific behavior. This strategy is called **noncontingent reinforcement** (**NCR**; see Carr et al., 2008, for a full discussion). With NCR, you first identify the function of the student's contextually inappropriate behavior and what is most likely reinforcing that behavior (e.g., a student frequently yells "I need help" during independent academic work to obtain adult attention). Then, you provide the reinforcer frequently—*not* contingent on any specific behavior, especially the targeted contextually inappropriate behavior—so that the student no longer needs to engage in the contextually inappropriate behavior to obtain reinforcement. For instance, if the perceived function of yelling "I need help" during independent academic work is to obtain adult attention, you may stop by the student's desk often while they are working to say hello and ask how the work is going (i.e., providing noncontingent attention).

If our students' contextually inappropriate behavior functions as a way for them to escape a task they find aversive (e.g., a difficult assignment), we could (1) modify the assignment, (2) give them a choice about which parts of the assignment they complete (or complete in which order), (3) reteach and provide frequent prompts about how to access help (i.e., modify antecedents), (4) offer or schedule frequent breaks (i.e., NCR) during aversive tasks, or (5) some combination of the above. In addition, we should review academic data to look for connections between specific subjects, task modalities, or other academic considerations and contextually inappropriate behavior.

As students age, a relationship between academic challenges and contextually inappropriate behavior is more likely (McIntosh et al., 2011). Because of this relationship, we may need to consider academic modifications and interventions when building supports to discourage contextually inappropriate behaviors. At the classwide level, look at data to determine if specific academic routines are associated with contextually inappropriate behavior. For any identified routines, determine if you're providing a high rate and variety of OTRs (as discussed in Chapter 5) and consider other ways to enhance or adjust your instruction to better meet the needs of your students.

If your students are not demonstrating contextually appropriate behaviors reliably and fluently, you should consider your students' phase of learning with your established classroom expectations. Were students able to move from acquisition to fluency, or do they need more practice? Are they engaging in contextually appropriate behaviors more often in some routines than in others? Revisit your teaching plan for social, emotional, and behavioral skills (or revisit Chapter 6 if you'd like a review of what this can look like) and consider reteaching or providing a booster session on some of the expected behaviors that aren't occurring regularly. Provide differentiated instruction as necessary for students who have more intensive social, emotional, or behavioral needs. Also, consider the contextual and cultural relevance and responsiveness of the behaviors you're asking from students: Are they respectful of individual and collective learning histories? Do they reflect the shared values of all members of the classroom community? Has the instruction been accessible to students whose first language is not the dominant one spoken in the classroom or students who need support with receptive language? You may wish to "circle up" with students and revisit the classroom expectations if you review collected data and determine that your current expectations may not be the right cultural or contextual fit—and solicit input from families, too. Students are more likely to demonstrate contextually appropriate behaviors if they understand the context and feel like valued members of the classroom community.

BEHAVIOR-SPECIFIC FEEDBACK: ERROR CORRECTION

We've mentioned behavior-specific error correction before; perhaps you remember our discussion in Chapter 3 about responding to low-intensity contextually inappropriate behaviors in the same manner you respond to academic errors. Because this is a critical concept in effectively supporting students' contextually appropriate behaviors and maintaining a supportive and helpful classroom environment, we'll provide another example here to illustrate this concept. Imagine the following scenarios:

- A student working an addition problem at the whiteboard makes an error. When the teacher sees the error, the teacher says, "Leona, why don't you try that problem again, using the strategy we just practiced, and see if you come up with a different answer? Let me know if you have any questions." The student tries again, applies the strategy, and when she comes up with the correct answer, the teacher says, "That's right! Nice work."
- A student yells out an answer in class instead of raising her hand. The teacher says, "Ashley, don't call out." Ashley raises her hand, but the teacher has already called on someone else.

In the first scenario, the student makes an academic error. The teacher provides feedback indicating a mistake was made, offers support to the student, and then provides contingent feedback and praise when the student demonstrates the correct academic response. In the second scenario, the teacher uses a "don't" statement in an effort to positively punish the behavior (i.e., by adding the statement to the environment in order to decrease the future rate of calling out). When the student does perform the desired behavior (i.e., raising her hand), the student receives no feedback or acknowledgment for engaging in the contextually appropriate behavior.

Why don't we treat low-level contextually inappropriate behaviors the same way we treat academic errors? When students make academic errors, we provide support, we reteach skills as necessary, we provide immediate feedback on student performance, and we frequently check for understanding. When students engage in low-level contextually inappropriate behaviors (i.e., they make minor social behavioral mistakes), we often add an aversive stimulus to the environment in the form of a "no, stop, don't" statement in an effort to (1) stop the occurrence of the contextually inappropriate behavior and (2) start the demonstration of an expected behavior. Imagine if a student made a spelling mistake and you said, "Stop spelling incorrectly," anticipating that your statement would produce a correctly spelled word—unlikely, right? We know this process doesn't work to increase correct academic responses, and it's unlikely to be an effective way to increase contextually appropriate social behaviors.

Here's something to think about, too: "no, stop, don't" statements are actually conditioned punishers. Loud noises and pain are two punishers that we naturally find aversive; if these occur contingent on a behavior, we usually stop engaging in that behavior. For instance, if you put your hand on a hot stove, it burns; in the future, you're less likely to put your hand on a hot stove—you've learned that particular behavior results in pain. With young children, when we see them in danger (e.g., they are about to walk into a busy street or pull a dog's tail), we may yell, "NO!" or "DON'T!" Even if the young child does not understand the word, they understand the volume and tone of the words, which are frightening and aversive, causing the child to stop the behavior. Eventually, the words "no" or "don't" can stop a behavior by themselves— even if they are not yelled—because of their previous association with the aversive volume and tone. Therefore, when we use "no, stop, don't" statements with students, we are actually using conditioned punishers whose value was learned through pairing with loud noises and sometimes even physical consequences (e.g., grabbing a child's arm while saying, "Don't do that").

Teachers who control the classroom through the administration of contingent aversive consequences risk increased power struggles with their students (Kerr & Nelson, 2006). As adults, we may take issue with being managed this way (e.g., "do this or else!") and recognize that it leads to a hostile environment; children are not immune to feeling stress, fear, or even fighting back if adults "establish control" through contingent aversive consequences. Students impacted by trauma and students with elevated social, emotional, or behavioral needs may struggle more with self-regulation and making progress in an environment where adults view their role as "controlling" or "managing" students rather than providing supports that meet their social, emotional, behavioral, and academic needs. In addition, forcing compliance by threatening aversive consequences when students make behavioral mistakes does not reflect a culturally responsive, equity-centered mindset: the "do as I say or else" approach does not reflect a collaborative, welcoming, or inclusive approach to supporting student needs and can actually increase disproportionality and widen the discipline gap (Leverson et al., 2021).

Another consideration: if teachers exhibit frustration through raised voices and frequent negative interactions with students, they are *not* modeling behaviors that align with creating a supportive, safe, and predictable classroom environment—and their behavior may actually function as a reinforcer for students' contextually inappropriate behaviors. (Picture a classroom where students encourage each other to break rules or intensify their contextually inappropriate behaviors to see how angry the teacher will get.) We have a choice: our classrooms can be places where we encourage students' contextually appropriate behaviors mainly through the availability of positive reinforcement in the form of teacher acknowledgement, good grades, and other pleasant stimuli added to the environment, or, our classrooms can be places where we encourage students' contextually appropriate behaviors mainly through the availability of negative reinforcement (e.g., avoiding aversive stimuli like reprimands, calls home to report behavioral "violations," detention, and so forth). One issue with primarily using negative reinforcement to discourage contextually inappropriate behaviors—along with creating a potentially hostile environment that is not warm, welcoming, or inclusive—is that the aversive consequences to be avoided may not function as punishers for all students (e.g., some students enjoy being suspended, as they do not have to attend school), thereby decreasing the likelihood that students will engage in behaviors that result in avoiding these consequences.

Rather than introducing a "no, stop, don't" statement into the environment, we suggest approaching low-level, nondangerous contextually inappropriate behaviors with the same mindset you'd have when responding to academic errors. Think back to our previous scenario, and look at how it could unfold differently by using this approach:

A student yells out an answer in class instead of raising her hand. The teacher says, "Ashley, remember what it looks like to be responsible during class. Can you show me how to share your comment responsibly?" Ashley raises her hand, and the teacher says, "That's exactly right. Now, what did you want to add to our discussion?"

Here, we have turned a potentially negative interaction (and any negative interaction, however minor, has the potential to escalate into a power struggle) into a positive interaction, where the student receives contingent feedback on her use of the expected behavior rather than just a contingent aversive statement when she yells out. If error corrections are our dominant type of interaction with students, more misbehavior is likely (Kerr & Nelson, 2006). Research indicates that teachers who have a higher ratio of positive to negative interactions with students (e.g., ≥5:1, with a higher ratio for students with elevated social, emotional and behavioral needs; Cook et al., 2017; Downs et al., 2019; Center on PBIS, 2022a) see improved student behavior and a decrease in inappropriate behaviors.

When you have to deliver an error correction for a low-intensity contextually inappropriate behavior, speak calmly and clearly; always consider the behavioral model you are providing. Explicitly state the behavior that did not align with the established expectations (e.g., "Adam, poking Chaz is not safe. Please keep your hands to yourself in the hallway.") When Adam demonstrates the expected behavior, acknowledge him for doing so ("That's what being safe looks like—thank you"). Like most adults, students tend to prefer error corrections being delivered quickly and quietly, rather than publicly (Infantino & Little, 2005). While some may find value in public reprimands serving as a reminder about expected behaviors for other students, reducing the potential for student embarrassment and preserving student dignity are both more important considerations. We want to model contextually appropriate behaviors; discretion and compassion when correcting errors is almost always contextually appropriate. Remember, people make behavioral mistakes for a variety of reasons—setting events, unclear expectations, unmet needs—and introducing humiliation when errors are made is not being supportive and helpful. When you correct an error, remember to acknowledge the expected behavior as soon as it occurs. After all, if we're providing contingent attention for a contextually inappropriate behavior, we should do the same when the expected behavior occurs, as that's the behavior we want to see again in the future.

Remember, behavior-specific error corrections is a relatively simple and low-effort strategy to implement and can be used for students of all ages and ability levels; like praise, we consider behavior-specific error correction a "nonnegotiable" strategy for your classroom. However, simple error corrections aren't effective or appropriate responses for higher magnitude, unsafe, or chronic contextually inappropriate behaviors. Whenever possible, low-intensity contextually inappropriate behaviors should be treated like academic errors, with reinforcement for the expected, contextually appropriate behavior as soon as it occurs.

DIFFERENTIAL REINFORCEMENT

Another strategy for responding to contextually inappropriate behavior is **differential reinforcement.** "What's that?" you may be thinking. "Reinforcement to *decrease* behaviors?" Well, kind of. Differential reinforcement is a special schedule of reinforcement designed to lower the frequency or reinforce the absence of certain contextually inappropriate behaviors and/ or reinforce contextually appropriate behaviors that can replace them. Differential reinforcement is traditionally used at the individual-student level; classroom application is possible, but challenging, given some of the considerations and caveats. There are a few different kinds of differential reinforcement, two of which we discuss in detail below.

Differential Reinforcement of Lower Rates of Behavior

Differential reinforcement of lower rates of behavior (DRL) is the application of a specific schedule of reinforcement designed to decrease behaviors that are contextually inappropriate primarily due to their frequency (Alberto et al., 2021). For instance, participating in class is usually a contextually appropriate, even desired, behavior. However, participating too frequently (e.g., answering every time the teacher asks a question or offering a thought after every fact mentioned by a peer) is not contextually appropriate. Therefore, a teacher could apply DRL as follows, by discreetly addressing the too-frequent participation as follows:

> "Matt, I appreciate that you are eager to share your answers and thoughts with the rest of the class. However, everyone in the class needs a chance to participate, so I'd like you to raise your hand only four times during a class period. I'll put four sticky notes on your desk, and each time you participate, take one off, so you can keep track. If you keep it to four, you can be my helper this afternoon and we can discuss any other questions you had."

With DRL, teachers reinforce lower rates of a target behavior. To use DRL effectively, collect data on the contextually inappropriate behavior you wish to target to establish a baseline rate of that behavior. Then, use reasonably spaced criteria to decrease limits (Alberto et al., 2021). If a student is currently calling out 20 times per class, differentially reinforcing four or fewer callouts per class is probably an unreasonable criterion to start—15 or 10 per class might make more sense. In addition, if you plan to use DRL for a behavior that is inappropriate at any level, remember that reinforcement is still provided after occurrences of the target behavior, even though the frequency has decreased. For example, if you have a student who currently averages 15 curse words during class and you tell them that they will receive a reinforcer for swearing 5 or fewer times, there's a risk of interpreting that as "Swearing 5 times is okay!" A better option may be to eschew transparency in this case; if your data show a decrease in the target behavior (i.e., the use of curse words), you can say to the student, "You're making a real effort with your language, and I think you've earned this Bernard Buck for that." (You could also reinforce an amount of time they go without swearing, using differential reinforcement of zero target behaviors.)

Differential Reinforcement of Alternative Behaviors

Good news! If you've been implementing the strategies you've read about in this book (specifically those for encouraging contextually appropriate behaviors, discussed in detail in Chapter 7), you're already using differential reinforcement of alternative behaviors (DRA). With DRA, you reinforce contextually appropriate behaviors that take the place of (i.e., compete successfully with) the targeted contextually inappropriate behavior. You can reward a student for decreased rates of swearing (i.e., with DRL), while also providing contingent reinforcement on using kind words. (That is, you are differentially reinforcing their alternative behavior. Using kind words is a contextually appropriate alternative to swearing in the classroom.) If you are rewarding Matt for participating less frequently (i.e., DRL), you can also provide contingent reinforcement if he writes down what he'd like to contribute instead (i.e., DRA). You can also use DRA without DRL. For example, if you want to decrease off-topic comments and increase on-topic comments, you can praise (and perhaps give a token) after each on-topic comment, and resume instruction without commenting on off-topic comments. Any contextually appropriate behavior that serves the same function as the target contextually inappropriate behavior can be reinforced; make sure that your students know the contingency and that you are prompting and teaching the expected behaviors.

Differential reinforcement can be an effective way to increase contextually appropriate behaviors and decrease contextually inappropriate behaviors without introducing aversive stimuli into the environment (or removing something pleasant) contingent on contextually inappropriate behavior. We want to keep our interactions with students as supportive, positive, and helpful as possible, and we want to talk about and provide attention to contextually appropriate behavior far more often than we talk about or provide attention to contextually inappropriate behavior. Differential reinforcement is one option on the continuum of strategies to discourage contextually inappropriate behavior.

PLANNED IGNORING

In Chapter 2, we discussed the behavioral principle of "extinction," in which you withhold reinforcement for a behavior that was previously reinforced. For example, if Jacob's callouts function to obtain teacher attention (currently delivered in the form of statements like "Stop it, Jacob" or "Don't call out, Jacob"), the teacher can ignore Jacob's callouts (i.e., stop providing attention contingent on his callouts) in an effort to put the behavior on extinction. Of course, the teacher should beware the extinction burst: when Jacob's callouts are not met with teacher attention, he is likely to increase the volume, frequency, and intensity of his callouts. To decrease the likelihood of the extinction burst, the teacher should simultaneously be reinforcing any relevant contextually appropriate behaviors with a *lot* of contingent attention to increase the likelihood that Jacob will use those behaviors (e.g., raising his hand, orienting his body toward the teacher) to obtain attention in the future, decreasing the likelihood of him calling out. The teacher should also employ antecedent strategies, like checking in frequently with Jacob and providing periodic attention (i.e., NCR) throughout the class, to decrease the likelihood he will need to seek teacher attention—it's already being provided!

Planned ignoring can be considered extinction when applied to behaviors that function to gain attention. (If you ignore a behavior that functions to provide escape from an aversive stimulus or condition—like a student who puts their head down to avoid doing work—it's highly unlikely that you will extinguish that behavior!) Planned ignoring is often difficult to implement effectively, and it should *not* be used in isolation. If you intend to withhold reinforcement for a behavior that functions to obtain attention, it is critical that you teach and reinforce an alternative behavior that meets the same function—as in the example with Jacob. The teacher must make sure Jacob receives contingent attention for appropriate behaviors (and even some noncontingent attention in the form of frequent check-ins) that matches or exceeds the intensity previously provided when Jacob called out. The teacher makes the calling-out behavior irrelevant (because Jacob already is provided with ample attention and has clear, efficient ways to earn more attention when demonstrating relevant contextually appropriate behaviors) and ineffective (because the calling-out behavior no longer results in attention).

If you are using planned ignoring, remember that the behavior targeted for extinction is likely to get worse before it gets better; consider how disruptive a potential extinction burst may be and if the risk is too high, select a different strategy or strategies to discourage the target behavior. For example, your collaborative classroom norms include calling staff members by their selected formal title (e.g., Mr., Ms., Miss, Mrs., Dr., Mx.) and last name. One student routinely calls you by your first name and you've been responding with contingent attention in the form of "Don't call me that! It's Miss Smith" or a similar verbal reprimand. After reading to this point in our book, you might consider planned ignoring. However, be forewarned that the student's behavior is likely to get worse before it gets better. When the student says, "Hey, Norma" and you do not respond, the student may try again. Because the behavior has previously resulted in contingent attention from you (remember our discussion about learning histories?), the student may try again and again, and she may increase the frequency and intensity of the behavior: "Hey, Norma! NORMA! What's up, Norma? I know you can hear me! Hey, Norma!" Will you be able to withstand that kind of an extinction burst? Consider what happens if after the 100th "Norma!" you turn around and yell, "CALL ME MISS SMITH! DON'T CALL ME NORMA!" You've just reinforced an entirely new level of the contextually inappropriate behavior and demonstrated to the student that the behavior eventually will result in contingent attention—it just may take a while. So, only use planned ignoring—or any extinction procedure—if you can use it consistently and withstand a temporary increase in behavior.

One last caveat about this strategy: planned ignoring means removing *all* attention contingent on the contextually inappropriate behavior targeted for extinction. Therefore, when a student directs an unkind remark at a teacher, the teacher should *not* say, "I'm ignoring you," or "I don't respond when students say unkind things." That is not ignoring the behavior; that's simply providing attention in a different way. Similarly, teachers who start "ignoring" contextually inappropriate behaviors but put a check mark on a board next to a student's name or give the student a "look" contingent on the contextually inappropriate behavior are not putting those behaviors on extinction; they are just providing a different kind of attention. The teacher should provide attention *only* when the student is engaging in the expected behavior, and only in the absence of any related contextually inappropriate behaviors.

OVERCORRECTION

Overcorrection is a consequence strategy that requires students to engage in exaggerated practice of the appropriate behavior (Alberto et al., 2021). While intended to reduce future occurrences of contextually inappropriate behavior through the application of positive punishment (i.e., adding something to the environment to decrease the future likelihood of a behavior), overcorrection actually requires that students engage in extended practice of a contextually appropriate behavior. In overcorrection, the punishment truly does "fit the crime."

There are two types of overcorrection. In **restitutional overcorrection,** the student who has disturbed the environment in some way through their contextually inappropriate behavior is required to restore the environment to its original condition—and then some (Alberto et al., 2021). For instance, Keisha writes her name on her desk with markers, which does not align with your classroom's agreed-upon expectation of respecting property. In this case, a response using restitutional overcorrection may look like asking Keisha to clean her own desk and the other desks in the classroom. Keisha corrects her own behavioral error and engages in *overcorrection* through cleaning the other desks.

The other type of overcorrection is **positive-practice overcorrection.** In positive-practice overcorrection, the student or students who engage in contextually inappropriate behavior are required to engage in the relevant culturally appropriate behavior—and then some (Alberto et al., 2021). For example, you see a group of students running in the hallway when your school-wide norm is to walk in the hallway. To apply positive-practice overcorrection, you could have these students walk through the hallway several times, thus "positively practicing" the expected behavior. The behavioral mechanics are hopefully calibrated so that students find the overcorrection just aversive enough to decrease the likelihood of engaging in the contextually inappropriate behavior in the future, but you do not have to introduce traditional or novel aversive stimuli (e.g., yelling, "Don't run!" or issuing demerits or detentions) into the environment; you are simply having them practice the expected behavior several times.

There are a few caveats to consider when implementing overcorrection procedures. First, as with any consequence, you do not want to use it too often, lest it lose its effectiveness. In addition, we don't want students associating a contextually appropriate behavior with an aversive experience. If you make students line up 30 times as part of a positive-practice overcorrection response, when you ask them to line up in the future, you may hear sighs and groans as students recall their last experience with lining up. Also, if you are using restitutional overcorrection responses, ensure that you are doing so within the guidelines of school policy and that your intent to use restitutional responses is shared with your students and families; students and families may have questions about and may even be uncomfortable with some restitutional tasks, so be transparent and willing to adjust (or abandon) your application of the practice accordingly.

Overcorrection can be an effective consequence to reduce future occurrences of contextually inappropriate behaviors, and it requires practice of desired behaviors (in positive-practice overcorrection) or building fluency with the social skill of taking accountability for one's actions (in restitutional overcorrection). We will talk more about another—and potentially more effective—way to encourage accountability through restorative practices later in this chapter. As with all responses to contextually inappropriate behavior, overcorrection should be used judiciously and in conjunction with ongoing reinforcement for contextually appropriate behavior.

RESPONSE COST

With **response cost** a stimulus is taken away contingent on contextually inappropriate behavior (Simonsen et al., 2008). The use of response-cost measures is designed to negatively punish contextually inappropriate behaviors; that is, the removal of desirable stimuli contingent on contextually inappropriate behavior is intended to reduce future occurrences of that behavior. Of course, response cost isn't actually punishing (in the behavioral sense of the word) unless occurrences of the contextually inappropriate behavior decrease after the pleasant stimulus is removed from the environment.

Response cost, if used at all, is usually used in conjunction with a token economy (see Chapter 7 for a full discussion of token economies). In a token economy, students earn tokens (i.e., generalized conditioned reinforcers) contingent on contextually appropriate behavior. Response cost is the loss of previously earned reinforcers or the loss of the ability to earn reinforcers; that is, the student is "fined" for contextually inappropriate behavior. Whether or not the response-cost strategy is effective depends on (1) whether the students find the tokens and backup reinforcers valuable and (2) the rate and schedule of students' token accumulation (Alberto et al., 2021).

The following are examples of response-cost application:

- Mr. Belvedere gives out "Way to Go!" tickets for a variety of contextually appropriate behaviors. When students engage in contextually inappropriate behavior, Mr. Belvedere removes a specific number of tickets from students' totals. For example, when a student uses inappropriate language, they lose two tickets. The fines are preestablished; students know that certain behaviors that don't align with their agreed-on classroom norms will result in the loss of a certain number of tickets.
- Mx. Chin puts stickers on a chart whenever their students engage in certain contextually appropriate behaviors (e.g., helping others, cleaning up, or volunteering in class). When a student demonstrates contextually inappropriate behaviors (e.g., saying something unkind to a peer or not being prepared for class), Mx. Chin removes a preestablished number of stickers from the student's chart.

Both Mr. Belvedere and Mx. Chin have made it clear which contextually inappropriate behaviors will result in the loss of tokens and how many tokens will be lost. If you decide to use a response-cost system (and please note that we are *not* suggesting you do; we are simply providing you with another possible strategy for your continuum of responses to contextually inappropriate behavior), be sure that you establish the "fines" up front, so students know which behaviors will result in the loss of their earned rewards and how much they will lose. Response cost has been successful at reducing certain behaviors like swearing (Trice & Parker, 1983) and aggressive behavior (Forman, 1980).

There are many caveats when using a response-cost strategy; we encourage you to reflect carefully on each if you're considering using response cost in your classroom. First, response cost is more intrusive than the strategies discussed thus far, as it requires the active removal of something the student has already earned. Unlike overcorrection, there is no engagement in contextually appropriate behavior when applying response cost. With response cost, you are actively administering a (potentially) punishing consequence (i.e., the loss of an earned reward), whereas with differential reinforcement and planned ignoring, you are manipulating your reinforcement of contextually inappropriate (and appropriate) behavior. With error correction, the student receives feedback on the contextually inappropriate behavior and is provided with a chance to demonstrate (and receive feedback on) the expected contextually appropriate behavior.

Second, there are logistical issues to think about when implementing response cost. For example, imagine the following scenarios in a classroom that uses "Care Coupons" for tokens:

- Nicole is chewing gum in class. Her teacher says, "Nicole, you signed our classroom behavioral contract and you know chewing gum isn't allowed in class. Please spit out the gum, and I'm taking away two Care Coupons." Nicole says, "I don't have any Care Coupons. I haven't earned any."
- August is making noises and faces at classmates. His teacher says, "August, that's not kind behavior. You owe me three of your Care Coupons." August replies, "I earned those! They're in my desk. If you want them, you'll have to come and get them."

In both of these scenarios, there are clear issues with using the response-cost strategy. In the first one, Nicole hasn't earned enough tokens to pay the fine, forcing the teacher to make an awkward decision—either forgo the consequence or have Nicole hand over the next two she earns, which may make earning them less appealing. (And this situation can happen more often than you might think, since those students who earn the fewest tokens are often the first to engage in contextually inappropriate behaviors that result in tokens being taken away.) You have to guard against students having a low or zero "token balance" if you intend to use response cost; otherwise, these scenarios will happen. We have seen response cost work in a math classroom where students kept a "checkbook" where they kept track of their "money" (i.e., tokens). The teacher did implement a response-cost strategy, but because he was using a system analogous to a real-life checking account the teacher was able to incorporate having a "negative balance" into his system and took it as an opportunity to teach his students about negative numbers. (Please note that he didn't encourage students to have a negative token balance; he simply planned for the possibility and used the possibility as a teachable moment for his class.)

In the scenario with August, the teacher has to physically remove tokens from a student who does not willingly hand them over. If you are considering using response cost, how will you physically retrieve tokens from students who do not hand them to you? If you are using a point system or if you manage the tokens yourself, that situation won't happen, but many token economies are based on tangible tokens the students collect and manage. We certainly don't want you or your students to be in a standoff over tokens, nor do we want to set the stage for a potential power struggle. Remember that the students most likely to lose tokens are those with more frequent contextually inappropriate behaviors; are you certain that you want to use a strategy with the potential to lead to this kind of uncomfortable situation (for both you and the student)? Please, please consider the impact of using response cost before selecting it as a strategy to discourage contextually inappropriate behaviors, and be thoughtful and careful if you do.

Our last caveat about using response cost is the potential impact on your reward system. When you collaborated with your students and families to design your classwide reinforcement system, the goal was to create an effective, efficient system to encourage your students' contextually appropriate behaviors. You carefully selected tokens and backup reinforcers, planned the exchange system, and created a thoughtful schedule of reinforcement. By implementing response cost, you introduce a potentially aversive aspect to your reinforcement system. That is, something that you've designed to be part of your positive, welcoming, predictable, and safe classroom climate is associated with potentially punitive and unpleasant consequences. As we mentioned in the previous paragraph, it is the students with the most frequent contextually inappropriate behaviors and those with elevated social, emotional, and behavioral needs who are (1) least likely to earn tokens and (2) most likely to have them taken away, a combination that almost guarantees frustration and loss of interest in the reinforcement system if the student is unable to keep the tokens they have earned (or is constantly threatened with loss of tokens).

As adults, we would likely be uncomfortable (and downright outraged) if a response-cost strategy were applied to our paycheck. If you are paid by the hour, you earn wages for the hours that you work. If you call in sick, you do not get paid for the hours you do not work; your supervisor does *not* go into your bank account and remove the money you've previously earned. Think about how upset you would be if that happened and remember that when considering the use of response cost. Our advice is to focus primarily on reinforcing contextually appropriate behaviors; if students do not engage in contextually appropriate behaviors (or engage in contextually inappropriate behaviors), they simply do not earn reinforcement.

TIME-OUT FROM REINFORCEMENT

Time-out from reinforcement is another strategy for responding to contextually inappropriate behavior. Please note that we have not simply used the phrase "time-out"; we used "time-out from reinforcement." In order for time-out to be effective, the student needs to be prevented from accessing reinforcement or removed from an environment where they want to be—otherwise, the time-out will not reduce future occurrences of the contextually inappropriate behavior. In fact, we may inadvertently reinforce the contextually inappropriate behavior if the "time-out" takes place in a preferred environment (or allows the student to escape from an unpreferred environment or activity).

For instance, think about a child who is sent to his room for swearing and yelling. The child's room contains a video game system and a tablet he can use to text and talk with friends—the child likes it there, which decreases the likelihood of this consequence reducing future occurrences of swearing and yelling. Now, think about the student who is engaging in behaviors that do not align with the agreed-upon norms for science class by refusing to get to work and mocking the teacher. Finally, the teacher says, "That's enough, Jimmy! Get down to the principal's office." Jimmy leaves to the sound of his peers cheering and goes to the office, where he chats with the secretary and eventually has a one-on-one conversation with the principal. Jimmy receives a lot of contingent attention for his contextually inappropriate behavior, and he escapes a class where he may not have wanted to be (negative reinforcement at work!). This "time-out" is not time-out from reinforcement at all; in fact, the next time Jimmy doesn't feel like being in science, the likelihood of him repeating the same contextually inappropriate behavior is high, as that behavior previously resulted in a lot of contingent attention and escape. As you continue reading, remember that every time we say "time-out," we mean "time-out from reinforcement."

Time-out from reinforcement can be administered in a variety of ways; time-out can be either "nonexclusionary" or "exclusionary" (Alberto et al., 2021). One type of nonexclusionary time-out is **contingent observation,** which you may remember from your own days in elementary school; a popular usage of this kind of time-out is having students stand "on the wall" at recess. That is, when students engage in contextually inappropriate playground behavior (e.g., not sharing equipment, pushing in line for the swings), they may be told they are "on the wall," and they report to a bench or lean against a wall, where they can see their peers continuing to enjoy recess. With contingent observation, students remain in the environment where the contextually inappropriate behavior occurred, but they cannot access reinforcement or take part in the activities. After a predetermined amount of time, the student can return to the environment (and should praised for expected behavior as soon as it occurs).

In the classroom, nonexclusionary time-out may look like being told to "sit and watch" while peers engage in an activity, being asked to put your head down, or simply being unable to earn reinforcement (e.g., tokens) for a specific period of time. We did say "specific." The administration of time-out should not be arbitrary or until you "feel" the student is ready; there should be consistent time limits that are specified beforehand (e.g., "Pushing and shoving at recess will result in 2 minutes on the wall," or "Being unkind to a peer when they are sharing during group activities will result in a freeze on earning tokens until the end of the period"). To recap, if the student remains in the educational environment but is denied access to the activity or to reinforcement, that is nonexclusionary time-out.

In **exclusionary time-out,** the student is removed from the activity altogether; they may be moved to a different part of the classroom, or the student may be removed from the environment itself. Examples of exclusionary time-out include the following:

- Beverly is singing loudly during independent seatwork and her peers are laughing. After the third warning, the teacher moves Beverly's seat to the back of the classroom, where she cannot see her peers (but the teacher can still see Beverly). The teacher tells Beverly that she needs to sit there quietly for 6 minutes before she can rejoin the class.
- Kenny is asked to write a math problem on the board. He begins drawing pictures instead, and his classmates begin to laugh. The teacher issues a verbal warning, but Kenny persists, adding captions (including contextually inappropriate language) to his pictures. The teacher walks Kenny to the principal's office, where he is to remain until the end of the class.

Remember, in order for time-out to be effective (i.e., in order to decrease the future likelihood of a behavior), a student must be removed from reinforcement. If a student throws her papers on the ground, refuses to do work, and puts her head down, removing her from the environment is likely not time-out from reinforcement. In fact, removing her from the environment might negatively reinforce her behavior if she desires escaping from that class. In addition, the teacher may be negatively reinforced for removing the student from the classroom (i.e., the student's contextually inappropriate behavior—likely aversive to the teacher—is removed when the teacher tells the student to leave the classroom). This misuse of time-out can result in a **coercive cycle,** in which a student engages in contextually inappropriate behavior and is removed from the environment (which is negatively reinforcing to the student), and the student's removal is negatively reinforcing to the teacher (Sutherland & Singh, 2004). The next time the student doesn't want to be in class, they are likely to engage in the same behavior, and the next time the student engages in the behavior, the teacher is likely to remove the student from the environment.

As you may have surmised by now, using time-out effectively is challenging (and it is incumbent on us to mention here that positive practices *are* easier and more ethical). Time-out requires a lot of consideration and careful management on the part of the teacher, and it is easy to overuse. Also, removing students from the educational environment poses a significant disruption to their learning; the students who engage in frequent contextually inappropriate behaviors are likely those who need the structure and instruction in the classroom the *most*. There is no opportunity for the student to practice contextually appropriate behaviors while experiencing a time-out; they only learn which behaviors result in time-out from reinforcement. If you implement time-out procedures and the same students receive the consequence repeatedly, you aren't punishing the behavior (i.e., the contextually inappropriate behavior doesn't decrease or stop)—and that's true for all consequences. Whether you believe that you are "punishing" a behavior or not is irrelevant; the only way we know if a consequence is truly punishing is if the target behavior decreases or stops in the future. In addition, a critical concern with the use of exclusionary time-out (and any exclusionary discipline responses, like suspension) is the long history of exclusionary practices being used disproportionately with students of color, especially if they have disabilities (Losen & Martinez, 2020). Exclusionary practices are not culturally responsive or inclusive; they widen the access and achievement gap for students of color and are associated with *lower* schoolwide achievement and perceived safety (American Psychological Association, 2008; Nese et al., 2023). As we work to center equity in our behavioral support framework, reducing the use of exclusionary discipline tools is a necessary consideration.

RESTORATIVE PRACTICES

Given that many of our "traditional" responses to contextually inappropriate behavior (e.g., response cost, exclusionary time-out) are misaligned with culturally responsive, positive, and proactive behavioral supports, we should seek ways to incorporate instructional, restorative responses to contextually inappropriate behaviors. Luckily, multiple resources exist to help with implementation of restorative practices as part of a schoolwide prevention-focused behavioral support framework. For example, the Learning Policy Institute (*www.learningpolicyinstitute.org*) has several informative and helpful tools on their website, and Nese et al. (2023) developed the Inclusive Skill-Building Learning Approach (ISLA; *www.neselab.org/isla*). Below, we offer a quick overview of how restorative practices can be implemented in your classroom.

Restorative practices are centered on the concept of repairing harm. In the context of our classroom PBIS, we can implement restorative practices as a way to help students recognize the impact of their behavior on others, on the environment, and on themselves, help them take accountability for their behaviors, work with them to restore any harm done by their behavior, and create a plan to help the student make more positive choices the next time a similar situation occurs.

Restorative responses to contextually inappropriate behaviors can be a regular part of our classwide PBIS model. Building out your restorative process should involve collaboration with your students and their families and teaching any prerequisite social, emotional, and behavioral skills (e.g., coping and tolerance skills for uncomfortable situations, self-awareness, self-reflection, goal setting). Think back to Chapter 4—these are skills that should be included in your classroom matrix. Any behavior that causes harm to others, the environment, or the student themselves lends itself to a restorative response.

The restorative process begins with a **restorative conversation.** The conversation should center on a few key questions. First, ask the student what happened—and listen to their account without interruption or judgment. Then, ask about the impact they think their behavior had on others, on the community, on the environment, or on themselves. This provides an opportunity for students to recognize how their behavior affects the world around them. This conversation is a chance for the student to see the consequences of their behavior, and help them see how their behaviors may trigger (be an antecedent for) others' responses. These restorative conversations are likely to be more impactful if the student feels like a valued member of the classroom community (i.e., has a learning history of your classroom community being positively reinforcing rather than punishing). If you've followed our guidance and created a welcoming, safe, and predictable space for all of your learners, students feeling connected to their community is more likely! If the student has identified specific ways that their behavior resulted in harm, this may present an opportunity to identify an appropriate, relevant restorative task. For example, if the student's behavior hurt the feelings of a peer, the student may identify an act of kindness they could do for that peer. Follow up with questions about what the student could have done differently to reduce any negative impacts of their behavior and begin to develop a plan for how the student can take different actions if a similar situation arises in the future. Finally, ask the student what they need from you to be successful in executing the plan—what supports will increase the likelihood of future success?

There are a few additional considerations if you plan to implement restorative practices in your classroom. First, anyone who was impacted by the behavior should be part of the restorative process and take part in the conversation, including staff members. The goal is to restore harm done, which includes any harm to relationships. Keep in mind that staff members may also need to actively restore harm—sometimes, we make mistakes when responding to contextually inappropriate behaviors, and we can use the restorative conversation to take accountability and model self-awareness and responsibility to our students.

Second, consider logistics. If a restorative conversation needs to take place, it may be challenging in a classroom with other students and a schedule to keep; consider enlisting the help of other staff (e.g., a social worker or counselor) to partner with you and think through some of the operational challenges. Be sure to also involve families in the process (if they are willing and able to participate); restorative practices provide unique opportunities to build and strengthen relationships, establish (or reestablish) a positive and supportive community, and help students create connections between how their behavior at school relates to the larger community and their lives at home.

Finally, consider each student's unique learning history and the function of their behavior. For example, if a student has a history of trauma, especially associated with one of the members of your classroom community (e.g., if they were assaulted by a peer), a restorative conversation may not be appropriate without significant support from clinicians. It is also important to make sure restorative conversations do not inadvertently reinforce the behaviors that resulted in the conversation. For example, if a student engages in contextually inappropriate behavior to obtain adult attention and a restorative conversation with an adult quickly follows that contextually inappropriate behavior, it's possible that the conversation could inadvertently reinforce that behavior. Thus, it is important to "think functionally" and consider students' learning histories when planning a restorative conversation.

Restorative practices provide a positive, instructional, and culturally responsive way to encourage contextually appropriate behavior and discourage contextually inappropriate behavior—please apply what you've learned earlier in this text and explore available resources as you consider how a restorative approach might benefit your responses to contextually inappropriate behavior as part of your classwide PBIS implementation.

ADDITIONAL CONSIDERATIONS WHEN RESPONDING TO CONTEXTUALLY INAPPROPRIATE BEHAVIOR

We have offered a lot of caveats with the more intrusive strategies described in this chapter, and we would be remiss if we didn't recap some of our concerns with using punishment and exclusionary practices in the classroom. First, please understand that we are not advocating for a classroom devoid of accountability when students engage in contextually inappropriate behaviors; we just want you to respond to those behaviors judiciously, thoughtfully, and through the lens of equity and cultural responsiveness (and we urge you to explore restorative practices as a way to do this). We also encourage you to spend most of your time on prevention and setting your students (and you!) up for success by implementing what you learned in Chapters 5, 6, and 7 of this book.

Please remember that positive and proactive interventions are necessary—we'd say *critical*—when using punishment. We already know that all behavior serves a purpose; we discuss function at great length in other chapters. Therefore, we know that all contextually inappropriate behavior serves a purpose; a student is trying to get/obtain something or escape/avoid something. If we punish a student's behavior, we deprive that student of a way to get their needs met: we must provide (i.e., teach) the student a replacement behavior that serves the same function. If a student is constantly shouting to gain teacher attention, saying "Stop shouting" might temporarily stop the behavior (since saying "stop" is a conditioned aversive consequence), but it doesn't teach the student how to gain attention appropriately (e.g., by raising their hand, asking a peer for help, having an appropriate conversation in the cafeteria). Our focus should *always* be on increasing students' use of contextually appropriate behaviors; in order for students to choose contextually appropriate behaviors over contextually inappropriate behaviors, the students must be reinforced only for the contextually appropriate behaviors (and not be able to access reinforcement through using the contextually inappropriate behaviors).

Often, we don't think functionally about the consequences for contextually inappropriate behavior. For instance, sometimes skipping school or cutting class results in students being suspended, which is *clearly* not a function-based approach. Students usually skip school and class because they don't want to be there; using suspension as a consequence is hardly punishing! Similarly, traditional consequences such as detention and withholding privileges (e.g., denying recess) don't always function as punishers (and may be inconsistent with district or state policy). Consider detentions that are served long after the contextually inappropriate behavior takes place (i.e., not contingent) once everyone's schedules are worked out. Consider the group detentions served after school, when many of students know one another and spend their time chatting. Consider detentions where students complete homework. None of these is likely to effectively punish a contextually inappropriate behavior. Withholding privileges is only an effective punisher if students are interested in the privilege; some students don't value recess or lunch in the cafeteria or field trips, so losing those privileges has a minimal impact (and is certainly not punitive) for these students.

The most important concern with using punishment is the potential to abuse it. Frequent use of punishment in the classroom can lead to a hostile learning environment (Darch & Kame'enui, 2004). Think about the kind of classroom climate you want to have: do you want students who engage in expected behaviors because of their commitment to classroom norms; fluency with social, emotional, and behavioral skills; and available reinforcers (which can include teacher praise, good grades, positive notes home, and other natural reinforcers in addition to a token economy), or do you want students who engage in expected behaviors because they want to avoid punishment—a fear-based model?

We think you and your students would be happier and more productive in an environment where contextually appropriate behavior is encouraged and reinforced, rather than in an environment that only discourages and punishes contextually inappropriate behavior. When faced with aversive control, students (like adults) often push back, which can lead to increased behavioral problems and power struggles. Remember that using punishment only teaches students which behaviors result in punishment and leads them to figure out how to avoid punishment—it doesn't teach them to behave in contextually appropriate ways, and it doesn't help them develop the social, emotional, and behavioral skills they will need to succeed in school and beyond. If you've ever gotten a speeding ticket, you can relate to this: the ticket was likely punitive in the short term, and you slowed down (but you didn't learn how to get where you were going any faster!). Then, if you're like most people, the effects of the ticket wore off, and you began speeding again (but you may have learned to slow down around the area where the police car waits for speeders). The effects of punishment often don't last. If, however, you had learned to get up earlier or manage your time more effectively, you may not have needed to speed in the future. Stay focused on encouraging the contextually appropriate behaviors you and your students have agreed upon for your classroom expectations, and you'll see fewer contextually inappropriate behaviors by default.

Remember to inform all students and their families about all of your classroom PBIS strategies from the first day of school (or from the first day a student enters your classroom, if a new student arrives during the year). Share your established classwide expectations (and invite input, if you haven't done that yet), share documentation of what happens when students demonstrate those expected behaviors (i.e., your classwide reinforcement system), and share documentation of what happens when students make mistakes (i.e., your continuum of responses to decrease contextually inappropriate behavior and your explanation of which behaviors result in which responses). If students and families have an opportunity to participate in designing and awareness of all aspects of your classroom PBIS approach ahead of time, you increase the potential for partnership and collaboration when contextually inappropriate behaviors occur. Students and families should not be surprised by certain responses to contextually appropriate or contextually inappropriate behaviors. Fair and consistent application builds trust, positive relationships, and collaborative partnerships.

If you are in a school that is implementing PBIS and using a supportive, instructional, and restorative approach to discipline, be sure to align your approach with district policies and procedures. In this case, you may be able to rely on their documentation and explanation of a continuum to respond to behavior. If not, you may need to have a simple strategy for communicating your classroom PBIS approach with families. In the context of an overall positive and proactive approach, describe how you will respond when students make social, emotional, and behavioral errors. For example, "If students make a mistake with their behavior, I will be there to support them with a reminder of how to correct that mistake. If students continue to make mistakes, I'll provide further support—we may have additional opportunities to practice the behavioral skills they need and more opportunities for them to be recognized for their safe, engaged, and thoughtful behavior. If the mistakes persist, I will reach out to you to discuss how to better support your child. In our classroom, we will make efforts to repair any harm created by our actions and restore our classroom to a positive, caring, and safe environment where all students can learn and feel they belong." If your students have more complex or elevated social, emotional, and behavioral needs, your communication with families may need to be more detailed and explicit about how you will support and respond to students' behavioral mistakes.

Consider developing a chart to help you (and anyone else who comes into your classroom, like paraprofessionals, volunteers, or substitute teachers) respond to student's behavioral mistakes consistently and fairly (see Figure 8.1 for an example).

Remember, the use of punishment strategies should be a last resort. Always consider what you can do differently to prevent the contextually inappropriate behaviors from occurring (and increase the likelihood of contextually appropriate behaviors!). Reflect on what you may be able to change in the environment to encourage behaviors aligned with your agreed-upon classroom expectations and to discourage contextually inappropriate behaviors. Are your lessons and task dimensions appropriate for your learners? Is your instruction engaging and culturally responsive? Are the academic and behavioral expectations clear? Do you prompt frequently for contextually appropriate behaviors? Have you evaluated the effectiveness of your reinforcement system and considered any adjustments (e.g., schedule of reinforcement, selection of backup reinforcers)? Have you taught students how to get their needs met? Do you model the behaviors you want to see? Have you included students and families as authentic partners in your classroom community and reflected their voices in your daily practices? Before implementing any punitive consequences, reflect on if you've done *everything* possible to prevent the contextually inappropriate behavior from occurring. Review Chapters 5, 6, and 7 and evaluate your application of those strategies. After all, the most effective way to discourage contextually inappropriate behavior is to prevent its occurrence in the first place.

SUMMARY

As with our responses to contextually appropriate behaviors, our responses to contextually inappropriate behaviors should occur along a continuum, where the intensity of the response matches the intensity of the behavior. More intensive, intrusive consequences should be reserved for contextually inappropriate behaviors that significantly impact the student, others, or the environment, and we should always consider the *function* of the problem behavior when responding. Restorative practices provide a culturally responsive mechanism for promoting student accountability and self-awareness while repairing harm and preserving (and often strengthening) relationships. When contextually inappropriate behaviors occur, reflect on our proactive and positive strategies and adjust if needed. With a consistent, instructional focus on encouraging contextually appropriate behaviors, many contextually inappropriate behaviors will be prevented.

Student engages in contextually inappropriate behavior.
First, determine if the behavior constitutes a major (i.e., handled by administration) or minor (i.e., handed in the setting) mistake.

If it's a major behavior mistake (as defined in the school handbook), the student is sent to the office with an ODR.

If it's a minor behavior mistake (as defined in the school handbook), the staff member follows these steps:

Ask: is this the student's first behavioral mistake of this kind?

If **yes,** consider the type of error.

If it's an **acquisition** error (i.e., the student doesn't have the social, emotional, or behavioral skills to perform the behavior), reteach the expected behavior.

If it's a **fluency** error (i.e., student can perform the skill but doesn't do so consistently), provide opportunities to practice and received specific feedback on the expected behavior.

If it's a **maintenance** error (i.e., student does not maintain the same level of the behavior after a break from the instructional environment), provide a brief reminder of the expected behavior; reteach as needed, and reinforce occurrences more frequently.

If it's a **generalization** error (i.e., student cannot reliably perform the skill in different settings or with a different S^D), provide practice and acknowledgment in other settings and with other people.

Also, identify possible **setting** events and intervene accordingly.

If **no:**

Reteach expected behavior as necessary, according to phases of learning.

Remind student about the expected behavior (i.e., provide brief and specific error correction).

If behavioral mistake continues:
- Employ a **function-based response** (e.g., remove them from peer group if behavior functions to obtain peer attention).
- **Pause access to rewards** (e.g., "freeze" on earning tokens and access to incentives).
- Have a **restorative conversation** with the student to identify harm done and solutions to repair that harm.
- **Partner with families** to talk about the mistakes and brainstorm solutions.
- **Intensify proactive supports** as needed (e.g., more frequent prompts, increased reinforcement opportunities).

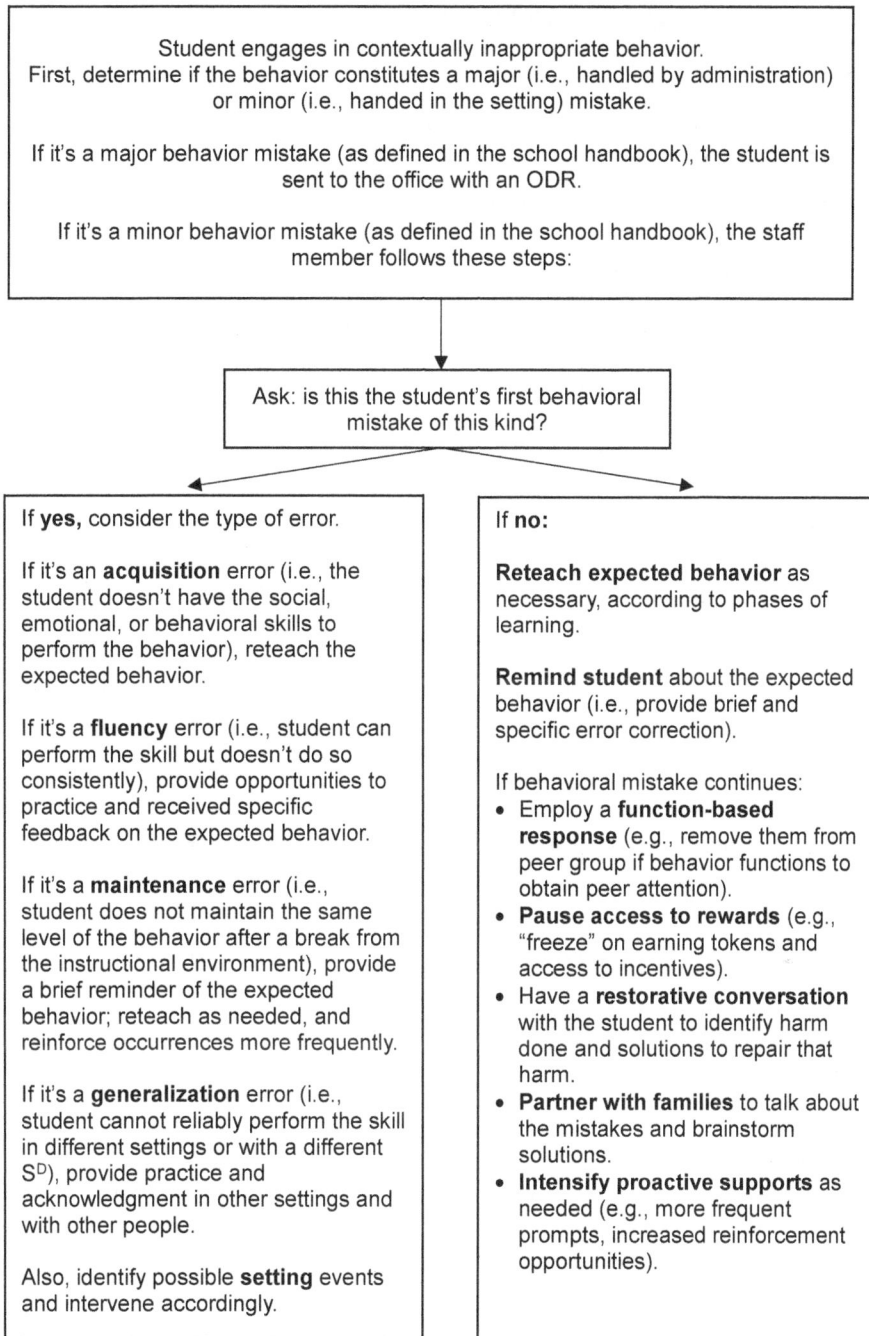

FIGURE 8.1. Response chart: having a predetermined continuum of responses to decrease contextually inappropriate behaviors promotes consistency and predictability.

PHASES OF LEARNING ACTIVITIES: CHAPTER 8

Acquisition

1. What makes error correction specific and contingent? Give an example of a specific, contingent error correction and describe the rationale for responding to minor behavioral errors this way.

2. Describe two different types of differential reinforcement and give a specific example of each.

Fluency

1. What does having a "continuum of responses" to respond to contextually inappropriate behaviors mean? Why should you have more than one ready response?

2. Define *overcorrection* and give an example of restitutional overcorrection and positive-practice overcorrection (other than the ones given in the chapter).

Maintenance

1. Describe the principles of positive and negative punishment (discussed in Chapter 2) and how they relate to the response strategies shared in this chapter.

2. What are the pros and cons of using a response-cost system in your classroom? How will these pros and cons impact your decision about whether to use response cost or not?

Generalization

1. How can you effectively reflect the voices and identities of your students and their families when developing a continuum of strategies to decrease contextually inappropriate behavior? How would you structure the process?

2. How can you ensure that your system for decreasing contextually inappropriate behavior is culturally responsive? How will you know if your system centers equity? Provide specific examples in your response.

Other Skill-Building Exercises

1. You want to design and implement a continuum of strategies to respond to contextually inappropriate behaviors in your classroom. Create a document that details (1) the steps in the process, (2) the strategies in your continuum and your rationale for selection, and (3) how you will engage all stakeholders in the process.

2. Do some research on restorative practices (you can begin with the suggestions in this chapter) and develop a plan for piloting restorative practices in your classroom. If you're already using restorative practices, consider whether you should make any adjustments based on your understanding of behavioral science (i.e., considering students' unique and collective learning histories, including the function of their contextually inappropriate behaviors).

3. Describe (or design) your evaluation process for assessing the effectiveness of responses to students' behavioral mistakes. For example, how are you measuring the impact of restorative practices, and how do you use the results of your assessment to tweak, shape, or change your practices?

PART III

ADDITIONAL TIERS OF SUPPORT FOR STUDENTS

CHAPTER 9

Overview of Tier 2 Supports in Your School and Classroom

CHAPTER OBJECTIVES

By the end of this chapter, you should be able to . . .

1. Identify the defining characteristics of Tier 2 (i.e., targeted) supports and interventions.
2. Determine which students may benefit from Tier 2 supports.
3. Describe evidence-based Tier 2 interventions.
4. Integrate Tier 2 interventions within your classwide PBIS system.

Imagine This: *Mrs. Gaines has been reading this book and implementing all of the practices described within. She has collaborated with her students and their families to establish and define classroom expectations, she has taught the contextually appropriate behaviors across all of her different classroom routines, and she prompts for and reinforces expected behavior. In her class of 25 students, though, there are four students who continue to have lower rates of contextually appropriate behaviors than their peers and have some frequent contextually inappropriate behaviors that disrupt their learning. Mrs. Gaines has been talking to these four students, using specific error corrections, and, when more intensive behavioral mistakes occur, writing ODRs, but she wants to find a way to differentiate the positive, proactive interventions she already has in place to support these four students. She does some research and discovers several studies in which teachers have implemented a secondary level of support (that complements a universal PBIS framework) in their classrooms with a Check-In/ Check-Out (CICO) model. Excited by what she has read, Mrs. Gaines develops a CICO system for her classroom.*

She orients the four students to the CICO system, which involves checking in with Mrs. Gaines in the morning, receiving a point sheet listing the class expectations and the students' individual goals, and checking out with Mrs. Gaines in the afternoon. After a few weeks, Mrs. Gaines notices marked improvement in three out of the four students' behavior. "This is great," she thinks. "Since three of those students are meeting their goals and are experiencing fewer disruptions to their learning, I can focus my attention on the fourth student, who might need a more intensive intervention." (Luckily for her, we explore individualized interventions in Chapter 10!)

WHAT ARE TIER 2 INTERVENTIONS?

While carefully designed, culturally responsive schoolwide PBIS and classwide PBIS systems can support the social, emotional, and behavioral needs of most of our students, there will be some students who have social, emotional, or behavioral needs that require more than the universal level of prevention and support. Researchers estimate this number to be at around 15–20 percent of students in a school (with a slightly higher percentage for high schools; Spaulding et al., 2010). If more than 15–20 percent of students are demonstrating elevated needs, the solution should be to intensify Tier 1 supports (*not* to increase the number of students receiving Tier 2 supports). Remember, Tier 1 supports are intended to meet the social, emotional, and behavioral needs of approximately 80 percent of students; in settings or times when needs are more intensive (e.g., students returning from a pandemic, students returning after crisis), we must intensify Tier 1 supports to meet those needs.

For students who exhibit chronic, low-intensity, nondangerous contextually inappropriate behaviors (e.g., being off task, tardiness, not following directions) that disrupt learning but do not warrant more intensive intervention (i.e., Tier 3; see Chapter 10), Tier 2 interventions may be an appropriate addition to the universal Tier 1 supports. Students with elevated social, emotional, and behavioral needs may also benefit from targeted Tier 2 interventions that provide additional support (e.g., more frequent prompts and opportunities for behavior-specific feedback; increased adult attention). While a complete review of empirically supported Tier 2 interventions is beyond the scope of this book, we discuss several options later in the chapter that can complement existing schoolwide and classwide PBIS approaches.

Whereas the universal (i.e., Tier 1) level of support in schoolwide and classwide PBIS is designed to increase contextually appropriate behaviors and promote social, emotional, and behavioral wellness for all members of the community, Tier 2 interventions focus on supporting students who have more intensive levels of need. These may be students who are considered "at risk" of developing behaviors or needs that may interfere with their learning, including a previous history of contextually inappropriate behaviors that did not decrease in response to universal supports, frequent ODRs, withdrawn or internalizing behaviors that disrupt learning, or difficulty with academics that manifests in contextually inappropriate behaviors. Teachers or other staff who regularly interact with and observe students may also notice increases in internalizing or externalizing behaviors that are impacting student learning; these students may be appropriate candidates for more intensive Tier 2 interventions. Tier 2 interventions are targeted; that is, the teacher (or behavioral support team responsible for assessing students and implementing or assigning supports) can select and implement interventions to provide *focused* support (e.g., increased reinforcement contingent on contextually appropriate behavior for the student who has numerous ODRs; more academic scaffolding for the student who is struggling with her work). The type, intensity, and design of Tier 2 interventions should be based on collected data and reflect and respect existing culture and context. Tier 2 interventions will only be effective in environments where a strong foundation of proactive, positive behavioral support is in place, whether at the classwide or (ideally) at the schoolwide level. Sometimes, providing Tier 2 support is as simple as differentiating the practices implemented at the universal support level—we'll start there.

FURTHER DIFFERENTIATING AND INTENSIFYING TIER 1 PRACTICES

Hopefully, you've implemented many of the critical practices we've discussed so far in this book (refer back to Chapters 5, 6, 7, and 8 if you need a refresher!). If you have, your universal level of classroom behavioral support consists of robust, effective, evidence-based, and contextually relevant practices that support your students' social, emotional, and behavioral needs. Great news: those practices can be differentiated and intensified to meet the needs of students who may require an elevated level of support (Simonsen, Robbie, et al., 2021). Let's explore what this can look like.

Think back to our discussion about creating an inclusive, predictable, safe, and engaging classroom in Chapter 5. Students with elevated social, emotional, and behavioral needs may benefit from **increased structure and opportunities for connection,** which could be provided in multiple ways, depending on student-specific needs. For example:

- Use strategic and purposeful seat assignment to increase proximity to mentor peers, improve access to materials, or facilitate monitoring and the ability to deliver behavior-specific feedback.
- Create a designated space and teach specific routines for students to practice and use calming or self-regulation strategies.
- Provide additional opportunities for intentional peer-to-peer (e.g., tasks completed in pairs; peer-to-peer praise), student-to-educator (e.g., lunch conversation; 1:1 walk during a break), and family (e.g., open door policy; virtual Q and A) connections.

Next, reflect back on what you learned in Chapter 6 and how to establish and teach positively stated norms or expectations in your classroom. We can **differentiate how we define and teach our expectations** to provide an additional layer of support to students with more intensive social, emotional, or behavioral needs. For example:

- Increase visual and verbal prompts for key social, emotional, and behavioral skills.
- Reteach existing routines and introduce and teach new routines to provide additional support (e.g., how to take space when needed, specific mindfulness activities).
- Increase the specificity and clarity of existing classroom routines or add specific dimensions to an expected behavior based on students' needs (see Figure 9.1 for an example of what this can look like).
- Build in more frequent opportunities for practicing, reviewing, monitoring, and providing feedback on targeted social, emotional, and behavioral skills.

	Classroom Routines				
	Group work	Desk work	Quizzes and tests	Arrival	Dismissal
Expectation: Responsibility	**Tier 1 (*expected behaviors for all students*)**				
	Offer ideas. Complete all tasks.	Sit with feet on the ground. Get up and stretch if necessary.	Study for all assessments. Read through and double-check all work.	Get all supplies for the day. Lock belongings in locker.	Check on homework. Pack necessary materials.
	Tier 2 (*expected behaviors for some students*)				
	Make a list of three ways to contribute to the group.	Keep all materials in designated bin on desk.	Write down questions for teacher on scrap paper during exam.	Turn in point sheet with family signature.	Put point sheet into homework folder.

FIGURE 9.1. Example of differentiated classroom expectations.

Finally, review Chapters 7 and 8 and the evidence-based practices you can implement to encourage contextually appropriate behaviors and discourage contextually inappropriate behaviors. We can **intensify and adjust responses to target behaviors** for students who may benefit from additional social, emotional, and behavioral support. For example:

- Teach necessary skills and create intentional opportunities for students to provide behavior-specific feedback to each other.
- Expand acknowledgment practices across form and function (e.g., social attention, activities, sensory experiences, breaks, raffles) and availability (e.g., "special occasion" items, daily rewards, variable schedules of reinforcement).
- Provide more frequent behavior-specific feedback and targeted error correction, add more specific prompts for alternative behaviors when using differential reinforcement, and increase strategic use of proximity and active supervision to redirect contextually inappropriate behaviors and recognize contextually appropriate behaviors.

In short, if your data indicate that some students may benefit from more intensive social, emotional, and behavioral support, begin by looking for opportunities to enhance the foundational practices you already have in place rather than rushing to create new systems. No need to reinvent the wheel when some simple adjustments can make a difference! If you need to expand your Tier 2 supports beyond further differentiating your universal practices, we discuss additional Tier 2 interventions in the next section.

EMPIRICALLY SUPPORTED TIER 2 INTERVENTIONS

Providing additional layers of support in a systematic, tiered fashion can benefit all students in a classroom. Several Tier 2 interventions have empirical (i.e., research-based) support; we provide an overview of some of the most familiar interventions below.

Social Skills Instruction

Explicit social skills instruction is an evidence-based practice critical to all three tiers of a PBIS framework, and small-group social skills instruction can be used effectively as a Tier 2 intervention (e.g., Cho Blair et al., 2020; Kern et al., 2020). When used as a Tier 2 intervention at the schoolwide level, social skills groups may be run by school clinicians (e.g., counselors, psychologists, social workers) and can provide general social skills instruction and/or instruction targeted to students' specific needs (e.g., anger management, conflict resolution, initiating conversation). Group social skills lessons can be delivered on a weekly, monthly, or as-needed basis; often, students with emotional and behavioral disorders will have targeted group or individual social skills training mandated by their individualized education plans (IEPs). These lessons may be conducted outside of the classroom (so collaborating with the clinicians delivering the instruction and planning for generalization is essential); the lessons may be written by clinicians or teachers, or they may include lessons from packaged curricula. For example, **Second Step** is a prepackaged curriculum focused on building social and emotional competence that has been used successfully for social skills training in schools (e.g., Frey et al., 2005; Grossman et al., 1997).

Considerations for Using Small-Group Social Skills Instruction at the Classroom Level

Using explicit social skills instruction as a Tier 2 intervention will be most effective if aligned and integrated within your existing classwide PBIS system. Consider the following as you design a plan for implementation (Simonsen, Robbie, et al., 2021):

- Provide targeted social skills instruction in a quiet place that maximizes structure and minimizes distractions.
- Create intentional opportunities for students to practice and receive feedback on the specific social skills being taught.
- Provide targeted visual and verbal prompts to increase the likelihood of students using the specific social skills they've been taught.
- Connect social skills instruction to classroom norms or expectations. For example, if social skills instruction focuses on responsible decision making, you can work with students to make connections between the skills required for responsible decision making and the broader classroom norm of accountability.
- Teach targeted social skills that can replace contextually inappropriate behaviors; for example, teaching a student how to request help instead of putting their head down or withdrawing when encountering a challenging academic task.
- Provide social skills instruction and practice opportunities in the natural setting to promote generalization and help establish connections between the social skill being taught and naturally occurring reinforcers; for example, practicing tolerance skills (i.e., skills that help an individual endure distress in situations they cannot escape) in an environment where they're needed—like a long, boring bus ride with a natural reinforcer of getting where you're going afterward—is more impactful than practicing them by sitting still in the classroom for a specific number of minutes.

Check-In/Check-Out

The **Check-In/Check-Out intervention** (CICO; see Hawken et al., 2021, for a comprehensive guide to CICO) is a standardized Tier 2 intervention that complements schoolwide PBIS models (e.g., Simonsen et al., 2011). Key features of CICO as a schoolwide Tier 2 intervention include a core CICO implementation team, an established student referral process, a brief functional assessment, training in CICO procedures for all staff and participating students, a daily progress report (DPR) rating demonstration of expected behaviors, morning and afternoon check-in and check-out (respectively), reinforcement, family connection, and ongoing data collection and evaluation. CICO is designed to be a comprehensive, effective Tier 2 intervention within a schoolwide PBIS model; the DPR should reflect language from the schoolwide expectations, and the reinforcers should align with the schoolwide system of reinforcement. You can also implement elements of CICO within a classwide PBIS model (see Fairbanks et al., 2007, for an example)—continue reading to learn how, and notice how the key words in **bold print** are already elements of your classwide behavioral support model.

Considerations for Implementing CICO at the Classroom Level

When designing CICO for use at the classroom level, begin by building on your existing **foundational classroom practices.** Students participating in CICO will check in at the beginning of the day, before and after activities during the day, and at the end of the day (as well as with their families at home). The check-ins are designed to provide additional opportunities for **connection** and feedback. Design a DPR where adults (including family members) can provide feedback and positive comments (adding even more opportunities for connection and feedback). Ensure the DPR reflects your classroom **expectations or norms** and is developmentally appropriate—consider smiley faces and minimal text for a younger student (see Figure 9.2) and points for older students (see Figure 9.3). Establish clear procedures and **routines** to facilitate these check-ins, and design your physical **classroom environment** to facilitate CICO practices (e.g., providing bins to collect DPRs; designating an easily accessible space for check-ins and end-of-day check-out). Teach these new routines to participating students and communicate them to families; make connections to your classroom norms and existing routines (Simonsen, Robbie, et al., 2021). During morning check-ins, provide **prompts and precorrections** for the day, check that the student is prepared for the day with all necessary materials, and provide a blank DPR, which includes a written reminder of the expected behaviors. Remind the student about available **reinforcers** for meeting goals, and ensure they have their necessary materials for the day (e.g., pencil, paper, charged electronic device if required by your district).

During the brief check-ins at the beginning of activities throughout the day, provide micro-lessons or reminders about the expected behaviors, always connecting targeted social, emotional, or behavioral skills to the broader classroom **expectations.** During check-ins after activities, provide **behavior-specific feedback** and rate the student's behavior (relative to the expectations) on the DPR. Ratings may convert to tokens for participation in the classroom **token economy,** or there may be a specific reinforcer menu for CICO participants (Simonsen, Robbie, et al., 2021). Collect and evaluate **data** to determine if students should continue participating in CICO, if supports can be faded (e.g., check-ins happen less frequently), or if sup-

Student Name: _____ Date: _____

Classroom Norms: We are **kind** to ourself, others, and our environment

Activity	Needs to be better	OK	Good	Great!	Comments
Reading		☺	☺☺	☺☺☺	
Math		☺	☺☺	☺☺☺	
Center Time		☺	☺☺	☺☺☺	
Lunch and Recess		☺	☺☺	☺☺☺	
Social Studies		☺	☺☺	☺☺☺	

Student's signature: _____

Teacher's signature: _____

Guardian's signature: _____

Guardian's comments: _____

_____

_____

_____

_____

_____

_____

_____

_____

FIGURE 9.2. A DPR for an elementary student.

Student Name: _____ Date: _____

Period	Kind	Responsible	Ready	Positive Comment	Teacher Initial
1	0 1 2	0 1 2	0 1 2		
2	0 1 2	0 1 2	0 1 2		
3	0 1 2	0 1 2	0 1 2		
4	0 1 2	0 1 2	0 1 2		
5	0 1 2	0 1 2	0 1 2		
6	0 1 2	0 1 2	0 1 2		
7	0 1 2	0 1 2	0 1 2		
8	0 1 2	0 1 2	0 1 2		
Total:				Daily Total:	

Previous day's sheet returned? If yes, add 2 points to total.

Daily behavioral goal: _____ out of 50 Goal met today? _____

Student's signature: _____

CICO representative's signature: _____

Guardian's signature: _____

Guardian's comments: _____

_____

_____

_____

_____

_____

_____

FIGURE 9.3. A DPR for a high school student.

ports should be intensified (e.g., check-ins happen more frequently or more specific and explicit teaching and prompting occurs).

Further, consider function when designing, implementing, and adapting CICO for your students. For example, CICO may best support students whose contextually inappropriate behaviors function to get or obtain attention, and may not work as well for students whose behaviors function to escape or avoid work or attention (e.g., McIntosh et al., 2009). However, simple adjustments, like allowing students to earn brief breaks (i.e., Breaks are Better; Boyd & Anderson, 2013; Majeika et al., 2022) may increase the potential for CICO to support a wider range of students.

Self-Monitoring

Self-monitoring is another strategy that may be an effective Tier 2 intervention within your classwide PBIS model. Self-monitoring has been an effective strategy for students with and without disabilities (e.g., Hunter et al., 2017; Wills & Mason, 2014) and has been associated with increases in on-task behavior, academic performance, task completion, and prosocial behaviors (Amato-Zech et al., 2006; Holifield et al., 2010; Legge et al., 2010; Wills & Mason, 2014). You can use self-monitoring on its own *or* use it in conjunction with other interventions; for example, self-monitoring can be used when fading support for students participating in CICO (i.e., they can move from DPRs completed by adults to DPRs they complete themselves; Figure 9.4 presents a sample DPR to support self-monitoring).

Considerations for Implementing Self-Monitoring at the Classroom Level

Self-monitoring interventions are highly customizable; we recommend using a simple form that is efficient, effective, and easy for students to complete. The most common format for self-monitoring is a checklist, usually divided into equal intervals based on the classroom schedule (e.g., every 15 minutes; the end of every class period), where students indicate if they met or did not meet established target behaviors during that interval. For example, you've identified four students in your high school English class who could use additional support to stay on task during classroom instruction. You meet with these students and tell them you'd like to try a new way to support their on-task behavior. You provide each student with a sheet that has the agreed-upon definition of on-task behavior from previous class discussions written at the top and a table like the one below that breaks the 50-minute class into 10 5-minute intervals:

Time	On task	Off task
10:05		
10:10		
10:15		

You then teach the students how the intervention works: They will each be provided with a silent timer to keep at their desks (or they can use a smartwatch, smartphone, or table if feasible and aligned with the agreed-upon classroom expectations) set to give a silent signal every 5 minutes. When they notice the signal, they assess if they are on task or off task at that moment and check the appropriate box. At the end of the period, they review the sheets, give themselves a

Student Name: _____ Date: _____

Period	Kind		Responsible		Ready		Positive Comment	Teacher Initial
	Teacher	Student	Teacher	Student	Teacher	Student		
1	0　1　2	0　1　2	0　1　2	0　1　2	0　1　2	0　1　2		
2	0　1　2	0　1　2	0　1　2	0　1　2	0　1　2	0　1　2		
3	0　1　2	0　1　2	0　1　2	0　1　2	0　1　2	0　1　2		
4	0　1　2	0　1　2	0　1　2	0　1　2	0　1　2	0　1　2		
5	0　1　2	0　1　2	0　1　2	0　1　2	0　1　2	0　1　2		
6	0　1　2	0　1　2	0　1　2	0　1　2	0　1　2	0　1　2		
7	0　1　2	0　1　2	0　1　2	0　1　2	0　1　2	0　1　2		
8	0　1　2	0　1　2	0　1　2	0　1　2	0　1　2	0　1　2		
Number of agreements							Total:	

Previous day's sheet returned? If yes, add 2 points to total.

Daily behavioral goal: _____ out of 26　　　Goal met today? _____

Student's signature: _____

CICO representative's signature: _____

Guardian's signature: _____

Guardian's comments: _____

_____

_____

_____

_____

_____

_____

FIGURE 9.4. A self-monitoring point sheet.

score (e.g., 6 out of 10 on task), and drop the sheet in the designated bin. That's it! After a week, you'll aggregate the data into a spreadsheet, look for any trends, and see if the student ratings align with your general observations of their on-task behavior.

Self-monitoring interventions do not necessarily require a reinforcement component, but, as we mentioned, self-monitoring interventions are highly customizable—so feel free to add one! Self-monitoring may increase the target desired behavior simply by increasing self-awareness. Any reinforcement component you add should be related to the accuracy of the rating (i.e., the student's assessment of their behavior "matched" yours) rather than the percentage of intervals with the target behavior to increase the likelihood of accurate self-assessment, at least until you are confident in the accuracy of their self-assessment.

Expanding beyond self-monitoring to self-management (where students manage their own antecedent and consequence strategies in addition to self-monitoring) can also be an efficient and effective way to support students (Briesch & Chafouleas, 2009). And, as you may have guessed, having a student self-monitor a contextually appropriate behavior (and earn reinforcement) that matches the function of their contextually inappropriate behavior is more likely to work than having them self-monitor a behavior that is not functionally relevant (Briere & Simonsen, 2011). For example, if a student is frequently engaging in low-level contextually inappropriate behaviors to escape work, having them monitor their engagement and earn a brief break may work better than having them monitor kindness toward peers and earn an activity-based reinforcer during lunch.

TIER 2 INTERVENTIONS: OUTCOMES AND DATA

We've given you four options to consider if you want to provide increased social, emotional, and behavioral support for some of the students in your classroom: (1) further differentiating or intensifying your existing behavioral support practices; (2) small-group explicit social skills instruction; (3) a classroom version of CICO; and (4) self-monitoring. Before you select an intervention, consider the **outcomes** you wish to see—and be sure to collaborate with other partners, including students and families, to ensure those outcomes are culturally relevant and reflective of shared values. Examples of outcomes include increasing specific contextually appropriate behaviors (and reducing specific contextually inappropriate behaviors) for students participating in their Tier 2 intervention; increasing the number of students who access Tier 2 supports (or those who "graduate" from Tier 2 supports and move back to the universal support framework); reducing the number of ODRs generated by Tier 2 intervention participants; reducing the number of students needing Tier 3 supports; and/or improving academic metrics. Have your outcomes clearly defined before you begin: as we've mentioned before, effective leaders (and educators!) know where they are going!

Once you have determined your specific outcomes, determine which **data** you will use to measure progress toward your outcomes and how you will collect those data. Examples of data sources include:

- Evaluation of social, emotional, and behavioral strengths and skills (e.g., brief rating scales, universal screeners)
- ODRs

- Absence and tardy information
- Earned reinforcers
- Visits to the school nurse or other time out of class (if relevant)
- Grades
- Daily points or other measure
- Frequency/duration/latency data related to behaviors targeted for decrease
- Frequency/duration/latency data related to behaviors targeted for increase

Several of these data sources (e.g., absence and tardy information, grades, ODRs) are extant, meaning that the data exist outside of your Tier 2 supports—they are already being collected. Other sources of data may be easy to collect (e.g., using a strengths-based social, emotional, behavioral screener to monitor your students' strengths and skills; monitoring daily points earned in CICO). If you opt for a more observation-based data source (e.g., frequency of contextually appropriate behaviors), you may need to enlist the help of a paraprofessional or design an efficient data collection system that you can use (see "Case Study: Missy's Classroom" at the end of the chapter for an example of a teacher-friendly data collection system). Applications for tablets, computers, and smartphones can help you track behavioral data, too (try a quick App Store or Google Play search for "behavioral data" and see what's out there). Please refer back to Chapter 4 if you need a refresher or additional ideas for data collection.

Once you have decided on the data you will collect and how they will be collected, determine how you will manage your data. Will you use a program like Microsoft Excel to input and graph your data? Will you keep your data in a notebook on your desk, or as part of your gradebook? Will you share the data with the students and/or or their family? (We suggest that you share data with all relevant partners, including the student and their family.) How often will you review the data? In addition, determine the **decision rules** you will use to determine when to start, change, and stop additional Tier 2 supports for specific students. See Figure 9.5 for an example of decision rules related to Tier 2 behavioral interventions. Again, your decision rules will depend on the characteristics of your students and your classroom.

Data are also part of your **referral system.** Determining if students are appropriate candidates for targeted, more intensive interventions may include answering questions like:

- Does the student need additional social, emotional, or behavioral support? (You can operationalize some key indicators, for instance, "The student has not received a token contingent on contextually appropriate behavior in over 2 weeks" or "I am providing specific, repeated error corrections to this student several times per class period.")

- Are the student's behaviors intense enough (i.e., highly disruptive to all learners, unsafe) to warrant individualized, highly intensive (i.e., Tier 3) interventions? Some students may require more immediate and intensive intervention for behaviors like frequent acts of aggression, viable threats to others or self, or major and sustained property damage. Chapter 10 explores some options for providing Tier 3 interventions as part of your classroom PBIS system.

- Does the student have risk factors that may be mitigated by participating in a specific Tier 2 intervention? For instance, students with a history of behaviors that interfere with learning, students who have recently had family or community issues, or students who tend to be involved in conflicts with others may benefit from the increased structure and connection of CICO.

Data Pattern	Decision Rule
Student meets the goal for 8 consecutive days.	Increase the student's goal by 10%.
Student has met the highest possible goal for 8 consecutive days.	Student moves to self-management.
Student has met the goal on self-management for 8 consecutive days.	Student returns to Tier 1 level of support.

Student does not meet the goal for 3 consecutive days.	• Review the student's goal.
	• If the goal is too high, decrease.
	• If the goal is appropriate, determine:
	  ○ If program is being implemented with fidelity.
	  ○ If function of the behaviors could be different than what was assessed.
	  ○ If the program should be tweaked to include academic supports or other individualized support.

Student was meeting the goal consistently but has stopped meeting the goal.	• Determine if something has changed for the student (e.g., setting event). • Determine if the goal was raised too quickly. If so, decrease the goal. • Determine if rewards are still functioning as reinforcers.
Student meets the goal inconsistently.	Review the program. Determine if it is being implemented with fidelity. Look for common variables on days when student does meet the goal, and on days when they do not meet it. Consider tweaking the program (e.g., increasing reinforcement) based on information gathered.

FIGURE 9.5. Example of decision rules related to Tier 2 behavioral interventions.

• What is the *function* of the behaviors interfering with the student's learning? Consider completing the Functional Assessment Checklist for Teachers and Staff (FACTS; Anderson & Borgmeier, 2007). If it seems that the behaviors function to avoid adult attention, the increased attention in a typical CICO model may be aversive for that student, but a modified CICO (e.g., Breaks are Better; Boyd & Anderson, 2013; Majeika et al., 2022), small-group social skills instruction focused on contextually appropriate ways to ask for space, or self-monitoring of contextually appropriate and functionally relevant behaviors may be effective.

The answers to questions like these can help you determine which students may benefit from more intensive support. You should also develop a **system for fading supports.** You don't want to remove supports abruptly if a student makes the expected social, emotional, and behavioral improvements; support should be faded slowly in order to avoid extinction of any newly learned behaviors. Any decrease (or increase, for that matter) in supports should be based on data, following the decision rules that you've established.

Further, consider additional **systems** needed to effectively implement Tier 2 support. Does a schoolwide team exist to support you in all of the implementation steps (including centering equity in the practices, outcomes, and data we've already discussed)? If not, can you collaborate with others in your grade level, academic department, or even with others connected to your classroom (e.g., paraprofessionals, coaches, related service providers) to form a small team to share the work and data-driven decision making? Also, what level of knowledge and skills does each person who supports your student need to set them up for success? If you're using CICO, for example, have you shared your plan with specialized subject teachers (e.g., music, physical education, art, science, technology) so that they can also use CICO to support your student?

Do you need to provide (or request) additional training for staff in your classroom or school to support their implementation? Have you connected with any outside service providers (e.g., community mental health) who support your student(s) to align your classroom Tier 2 support with supports students may be accessing outside your classroom? In short, consider the systems needed to support educators' successful implementation of Tier 2 supports and interventions, and request implementation support from your school leadership as needed.

SUMMARY

Evidence-based, targeted Tier 2 supports and interventions can effectively deliver assistance to students who need an additional layer of social, emotional, and behavioral support. While we have a robust research base providing best practices at the Tier 1 and Tier 3 support levels, Tier 2 supports (echoing the long-standing complaints of many a middle child) have not always gotten the attention they deserve. Effective implementation of Tier 2 supports can reduce the number of student referrals for Tier 3 supports, which can free up resources (e.g., clinical staff, time spent writing individualized BSPs) for the students who need the most intensive level of support. Tier 2 supports are not intended to be permanent or long term; ideally, students build fluency with target behaviors and Tier 2 supports are faded so students return to receiving only universal prevention and support. Students who require a more intensive level of behavioral support will likely be referred for a Tier 3 intervention, discussed in detail in Chapter 10.

CASE STUDY: MISSY'S CLASSROOM (TRUE STORY!)[1]

Missy was a first-grade teacher enrolled in a graduate course on positive behavioral interventions and supports (taught by Diane) who eagerly applied what she learned in her course to her suburban public school classroom. Missy designed a classwide PBIS system with the expectations "Safe," "Responsible," and "Kind"; posters around the room served as a visual prompt to follow the expectations and included the reminder to "Be Spotted Using Good Behavior" (Missy loved dogs and had dog-themed decorations in her classroom). Missy designed a matrix for her classroom and explicitly taught the expected behaviors to her students. Each student in the class earned stickers contingent on demonstrations of expected behavior; when a student accrued 10 stickers, they could visit the "Treasure Chest." The system was effective; Missy noticed an immediate improvement in classroom climate and contextually appropriate behaviors after implementation.

There were three students, however, who earned significantly fewer stickers than their peers. These three students were frequently out of their seats and often did not complete assignments. After a night of class focused on Tier 2 interventions, Missy approached Diane and asked for some advice on implementing CICO in her classroom. They discussed the basics of implementation, and Missy began to develop her classroom CICO plan. She designed a point sheet appropriate for first grade; rather than numerical ratings, she chose to use smiley faces (Figure 9.2 is modeled after Missy's example). No smiley faces meant the expectation hadn't

---

[1] Used with permission from Melissa Duquette. Thanks, Missy!

been met, one smiley meant the expectation was met somewhat, two smileys indicated that the expectation was mostly met, and three smileys meant the expectation was met consistently. She divided the point sheet into blocks based on the structure of her day (e.g., Reading, Specials) and decided to focus on two of the expectations ("Being Safe" and "Being Kind"). Missy chose those two expectations because of the contextually inappropriate behaviors she was seeing most often (being out of seat and not following directions) and because two seemed manageable for 6- and 7-year-olds. She called the three students' families to engage them in discussions about implementing CICO (they were all very supportive) and prepared to introduce the "Smiley Face Chart" (hereafter known as "SFC") to the three students.

Never one to miss an opportunity for a potential case study, Diane suggested that Missy collect data on a dependent variable of interest (i.e., target behavior) and stagger the intervention to create a multiple-baseline design for investigating the effectiveness of the CICO intervention. Missy was all for the idea and chose a variable on which she could easily collect data: out-of-seat behavior. To track out-of-seat behavior, Missy moved a paper clip from her pocket into a container on her desk (she had a separate container for each student) every time a target student was out of their seat (and she defined out-of-seat behavior as "leaving seat without teacher permission, walking around the room, twirling around the room, or being in another area of the room [e.g., the book corner] when being in the seat is expected for a particular task"). She collected out-of-seat data on each student for 3 hours a day, alternating students every day. Missy staggered the implementation of the CICO intervention: She collected baseline data on all three students, then introduced CICO to the first student. When that student showed a stable trend in his data, she began CICO with the second student. When that student showed a stable trend in his data, she began CICO with the third. The students' data are shown in Figure 9.6.

Here's how Missy described her CICO implementation steps. On a daily basis, each student in CICO would meet with Missy upon arrival at school, turn in the previous day's SFC, and receive a new SFC. Missy would remind the student how they could earn smiley faces and meet the daily goal. At the end of each subject, the student would meet with Missy and discuss how many smiley faces they earned. Before the end of the day, the student would meet with Missy for a few minutes to total up the number of smiley faces. During this meeting, Missy offered praise and a sticker toward the classroom reinforcement system if the student met their goal. If the student didn't meet the goal, Missy and the student would problem-solve and discuss how tomorrow could be a better day. After the meeting, both Missy and the student would sign the SFC and then walk to the office to make a copy of the sheet. (The office walk could be delegated to a paraprofessional if one was available.) The student would put the copy of the SFC into their homework folder, which went directly into the student's backpack. Missy kept the original for her records. On a weekly basis, Missy kept in contact with the students' families via email (making it a point to give at least three positive updates whenever possible), and she "checked out" with each student at the end of the week to talk about how the week went and cite any improvements so that the student would hear something positive before heading home for the weekend.

The CICO intervention was successful (which Missy defined as a reduction in the three students' out-of-seat behavior and an increase in work completion). In fact, Missy was so excited by the intervention that she shared the results with her principal. The principal, in turn, wanted to use Missy's CICO as a model for implementation in other classrooms in the school. What appealed most to Missy (and to most teachers with whom we have worked on Tier 2 classroom supports) is the efficiency of the system. Certainly, there is some effort in the initial design and

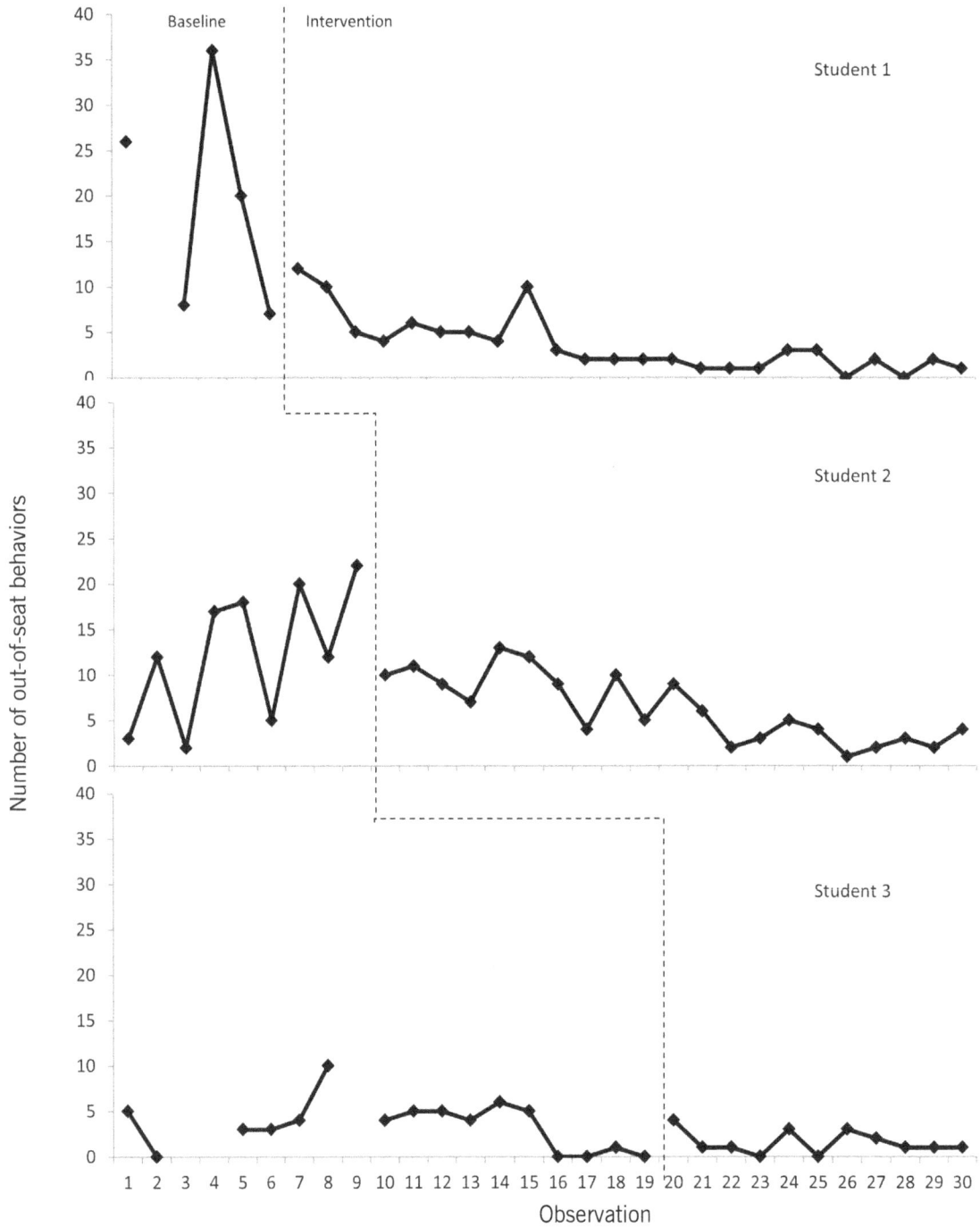

FIGURE 9.6. Missy's out-of-seat data from a CICO intervention done in her first-grade classroom.

implementation, but you need only develop a CICO intervention once. After that, CICO is continuously available for any student who requires a little extra support.

PHASES OF LEARNING ACTIVITIES: CHAPTER 9

Acquisition

1. You have a few students in your classroom who have not responded to your universal level of behavioral support. Describe, specifically, how you would select and implement a Tier 2 intervention in your classroom.
2. Another teacher tells you that Tier 2 interventions are a waste of time since you already have classroom behavioral supports in place. Provide at least three key talking points you'd raise in a discussion about the potential benefits of Tier 2 interventions.

Fluency

1. How do the behavioral principles you learned in Chapter 2 apply to Tier 2 interventions?
2. You have five students in your class about to begin a CICO program. Describe the specific steps you will take to orient them to your CICO intervention.

Maintenance

1. How do you ensure any Tier 2 interventions that you implement are culturally responsive and reflect student voice? Include specific examples of how Tier 2 interventions can center equity and incorporate input from the family and classroom community.
2. How can you use data to make decisions about Tier 2 interventions? Give at least three specific examples in your answer.

Generalization

1. How would designing a classroom Tier 2 intervention differ at the elementary, middle, and high school levels? Provide specific examples.
2. Describe how a self-monitoring intervention might look for use with younger students. Provide rationale for the way you design your self-monitoring intervention, and include an example of the self-monitoring tool you'd have students use.

CHAPTER 10

Overview of Tier 3 Supports in Your School and Classroom

CHAPTER OBJECTIVES

By the end of this chapter, you should be able to . . .

1. Identify the defining characteristics of Tier 3 (i.e., individualized and intensive) supports and interventions.
2. Describe the process of developing and implementing Tier 3 interventions.
3. Integrate individualized behavioral support within your classwide PBIS implementation.

Imagine This: Ozzy is a student in Mr. Butler's eighth-grade language arts class. Mr. Butler sees Ozzy for 60 minutes each day. At the beginning of the school year, the special education teacher met with Mr. Butler to share Ozzy's individualized education plan (IEP) and to talk about the supports Ozzy would have access to in the classroom (e.g., preferential seating, daily point sheet). Ozzy's current IEP goals target a reduction in aggressive behavior directed at peers and an increase in contextually appropriate social interactions with adults and peers. Ozzy enjoys writing, and Mr. Butler has made connections with Ozzy by providing feedback and encouragement on his writing projects. Mr. Butler also talked with Ozzy's aunt, who came by Mr. Butler's virtual coffee hour and mentioned that Ozzy's family would like him to have more positive relationships with peers and adults; the family had pushed to include the social interaction goal in Ozzy's IEP.

The special education teacher invites Mr. Butler to Ozzy's annual IEP meeting. At the meeting, Mr. Butler discusses the language arts curriculum and Ozzy's strengths as a student. Mr. Butler listens to the team's concerns and ideas. He shows some of Ozzy's writing projects to Ozzy's family. The team discusses new goals for Ozzy and develops a behavior support plan (BSP) based on a recently completed functional behavioral assessment (FBA). Data indicate that the function of Ozzy's aggressive behavior is to escape peer attention. Mr. Butler tells the team that Ozzy can ask to sit away from peers

200

and free write (if he needs a break from peers), and he can choose to work with a preferred peer (i.e., a peer chosen by Ozzy) several times a week to continue to work on peer relationship skills. Further, if Ozzy meets the classroom norm of being considerate (i.e., using kind words, actively listening—skills Mr. Butler has taught explicitly), Ozzy can earn an incentive, like lunch with Mr. Butler or a special writing project. The team likes this idea and incorporates it into the BSP. In addition, the team decides that Ozzy will meet weekly with the guidance counselor for individualized social skills training focused on peer relationship skills. Mr. Butler agrees to take whatever data he can on Ozzy's interactions with peers and agrees to reward Ozzy with praise and/or a break when he sees that Ozzy completes a collaborative task while demonstrating expected behaviors.

After a few weeks, the team reconvenes to review Ozzy's data. Data indicate an increase in positive peer interactions (as measured by what Mr. Butler recorded and three formal observations conducted by the school psychologist). Ozzy has been to all of his classes except for gym and he earned lunch with Mr. Butler three times. The team thinks about ways to encourage Ozzy's participation in gym but otherwise decides to leave the current plan in place.

WHAT ARE TIER 3 INTERVENTIONS?

Tier 3 interventions are individualized, intensive social, emotional, and behavioral supports. Students who require Tier 3 interventions demonstrate contextually inappropriate behaviors that (1) do not decrease in intensity or frequency when exposed to Tier 1 and Tier 2 levels of support or (2) require more immediate and intensive intervention. Consider these two scenarios:

• Tristan is a third grader in a school that's implementing a schoolwide PBIS framework with fidelity. Over the last 2 months, Tristan is sent to the principal's office repeatedly for behaviors including property damage, significant disruptions to others' learning, and walking out of the school building without permission. If he receives a schoolwide "High Five" ticket, he often tosses the ticket on the floor or into the trash as soon as the adult hands it to him. His teacher refers him to the school's CICO program, and Tristan begins checking in and checking out daily. He rarely checks in between activities; data from his daily point sheets indicate infrequent and inconsistent demonstrations of the contextually appropriate behaviors targeted on his CICO card. The school's behavioral support team reviews the data on Tristan (as part of their weekly review of all students in CICO), talks with Tristan's mother to learn more about his behavior at home and to solicit her input and feedback about additional help he may need in school, and decides to plan some more intensive supports for him, beginning with an academic assessment to determine if any academic skill deficits may be contributing to Tristan's behaviors of concern. In addition, the team and Tristan's mother plan for Tristan to begin individual counseling from the school social worker; Tristan's mother reports Tristan may be having difficulty adjusting to his parents' recent divorce and inconsistent schedules between each parent's new home.

• Bethany transfers into Oakmont High School during her sophomore year. Bethany receives special education services for an emotional disorder and attention-deficit/hyperactivity disorder; her IEP team at Oakmont met prior to her arrival, conferred with the team at Bethany's sending school, and talked with Bethany and her family. Oakmont has a robust schoolwide PBIS program and a CICO system, but Bethany's IEP team (which includes her father and grandfather) determines that these supports would not be enough given her history of self-injurious behaviors and the possible stress of the transition to a new school. The team decides to make some adjustments to Bethany's current BSP (based on an FBA conducted 6 months ago at her previous school) so it can be implemented in Oakmont as soon as she arrives. The team makes a plan to collect data on Bethany's self-injurious behaviors and class attendance (both behaviors that relate to current IEP goals) and reconvene 2 weeks after Bethany starts at Oakmont to assess contextual fit of the BSP and adjust as needed based on data.

Both Tristan and Bethany are appropriate candidates for Tier 3 interventions. Tristan's contextually inappropriate behaviors have not decreased in response to the school's Tier 1 and Tier 2 levels of support; Bethany has a history of requiring intensive, individualized behavioral support, so the team decides to continue providing individualized supports and collecting data on their efficacy.

Because a comprehensive discussion of Tier 3 support systems within a school's PBIS model is beyond the scope of this book, we suggest you explore some key resources (e.g., Crone et al., 2015; the Center on PBIS website content and resources focused on Tier 3 at *www.pbis.org/pbis/tier-3*). Our goal in this chapter is to help you support students with high-intensity social, emotional, and behavioral needs in your classroom, which will include (1) collaboration with your school's behavioral support team and any individual staff members who are working with the student and their family and (2) differentiating and intensifying your existing social, emotional, and behavioral supports. Let's dig in!

OVERVIEW OF TIER 3 SUPPORTS: CRITICAL FEATURES

A tiered prevention framework like PBIS supports the needs of *all* students. Students who experience intensive social, emotional, and behavioral needs that cannot be met with available Tier 1 or Tier 2 supports may benefit from intensive strategies matched to their individual needs (Center on PBIS, 2022b). These intensive needs may include internalizing (e.g., suicidal ideation, social withdrawal) and externalizing (e.g., physical aggression, property damage) behaviors and may be impacted by trauma, crisis, or mental health needs. Tier 3 supports are *not* the same as special education or a "last step" before a special education referral; the primary purpose of Tier 3 support is to help students with persistent needs receive the requisite interventions whether those students have an IEP, are in the process of special education evaluation, or have never been (and are unlikely to ever be) referred for special education evaluation (National Center on Intensive Intervention [NCII] & Center on PBIS, 2021).

The first core feature of Tier 3 support is **teaming** (Center on PBIS, 2022b). While a teacher or other individual staff member may be able to implement some components of intensive, individualized interventions, the process of building individual support plans, selecting relevant evidence-based interventions, and monitoring and evaluating supports requires a group of people with different areas of expertise, backgrounds, and perspectives. Team membership should include people who know the student well, who are familiar with the student's unique needs, who have behavioral expertise, who understand broader systems in the school and community, and who can make administrative decisions. When needed, the team should also include members with specific expertise related to academics, mental health, physical health, or other areas where supports are warranted and need to be developed (Center on PBIS, 2022b; NCII & Center on PBIS, 2021). Ideally, this individual student team is supported by a schoolwide team that monitors and supports Tier 3 for all individual students and their teams (Center on PBIS, 2022b).

The second core feature of Tier 3 support is **identifying and screening** students. Students may be referred for intensive supports in a variety of ways: family or teacher referral, regular data review of students receiving Tier 2 interventions, after a critical behavioral event, or resulting from a universal screening indicating the student has intensive social, emotional, or behavioral needs best met through individualized support. Most schools will have an established process for identifying students. Whatever process is used, *all* students in a school setting should have access to whatever level(s) of intervention they need. Students may only need the most intensive support in one or two specific areas (e.g., academics, peer relationships) and benefit from Tier 2 or Tier 1 supports in all other areas; for example, a student may access individualized counseling and a personalized incentive plan related to safe interactions with peers (Tier 3), a self-monitoring intervention to increase time on task in math class (Tier 2), and regular reinforcement for meeting the school's agreed-upon expectations (Tier 1).

The next core feature of Tier 3 support is **professional development and training.** All staff should be trained in PBIS and have working knowledge of how the different tiers of a schoolwide PBIS framework create a comprehensive system to support the social, emotional, and behavioral needs of all students. Related to Tier 3 supports, all staff should understand (1) the referral process and (2) their role if they are working with the Tier 3 team—for example, if a student whom a paraprofessional directly supports is referred for Tier 3 evaluation, the paraprofessional could be asked to provide their perspective on what the student may need and may be asked to help with developing contextually relevant supports. The paraprofessional may also have some data collection or implementation responsibilities once the student's Tier 3 BSP is rolled out. There should be additional, targeted training for those staff who are permanent members of the Tier 3 team and those staff (e.g., behavioral specialists) who frequently collaborate with teachers, students, and families around effective, efficient implementation of individualized behavioral interventions.

Another core feature (related to identifying and screening) is the initial and ongoing **assessment** of students determined to be appropriate candidates for Tier 3 supports. The goal of assessment is to identify specific needs and build effective, individualized plans. When determining an assessment plan, teams may develop individual assessments, use a collaborative problem-solving framework, and plan for coordinated implementation. Assessments should be done across all relevant domains (i.e., all domains where additional supports for the identified student may be warranted). Types of assessment include **functional behavioral assessment** (**FBA,** which we've referenced before; review Chapter 2 for a refresher on function, antecedents, and other behavioral concepts that are critical to the FBA process), **quality-of-life** measures, and **wraparound** assessment. Wraparound assessment and support (which usually include **person-centered planning**) include collaboration with other agencies and the community to build a comprehensive, complex, and multidimensional system of interventions across all areas of need to support the student in multiple settings. The type of assessment(s) selected will impact how the individual BSP is built for the student; the plan could be built on one assessment or multiple, and additional assessments could be part of ongoing monitoring and evaluation once the plan is in place.

The **behavioral intervention/support planning** aspect of Tier 3 brings together all of the previously mentioned features. Developing an individualized, positive, and function-based plan requires people who know the student, the student's family, and, ideally, the student themselves to ensure cultural responsiveness and contextual relevance. Plans that are the result of an FBA are often called behavior support plans (BSPs) or behavior intervention plans (BIPs). BSPs typically include an operational definition of any behavior(s) targeted for change and the criteria by which they will be measured; antecedent or prevention strategies based on any relevant antecedents or setting events; strategies for teaching alternative or replacement behaviors (i.e., contextually appropriate behaviors that meet the same function as the contextually inappropriate behaviors); strategies for teaching and shaping toward desired behaviors; consequence strategies that provide functional reinforcement for contextually appropriate behavior (and prevent reinforcement for contextually inappropriate behaviors); a crisis plan, if needed (i.e., if a student has a history of behaviors that present serious or imminent danger to themselves or others); strategies to match the BSP to the classroom and other settings to ensure cultural and contextual fit; and a plan for ongoing data collection to monitor and evaluate the effectiveness of the BSP and the fidelity of BSP implementation. (As we've mentioned, there is *a lot* that goes into designing an effective BSP with each of those components; we recommend reading Crone et al., 2015, and the Center on PBIS Tier 3 content and resources at *www.pbis.org/pbis/tier-3* for additional guidance.) In the next section, we talk about considerations for implementing some Tier 3 practices in the classroom, and we close the chapter with a closer look at the BSP process.

IMPLEMENTING TIER 3 PRACTICES IN THE CLASSROOM

As we've indicated, Tier 3 levels of support require a team-based approach to data collection, decision making, and designing effective individualized interventions. In your classroom, you may be able to individualize and intensify implementation of some of your existing behavioral supports (in collaboration with your school's Tier 3 team and your students' individualized Tier 3 team, including your student and their family). In the following paragraphs, we describe **individualization** and **intensification** of some specific practices that may help to support students with the highest level of need; again, we want to be clear that if you have a student whose social, emotional, and behavioral needs are intense enough to warrant consideration of individualized, intensive supports, you should work in tandem with your school's designated support team to ensure that the student gets all of their social, emotional, and behavioral needs met as efficiently and effectively as possible.

ORGANIZING MORE INTENSIVE SUPPORT: PREVENT, TEACH, AND RESPOND

Thinking about how to organize behavioral supports along a continuum from least-to-most intensive can be challenge. We like to keep it simple by thinking about how we can **prevent, teach, and respond** (e.g., Simonsen, Robbie, et al., 2021; based on prevent–teach–reinforce; Dunlap et al., 2010). Across all tiers of support, we're focused on **preventing** contextually appropriate behavior and proactively providing social, emotional, and behavioral supports to all learners. We're also explicitly **teaching** critical social, emotional, and behavioral skills that students need to access and benefit from academic instruction. Finally, across all tiers, we're **responding** in ways that encourage use of contextually appropriate social, emotional, and behavioral skills. As we think about how to intensify and individualize supports for students with elevated social, emotional, and behavioral needs, we'll use **prevent, teach,** and **respond** to organize our approach to differentiation.

Tier 3 Classroom Practices: Prevent

As we've said before (quoting Scott & Eber, 2003), "If you can predict it, you can prevent it." Setting the stage to prevent disrupted learning for students with the most intensive needs begins with **individualizing effective design.** That is, how do we use the space in classroom to encourage contextually appropriate social, emotional, and behavioral skills and discourage opportunities for contextually inappropriate behavior? First, examine the physical space itself: Do students with mobility needs have adequate room to easily navigate between activities? Is there a cooldown area or calming space available for students who may need a break? Can all students easily access materials? Once you've reviewed your physical space—including making sure you have plenty of visual prompts to help students remember how to access and use different spaces and materials in the classroom—think about any student-specific needs. Some students may need more space, a distraction-free place to work, access (or limited access) to sensory items or input, or safety-based individualizations (e.g., reducing unsupervised access to scissors for students who have a history of hurting others or themselves with sharp objects).

After you've considered and incorporated any individual design needs, think about how you can **individualize predictable routines** as needed. For example, some students who experience anxiety or have difficulty with transitions may benefit from an individualized schedule; the schedule can include visual reminders, if helpful, and also highlight when preferred activities will occur—you can even alternate easier and more difficult tasks to prevent frustration. If there's an unavoidable change to the schedule, provide as much advance notice to the student as possible, and also teach and practice coping and tolerance skills to help students for whom schedule disruptions are associated with increases in internalizing or externalizing contextually inappropriate behaviors. If any routines are particularly challenging for a student, you can tap into what you learned in Chapter 2 about teaching through shaping (i.e., reinforcing successive approximations) or chaining (i.e., breaking a task into separate steps and teaching each separately, then chaining them together). You can also incorporate what you learned in Chapters 7 and 8 and implement noncontingent reinforcement (e.g., attention, scheduled breaks) to minimize the likelihood of contextually inappropriate behaviors that serve related functions.

Another prevention consideration for implementing highly individualized supports in the classroom is **intensifying connections.** This can be done through more intentional engagement with students and their families in planning supports (which enhances cultural and contextual relevance—and effectiveness), increasing meaningful interactions with students (e.g., engaging with them around high-interest topics and activities), and setting up opportunities for students to build relationships with each other (e.g., structured community building time, mentoring) and practice their social, emotional, and behavioral skills with each other.

Finally, optimizing prevention means **intensifying and individualizing prompts, active supervision,** and **other antecedent interventions.** Examples include individualized prompts for classroom norms (e.g., a peer "buddy" who provides reminders about contextually appropriate behaviors, a self-management sheet or app that includes individual reminders), providing increased proximity and increased behavior-specific feedback when actively supervising students, and considering other factors that can impact social, emotional, and behavioral skill use. (Remember **setting events** from Chapter 2? If not, quickly flip back.) Those factors could be related to biological needs (e.g., history of hunger or limited sleep: our individualizations can include snacks and opportunities to rest) or to other antecedent conditions (e.g., difficulty transitioning from a preferred activity to a less preferred activity: our individualizations can include thoughtful sequencing of preferred and nonpreferred activities, additional prompting, and reminders of available incentives for successful transitions while starting a timer).

Tier 3 Classroom Practices: Teach

With our prevention strategies intensified and individualized to meet student needs, we can turn our attention to how to **intensify and individualize our social, emotional, and behavioral skills instruction.** First, we should ensure that our instruction in social, emotional, and behavioral skills aligns with the target skills in a student's BSP: are we teaching contextually appropriate behaviors that compete successfully (i.e., are a functional equivalent) with contextually inappropriate behaviors targeted for reduction? If a student has a history of biting when asked to stop engaging in a preferred task, for example, we can teach asking for a few more minutes, signing, "I'm not ready," or how to select one of two moderately preferred activities to do next. Again, you may need to use the shaping and chaining teaching strategies you learned in previous chapters.

As we're individualizing and intensifying our social, emotional, and behavioral instruction, we should align that instruction to our classroom norms and expectations to create intentional connections between individualized and universal supports, include students with the most intensive needs in the broader classroom community (i.e., reducing stigma), and promote generalization. Similarly, if students are participating in social, emotional, and behavioral skills instruction as part of their Tier 1 or Tier 2 supports, be sure to align the language and skills taught in their individualized plan with skills taught in other curricula or programs (which should also align with classroom expectations and norms!). For example, if a student is working on saying, "I'm not ready," instead of biting or hitting when asked to stop a preferred activity, that skill could connect to a classroom norm related to "accountability" and to whole-class lessons on "self-advocacy" from a social, emotional, and behavioral skills curriculum.

In addition to focusing on our instruction of social, emotional, and behavioral skills, we can **individualize and intensify our academic instruction.** Ensure that the academic instruction matches the student's level of need (as indicated by data), increase active engagement, and ensure task dimensions are selected intentionally to give the student the greatest likelihood of success. For instance, if a student is working on extending their capacity to remain on task, task duration should initially be short, especially for nonpreferred tasks. In addition, incorporating choice can be an effective way to individualize academic instruction and promote student engagement and autonomy; students can choose between assignments, their work partner, the order of tasks, and the preferred activity following task completion.

Tier 3 Classroom Practices: Respond

Finally, consider how to respond to the social, emotional, and academic behaviors of students with the highest level of need. First, we can **intensify and individualize behavior-specific supportive feedback.** This might include intensifying the frequency of our behavior-specific praise (either on its own or in relation to our corrective feedback; for example, we could work toward a 9:1 ratio rather than the recommended 5:1; Caldarella et al., 2023; Downs et al., 2019). Any error corrections should be calm, private, and helpful; we should intentionally include phrases like "Can I help you?" or "Let me know what you need from me to be successful" as appropriate to signify our intent to partner with the student to help meet social, emotional, and behavioral needs. In particular, we should provide specific feedback on any replacement behaviors (or any efforts toward using replacement behaviors; remember, we know how to shape!). If a student who has a history of eloping from the building continues to elope from the classroom but does not leave, we should provide specific positive feedback about that effort toward the eventual goal of remaining in the classroom and asking for a break.

We can also **intensify and individualize recognition strategies.** Your classroom continuum of acknowledgment for contextually appropriate behavior can be individualized to include more variety and additional consideration of the value of incentives: do they "match" the task and the function of students' behaviors? It may take more effort for students with the most intensive needs to demonstrate certain social, emotional, or behavioral skills; the reinforcer should also "intensify." You can also consider an individual token board (or an individualized version of your classroom token economy; remember, connecting individual practices to your broader system reduces stigma and promotes generalization) or individualized DPR to provide more frequent supportive feedback and acknowledgment. Any social, emotional, or behavioral skill that replaces a contextually inappropriate behavior should be followed by function-based reinforcement whenever possible; for example, if a student asks for a break (replacement behavior for eloping from the classroom), we should immediately honor the request and provide contingent reinforcement with specific praise or other more overt strategies. Finally, as we discussed at length in Chapter 7, be sure that your available incentives reflect individual preferences—provide preference assessments, observe what your students naturally gravitate toward when given multiple choices, and ask students what they want to earn. For students with the most intensive needs, asking them what they want to earn in the moment can be more effective than a conversation about what they'd like to learn "eventually."

Finally, we can **individualize and intensify strategies to decrease social, emotional, and behavioral challenges.** Preventing escalation should be a key focus; we can provide a brief private redirection when students don't use a contextually appropriate skill (rather than responding publicly or initiating a consequence) and reteach as needed. We can use differential reinforcement of lower rates of contextually inappropriate behaviors (e.g., decreased classroom elopement) and differential reinforcement of alternative behaviors (e.g., staying in class and asking for a break). If, despite our best efforts, contextually inappropriate behaviors escalate, we can use effective de-escalation strategies (see Strickland-Cohen et al., 2022). In addition, we should prevent reinforcement of contextually inappropriate behaviors as much as possible; for example, withhold (or limit as much as possible) attention for contextually inappropriate behaviors that function to obtain attention—but be sure to provide more intense and frequent attention for replacement behaviors. For example, if a student kicks and hits to obtain adult attention, we should minimize contingent attention for kicking and hitting as much as we can while maintaining safety—limit verbal interactions, evade as possible—and provide ample noncontingent adult attention and intensify our recognition of safe behaviors (e.g., feet on ground, observing personal space).

A CLOSER LOOK AT PLANNING AND IMPLEMENTATION

As a classroom teacher, you should never be solely responsible for assessing and developing a plan to support students with the most intensive social, emotional, and behavioral needs. As we discussed earlier in this chapter, a team made up of people with a range of expertise and perspectives—including people who know the student well—should work together to build a plan, based on collected data, that is culturally and contextually relevant. In the previous section, we provided some general considerations for supporting students with the most intensive needs in your classroom. Below, we talk about some of the specific considerations related to individual BSPs—when you are part of an individual student's support team, we want to you to be as prepared as possible!

INDIVIDUALIZED BSPs: APPLICATION

You may remember that in Chapter 2 we explained the *function* of behavior and how determining the function of a contextually inappropriate behavior that disrupts learning and safety can help us identify an equivalent, appropriate replacement behavior that serves the same function as the target behavior. When students exhibit intensive social, emotional, and behavioral needs, a support team will likely conduct an FBA to determine the function of the behavior(s) targeted for decrease, the antecedents that are likely to occasion the target behavior, and the consequences that are maintaining (i.e., reinforcing) the target behavior. The team should also collect information on the student's strengths and learn as much as possible about the student from the student themselves, their family, and other people who know them well. Then, the team develops a plan with targeted strategies across all relevant areas.

The BSP process begins with the development of objective, meaningful (to all partners), and measurable goals and objectives. Then, it's time for the team to start thinking about the actual interventions. First, the team considers **setting event strategies** (Horner et al., 1996). During the data collection process, the team may have discovered that the target behavior is more likely to occur when there is a specific setting event that makes a consequence more or less valuable. For example, Liam engages in withdrawal behaviors (i.e., putting his head down, not responding to teacher directions or peer communications) that result in him not completing his work (i.e., he escapes doing the work). If Liam has a fight on the bus (i.e., setting event), we hypothesize that he is more likely to want to escape doing work, so he is more likely to engage in the withdrawal behaviors. If the team is aware of any setting events, they can develop strategies to eliminate the setting events (if possible), mitigate the effects of the setting event, or increase reinforcement for contextually appropriate behavior. Here are some examples of setting event strategies:

Setting event

- Student frequently misses bus due to oversleeping; student is more likely to engage in behaviors that usually result in escaping class on these days.

- Student spends the weekend alone; student is more likely to engage in behaviors that usually result in peer attention on Monday.

- Student has an argument with guardian before school; student is more likely to engage in behaviors to avoid doing work on these days.

- Student has a fight with a peer on the bus; student is more likely to engage in behaviors that usually result in escaping peer attention on these days.

- Student's guardian works the night shift; student is more likely to engage in behaviors that usually result in adult attention on the following day.

Strategies

- *Eliminate.* Teach student how to use alarm clock, work with family to develop a morning routine.

- *Mitigate.* Schedule peer attention first thing Monday morning (e.g., partner work).

- *Increase reinforcement.* Tell student that they can earn a break for every assignment they finish.

- *Remove S^D for problem behavior.* Allow student to work alone during scheduled think/pair/share activity.

- *Increase prompting.* Increase the level of prompting for contextually appropriate behavior, including how to obtain adult attention according to classroom norms.

Sometimes, there will not be any setting events identified, and the team can move directly into developing **antecedent strategies.** Since the team has an idea of what events can occasion the contextually inappropriate behavior(s), it's likely that the team will be able to develop some strategies to *prevent* the contextually inappropriate behavior from occurring—much easier than trying to decide what to do after it happens! In addition, the team can also develop antecedent strategies that promote the use of new, more contextually appropriate behaviors. Any stimulus, event, or environment can be an antecedent that occasions a behavior, including transitions, peer attention, teacher attention, lack of attention, the cafeteria, a change in schedule, certain assignments and activities, a particular person . . . the list goes on and on. The specific antecedent depends on the student. While developing antecedent strategies, the team should keep the function of the contextually inappropriate behavior in mind. Since the student is engaging in the behavior to meet a certain function, we may be able to address through an antecedent modification (discussed in Chapter 8) and eliminate the need for the student to engage in the contextually inappropriate behavior. See examples below.

Antecedent	Strategies
• Transition to a different class (occasions yelling and poking that often results in peer and teacher attention).	• Student transitions alone, before peers. • Student transitions with a preferred peer. • Before the bell rings, student is reminded of (1) an appropriate way to transition and (2) what they can earn for following expectations.
• Being asked to work in a group (occasions contextually inappropriate verbalizations that often result in being able to work alone).	• Allow student to work alone. • Allow student to choose peers for group. • Remind student of expectations for working in groups and what they can earn for doing so.
• Math class (occasions asking for help and crying that often results in increased teacher attention).	• Give student a predetermined number of times that they can ask for help and remind them of what they can earn for meeting that expectation. • Check in with student regularly to offer help. • Remind student of strategies they can use to problem-solve on their own and what they can earn for doing so.

You may be thinking to yourself, "Wait a minute. Some of these strategies are just allowing the student to get what they want. If working in a group increases the likelihood of a student engaging in yelling and throwing items and that student is given the option to work alone, aren't you just reinforcing the behavior that doesn't align with your expectations?" Here's why we don't consider this "giving in" but rather "function-based behavior support": if you know a student will yell and throw items when asked to work in a group, you can eliminate the yelling and screaming by allowing her to work alone. For the teacher and other peers in the classroom, this is preferable to yelling and throwing items. This is not—not!—a permanent solution, though. Getting to a place where the student is calm and receptive to instruction is the first step to teaching contextually appropriate replacement behaviors. Antecedent strategies are designed to be faded so we can shape the contextually appropriate behavior. For instance, if we first provide the student with the option to work alone, we can add the option to work with a preferred peer (as the student becomes more fluent with the requisite social, emotional, and behavioral skills). Then, the student has the option to choose two peers. Then, the teacher chooses a peer and the student chooses a peer. Eventually, the student demonstrates contextually appropriate behavior no matter how the groups are selected; this is accomplished by increasing expectations, ongoing teaching and recognizing of the contextually appropriate behavior, and intensifying and individualizing prevention efforts (as we discussed in the previous section).

After the antecedent strategies are developed, the team shifts its focus to **behavioral strategies.** This is the most labor-intensive part of the BSP, as it usually requires explicit planning around the teaching and shaping of contextually appropriate replacement behaviors, as well as any intensive social, emotional, or academic instruction. To teach social, emotional, behavioral, functional, or academic skills, apply what you learned about teaching strategies in Chapter 2 and how to teach expected behaviors in Chapter 6. See the following examples.

Contextually inappropriate behavior that disrupts safety and learning	Behaviors to be taught
• Student walks out of class (hypothesized function: to avoid work).	• Teach student to ask for a break. • Teach student to ask for help. • Teach academic skills.
• Student makes noises and contextually inappropriate comments during class (hypothesized function: to obtain teacher attention).	• Teach student to raise hand to obtain attention. • Teach student to self-recruit praise after engaging in contextually appropriate behavior.
• Student puts head down and pulls hood over head when peers talk to him (hypothesized function: to avoid peers).	• Teach student how to ask to use calming space. • Teach social, emotional, and behavioral skills.

Notice that several of the behaviors above (e.g., "Ask for a break") are not long-term, permanent replacements for the contextually inappropriate behavior. While asking for a break is preferable now, breaks will not always be available—eventually, we want the student to access coping and tolerance strategies that help the student endure discomfort, as these are critical generalizable skills that will help the student in authentic situations (e.g., while using public transportation, waiting in a long line at a store, wearing clothes that occasionally pull or pinch).

See the following examples of how we can shape the replacement behavior into the desired behavior.

Current behavior	Replacement behavior	Shaping into contextually appropriate behavior
• Student walks out of class (hypothesized function: to avoid work).	• Teach student to ask for a break.	• Begin by allowing a break every time asked; slowly decrease the number of breaks provided (and incentivize "leftover" breaks; e.g., tell a student they have 10 to take and if they only take 8, they earn a reinforcer) and increase the amount of work required to earn a break, thereby increasing time between breaks, until student is able to stay in class and complete work.
• Student makes noises and contextually inappropriate comments during class (hypothesized function: to obtain teacher attention).	• Teach student to raise hand to obtain attention.	• Begin by giving attention contingent on every hand raise; slowly reduce number of hand raises permitted per class and move to an intermittent schedule of reinforcement until student's hand raising is contextually appropriate.

Current behavior	Replacement behavior	Shaping into contextually appropriate behavior
• Student puts head down and pulls hood over head when peers talk to him (hypothesized function: to avoid peers).	• Teach student how to ask to use calming space.	• Begin by reinforcing student for asking to take space; as you begin teaching social, emotional, and behavioral skills, build in reinforcement for interacting in a contextually appropriate way with peers and intermittently reinforce asking to take space.

After the team has documented how the contextually appropriate replacement behaviors will be taught and shaped, they can begin working on **response strategies.**

In order to be effective, any responses to replacement and new contextually appropriate behaviors must be *at least* as fast and as powerful as the responses to the contextually inappropriate behavior targeted for decrease; otherwise, why would the student use the new behavior, if the old one more effectively results in reinforcement? So, for a student who elopes from the classroom, we decide to teach them to ask for a break. Once the plan is implemented, the teacher must promptly respond to and grant every break request until the student is using the behavior predictably and reliably. If this sounds challenging, that's because it is: this is why implementing the BSP with fidelity (i.e., exactly as it is written) is so important. If the BSP is newly implemented and you forget (or need to build more fluency with the skills) to reinforce the new contextually appropriate behavior and inadvertently reinforce the target contextually inappropriate behavior, the plan is unlikely to work as intended.

If a student has a history of high-intensity unsafe behavior, a **crisis plan** should be developed as part of the BSP. The crisis plan should only be written for students whose past behavior, current behavior, or situation (e.g., threats and means to carry them out, signs of severe emotional dysregulation, unpredictable reaction to a setting event) indicates that they may experience a crisis. A crisis plan should be enacted when—and *only* when—the student's behavior has escalated to the point where they are not responding to any intervention and the student is in danger of harming themself or others. The crisis plan is *not* a consequence for responding to contextually inappropriate behavior (we cannot emphasize this enough!); it is a plan to ensure student and staff safety when implementation of the BSP has failed. The crisis plan might include instructions about whom to call if the behavior escalates to a point where it has become highly unsafe; also, the plan should include instructions related to other students (for instance, they may be removed if excess attention can exacerbate the situation). Although the crisis plan is written with the goal of never having to be used, its inclusion in the BSP and regular review is important (Simonsen, Sugai, et al., 2014); if you wait until a crisis to think about crisis planning, it's too late. (See additional guidance for crisis planning from the U.S. Department of Education, 2012).

The team also needs to determine how the BSP will be **evaluated and monitored** and make **decision rules** for making changes to the BSP. How big a decrease do we want to see in the target behavior before we begin fading supports? How often do we want to see the student engaging in contextually appropriate replacement behaviors before we thin the schedule of reinforcement? The decision rules will depend on the student, the baseline level of behavior, when a behavior is deemed "contextually appropriate" by the team (and especially the student and their family), and the objectives in the BSP. The following are examples of decision rules.

Baseline level of behavior	Decision-rule examples
• Student elopes from the classroom five times per day each class period.	• When elopement decreases to zero times per day for 3 consecutive days, move from continuous schedule of reinforcement for asking for a break to intermittent schedule (with increased reinforcement for staying in class for longer durations).
• Student has tantrums an average of three times each week.	• If tantrums do not decrease after 3 consecutive weeks, revisit function, review fidelity data (to see if components are being missed), and increase frequency of current reinforcer of one-on-one time with teacher.

The team should also assess **social validity.** Social validity is, essentially, "consumer satisfaction" with the intervention plan (Wolf, 1978). Any plan that is unsatisfactory to any of the partners—especially the student and their family—has little chance of being implemented or effective. In addition, if any plan or intervention is too complicated or unfeasible for implementation in a classroom setting, the plan is likely to fail; teacher feedback is critical when developing and monitoring the plan to ensure it can actually be implemented as designed (e.g., Benazzi et al., 2006).

SUMMARY

In this chapter, we provided an overview of Tier 3 supports. We identified key features of Tier 3 supports and described ways to intensify and individualize your classroom supports by using a prevent, teach, and respond approach. We wrapped up the chapter by looking at some key components of a BSP and some examples of what implementation might look like. When you have students with intensive social, emotional, and behavioral needs in your classroom, collaborate with your site's behavioral support team to develop a plan and use what you already know about effective, culturally responsive behavioral support to prevent, teach, and respond in ways likely to increase contextually appropriate behaviors.

PHASES OF LEARNING ACTIVITIES: CHAPTER 10

Acquisition

1. Provide four specific examples of how you could **intensify** current practices in your classroom.
2. Provide four specific examples of how you could **individualize** current practices in your classroom.

Fluency

1. Describe the core features of Tier 3 supports.
2. Describe what the core features of Tier 3 supports look like at your school.

Maintenance

1. How do the behavioral principles you learned in Chapter 2 apply to Tier 3 interventions? Provide at least three specific examples.

2. How can you use data (and what types of data would you collect) to make decisions about Tier 3 interventions? Provide at least three specific examples.

Generalization

1. You have a student with intensive behavioral needs in your class. Describe how you will engage the student and their family in developing individualized supports.

2. Describe a time when you experienced a lack of cultural relevance or contextual fit with an intervention (it could be academic, social, emotional, or behavioral, and it could come from your own experiences as a student or from your experiences as a teacher).

CHAPTER 11

Conclusion
Where Do We Go from Here?

CHAPTER OBJECTIVES

By the end of this chapter, you should be able to . . .

1. Summarize what you've learned from this textbook.
2. Generalize what you've learned into your own classroom and practice.
3. Access additional information on classroom PBIS and related topics.

Imagine This: *It's the first day of school and your first day as an official classroom teacher. Everything is in its place. While you wait for your students to arrive, you flip through your Classroom Behavior Support 101 notes and a dog-eared, well-worn version of this book. You remember your professor saying, "Generalization is the goal of all teaching," and now you understand what she meant. It's one thing to write papers and take tests on behavioral principles and proactive interventions, but it's another thing altogether to apply those concepts in your own classroom. The bell rings and you take a deep breath as you stand by the door, ready to smile and greet your students warmly as they enter your classroom. It's showtime!*

SAYING GOOD-BYE

Well, you've reached the end of our book. Whether you scoured the book as part of a course, read chapters as part of a professional development workshop, or referenced key sections when reflecting on your own classroom practices, we hope you found it useful. In this conclusion, we'd like to "take a walk down memory lane" and review what we've covered, revisit the essential elements of PBIS that framed our discussion (i.e., equity, outcomes, systems, data, and practices), and then talk about next steps for you as you move toward the generalization phase of learning and apply the content in your classroom and perhaps even other aspects of your life.

WHAT HAVE WE DONE?

In the early chapters of this book, we provided you with a theoretical foundation on which to base our discussions of behavioral support. We introduced you to PBIS, summarized the evidence for using a multi-tiered framework to support behavior, and described the behavioral mechanisms that form the basis for effective classroom PBIS. We taught you the ABCs (and the S^{D}s!) and provided examples of their application in real life and in the classroom, reminding you that the "tricks" you learn may fail you sometimes, but the underlying mechanisms of behavior never will. Then we provided an overview of Tier 1 schoolwide PBIS and demonstrated how outcomes, systems, data, and practices are all critical parts of providing proactive behavioral support to all students—and how we center equity throughout. Finally, we explained classwide PBIS in terms of equity, outcomes, systems, and data.

In the second part of the book, we took you on a tour of empirically supported, culturally responsive practices that can help you establish PBIS in your own classroom. We talked about how you can connect with your students and create welcoming, safe, predictable routines in your classroom and how to actively engage students in your instruction, and we provided you with ways to engage your students in establishing, defining, teaching, and prompting classroom norms or expectations. We highlighted evidence-based practices you can include in a continuum of supports to increase contextually appropriate behaviors and those you can use to decrease contextually inappropriate behaviors.

Finally, in the last part of the book, we walked you through ways to organize and implement targeted and individualized supports for students with more intensive social, emotional, and behavioral needs. We described ways to embed these supports within your classwide PBIS implementation and explained how the behavioral principles discussed in Chapter 2 apply at the targeted and individual intervention level.

But enough about what we did. What did *you* do as you read through this book? What strategies did you use to facilitate your understanding of our discussions? How did you move through the phases of learning with the content provided? Take a quick break from reading and answer the questions that follow, which are framed in our "Big Five" concepts.

WHAT HAVE YOU DONE?

Outcomes

1. What did you expect to get out of this book?
2. Did you meet your expectations?
3. What did you do to ensure you met the expectations?

Data

1. What data did you collect while you used this book (e.g., grades in the course, self-reflections, self-assessments of your implementation of described practices)?
2. How did your data guide the decisions you made about your learning?

3. How will what you learned about data impact your acquisition of classroom PBIS skills in the future?

Practices

1. What practices did you use while reading this book to increase your likelihood of becoming fluent with, maintaining, and ultimately generalizing this content?
2. What practices will you use in the future as you develop your classroom management skills?
3. What practices explained in this book will apply to areas of your life besides your classroom?

Systems

1. How did the system you used to learn about classwide PBIS work for you? What aspects could you improve?
2. What systems will you use in the future to ensure that you stay current with evidence-based practices in classroom PBIS?
3. What systems will you use to ensure that you maintain your classroom PBIS skills? How will you engage in ongoing professional development and stay a lifelong learner?

Equity

1. How did your own learning history affect your experience with this content?
2. How will you center equity in your classroom PBIS system?
3. How will you ensure your practices reflect the voices, identities, and shared (and individual) learning histories of your students and their families?
4. How will you ensure that your practices are and continue to be culturally responsive as you meet new students, change over time, and generational changes come through your classroom?

   Thinking about questions like these may seem strange (given that you're at the end of the book), but we believe in data-based self-reflection, and we think that framing your experience with what you've learned here (and future experiences with classroom PBIS content) in terms of the "Big Five" can help sharpen your focus and increase the likelihood for generalization of skills.

WHAT WILL YOU DO NEXT?

Two of the previous questions involve developing a system for staying current with evidence-based practices in classroom PBIS and developing a system for maintaining your classroom PBIS skill set, respectively. We can help you get started with your answers to those questions by providing you with a list of our favorite and most trusted resources for locating up-to-date and exciting advances in classroom management and positive behavioral support.

Websites

First, we recommend the following **websites related to PBIS.** Each of these sites has great information and many free downloads (e.g., presentations, resources, templates):

- **National Technical Assistance Center on PBIS** (*www.pbis.org*). This website houses the multitudes of free resources produced by the National Technical Assistance Center on PBIS. You may have noticed that we referenced it extensively in this book! Here you will find information about PBIS at every level, research and presentations related to PBIS, and examples of PBIS in practice. Trust us: if you can visit only one website to access information to supplement this book, this is the website to visit.
- **Regional and state PBIS websites.** PBIS is implemented in more than 27,000 schools across the United States, and most states have a dedicated PBIS initiative. Some states have been at it longer than others, some states are supported by regional networks, and some regions and states place a heavier emphasis on classwide PBIS. In particular, for great resources related to classwide PBIS, check out the following regional and state websites:
  - **Northeast PBIS** (*https://nepbis.org*). This regional network website contains resources to help school leadership teams implement a full continuum of support, and there is a tab dedicated to classroom implementation.
  - **Midwest PBIS** (*www.midwestpbis2.org/home*). This regional network website also provides resources to support classroom PBIS within their "training resources" click. In addition, they have important work on how to integrate mental health within a PBIS framework.
  - **Missouri PBIS** (*http://pbismissouri.org*). This state website contains helpful resources that can be used to supplement content from this book. In particular, see their modules and resources related to classroom behavioral support (*https://pbismissouri.org/tier-1-effective-classroom-practices*).
  - **Florida PBIS** (*http://flpbs.fmhi.usf.edu*). Researchers at the University of South Florida have put together a set of modules and resources to guide teachers and PBIS team members through implementation of classwide PBIS (*https://flpbis.cbcs.usf.edu/tiers/classroom.html*).
  - **Center for Instructional and Behavioral Research in Schools (CIBRS)** (*https://cibrs.com*). After reading about practices in classwide PBIS, you may be wondering what they look like in action. In addition to several relevant resources and even mini-courses you can take, CIBRS has an extensive video library to see practices in action (*https://cibrs.com/video-library*).

Second, we have found the following websites helpful for identifying **other evidence-based practices** related to PBIS, classroom instruction, and a variety of other topics:

- **What Works Clearinghouse** (*http://ies.ed.gov/ncee/wwc*). This website, hosted by the U.S. Department of Education's Institute of Education Sciences (IES), offers a rigorous review of educational research and a summary of the practices that do (and do not) meet the criteria for being an "evidence-based practice." In addition, the website features suggestions and strategies for implementing these practices in schools and classrooms (click on the link for "Practice Guides" and you will be amazed at what the site offers—for free!).

- **Regional Educational Labs (*http://ies.ed.gov/ncee/edlabs/regions*).** In addition to federal resources, IES sponsors the regional education lab (REL) Program. RELs offer fantastic resources and may be more sensitive to regional or local needs.

Books

Although there are many, many behavioral texts available, we'd like to highlight the books that we've found particularly useful in our own practice (and referenced throughout this book).

- **Alberto, P. A., Troutman, A. C., & Axe, J. (2021). *Applied behavior analysis for teachers* (10th ed.). Pearson Education.** This book is a classic reference for teachers interested in learning more about ABA. Although the book contains a wealth of theoretical information, the writing style and organization make the material accessible to readers in every phase of learning.
- **Cooper, J. O., Heron, T. E., & Heward, W. L. (2021). *Applied behavior analysis* (3rd ed.). Pearson Education.** Affectionately known as the "white book," this book is standard for any program in ABA; it provides a level of breadth and depth about behavioral theory and ABA that is unparalleled. (Our bookshelves wouldn't be the same without it!)
- **Crone, D. A., Hawken, L. S., & Horner, R. H. (2015). *Building positive behavior support systems in schools* (2nd ed.). Guilford Press.** This book is the companion to the previous text and is a user-friendly primer on Tier 3 support. Like the previous resource, it could be used as a text in a college course for preservice educators or as a guide for inservice educators who implement Tier 3.
- **Hawken, L. S., Crone, D. A., Bundock, K., & Horner, R. H. (2021). *Responding to problem behavior in schools: The Check-In, Check-Out intervention* (3rd ed.). Guilford Press.** This book is a user-friendly primer on Tier 2 support and an implementation guide for CICO. It is a useful resource for pre- and inservice educators who want to learn about an efficient and empirically supported approach to Tier 2 support.
- **McIntosh, K., & Goodman, S. (2016). *Integrated multi-tiered systems of support: Blending RTI and PBIS*. Guilford Press.** This has become a go-to resource for the field on how to integrate academic and behavioral support within a MTSS framework. This book dives further into many of the ideas about how to support students' academic, social, emotional, and behavioral needs; and it includes a stronger emphasis on school and district supports.
- **Myers, D., Simonsen, B., & Freeman, J. (2020). *Implementing classwide PBIS: A guide to supporting teachers*. Guilford Press.** Yes, that's us! While the book you're currently reading focuses on the "what" of evidence-based classroom support practices, our second book focuses on "how" to implement those practices. Specifically, we provide structure and strategies for delivering effective professional development to teachers to ensure the fidelity, generalization, and maintenance of effective classwide PBIS practices. In other words, this book is all about the systems!
- **Other titles from "The Guilford Practical Intervention in the Schools Series."** In addition to the specific titles mentioned in previous bullets, we suggest you peruse other

titles in this series (see *www.guilford.com/practical*). There are resources related to behavioral assessment, coaching teachers for classroom management, and other topics relevant to CWPBIS.

As we've said before, we believe the best educators are lifelong learners. The resources we offer above will help you stay in touch with the field, and you may want to start your own list of your favorite and most trusted resources (if you haven't already). As new editions of trusted resources come out, update your collection—the field is constantly evolving, and you want to evolve your own knowledge and practices, too. If you were familiar with the first edition of this book and took it upon yourself to get the second, first, thank you! And second, we hope you found the updated references, language, practices, and focus on equity helpful to your lifelong learning journey.

In addition to being a lifelong learner, consider the type of educator you want to be. What are the "big" things you want your students to learn and remember about you and your class? What do you hope students will say about you years from now? How do you want to leave your mark on the field? As you reflect on these questions, there are likely some responses that are clearly observable, measurable, and discrete (e.g., "I want my students to learn to integrate functions"); there may be some responses that are slightly more subjective (e.g., "I want my students to become active participants in a democracy"); and there may be responses that are harder to define ("I want to build and maintain positive relationships with my students across the years"). For those responses that are already clearly observable and measurable, you now know how to turn those into outcome statements, collect data to guide your decision making, select and implement practices, and build systems to support and sustain your implementation. We believe that the same can be done for any outcome, including building relationships. Because relationships are the cornerstone of teaching and classwide PBIS, we end our book by revisiting building and maintaining supportive, positive connections with students and their families.

BUILDING RELATIONSHIPS WITH STUDENTS

As we covered in Chapter 5, connecting and building relationships with students and families is critical to creating an inclusive and positive classroom environment; students with supportive relationships at school have better attitudes toward school, higher levels of academic achievement, and lower levels of disruptive classroom behavior and poor achievement, which can lead to dropping out and other poor outcomes (Burns, 2020). Of course, "building relationships" is less observable and measurable than we would like; do you remember our discussion around the key behaviors associated with building connections and relationships? If not, no worries—we summarize below.

Think back to your own teachers and reflect on those with whom you felt you had a strong relationship. What did those teachers do differently? In all likelihood, they engaged in at least some of the following behaviors:

- Knowing all students' names, and using student names frequently when interacting with students (including greeting students by name at the start of class and in other encounters throughout the day)
- Engaging in nonacademic conversations with students before and after class (e.g., asking about how a student's weekend was or if anyone watched a popular new show)

- Practicing active listening when students are talking by using body language that demonstrates engagement (e.g., nodding), being able to repeat back what students say, and remembering the conversation (and referring to it) at a later date
- Correcting errors in a supportive, positive manner so students understand that making mistakes is not only okay, it's normal, and they are not discouraged from participating
- Smiling and being enthusiastic about the subject(s) being taught in a manner that feels authentic (we talked about being authentic with praise in Chapter 7)
- Communicating that students and their families are valued members of the classroom community (i.e., letting students know that their academic, social, emotional, and behavioral growth is the primary focus every single day)

In addition to engaging in these behaviors, using the practices we've provided in this book will help you effectively build connections and relationships with your students, too. Students feel more comfortable (and thus, more likely to make connections with their teacher) in environments where they know what to expect, and you have learned to increase predictability and consistency. We've talked about incorporating student voices, choices, interests, and preferences into your activities and choices of reinforcement, and we've talked about acknowledging students' contextually appropriate behaviors as often as possible. Students will know that you are "paying attention" if you use these strategies (and attention can be a powerful reinforcer), which can help foster teacher–student relationships that can be rewarding for both parties. The goal is not to get students to "like" you (although that is definitely not a bad thing); rather, the goal is to establish an environment where there is mutual respect and accountability between teacher and students; where diverse opinions are solicited, voiced comfortably, and valued; and where the focus is on what is going well (and how we can keep things going well). Students who have strong relationships with school staff are more likely to find attending school reinforcing, and we certainly want to increase the likelihood of that behavior.

One last thought: the students who can benefit most from strong relationships with their teachers are likely those with whom there are the most barriers to building connections and relationships. These may be students with chronic or highly intensive contextually inappropriate behaviors, students (and families) whose learning history includes many aversive experiences with school, or students who have high levels of academic need who engage in behaviors to escape academic demands. Despite these barriers, relationships and connections with students who have intensive social, emotional, behavioral, and other needs are not just possible but necessary to help them reach their goals, whatever those may be. As you may guess by getting to know us in this text, we also find those relationships to be the most impactful and rewarding! Focusing on student strengths and what students are doing well—instead of looking for mistakes—is so critical, as is maintaining a supportive and helpful approach even when your interventions seem to not be making a difference. It's likely that students who frequently demonstrate contextually inappropriate behaviors are used to getting attention (especially a lot of "no," "stop," and "don't" statements) for their behaviors; providing attention contingent on contextually appropriate behaviors makes them more likely to happen again *and* fosters connection. Win-win!

In short, never underestimate the positive influence you may have on a student's life or the privilege it is to work in this field. Every day, we have the opportunity to help students and families reach their goals and live lives that they find fulfilling if we can teach out students the social, emotional, and behavioral skills to make that happen. That's no small achievement!

THANK YOU AND A PARTING GIFT:
A CHECKLIST OF CRITICAL CLASSWIDE PBIS PRACTICES

Now that you have considered how your classroom PBIS implementation can create a proactive, welcoming, safe classroom environment and help you build connections with your students, it's time to say good-bye and good luck. As we part ways, we leave you with one final piece of advice, based on our combined years of research and practice in classwide PBIS, in the form of a checklist (see Figure 11.1). You can use this tool to hold yourself accountable for implementing classwide PBIS; either complete it as a self-assessment or ask a peer or administrator to complete it during a brief (10–15 minute) observation.

Thank you for taking this journey with us, and we hope that you finish this book with greater knowledge and the ability to create a positive, safe, welcoming, predictable, and engaging classroom environment where (1) contextually appropriate behaviors are taught, prompted, and reinforced and (2) contextually inappropriate behavior is prevented or efficiently addressed and redirected with an instructional approach. We look forward to seeing you in the field!

Instructions: Completing this checklist will help assess your implementation of key classwide PBIS practices. Mark "yes" for each item you implement fully; mark "partially" if you are almost there; mark "no" if you are not implementing this item, and mark "?" if you need further information. Your goal is to be able to mark "yes" for each item across most (if not all!) of your classroom activities. For each item marked "no" or "?," consult with a behavioral expert (e.g., mentor teacher, support staff, administrator) to request assistance with that item.

Educator _____ Date _____

Instructional Activity _____ Time (start/end) _____

Classwide PBIS Practice	Extent of Implementation			
	Yes	Partially	No	?
Create an Inclusive, Predictable, Safe, and Engaging Classroom				
1. I positively greet students at the door and intentionally connect with them to foster positive relationships throughout the day.				
2. I post the schedule/routine for the day and/or class activity and prompt predictable routines, as needed, throughout the day.				
3. I physically arrange the room (seating assignments, furniture arrangement) to promote access and contextually appropriate behavior.				
Establish, Prompt, and Monitor Positively Stated Norms or Expectations				
1. I post a small number (3–5) of positively stated norms or expectations that are defined across classroom routines.				
2. I actively and supportively monitor my classroom (e.g., moving, scanning, positively interacting) during instruction.				
3. I effectively prompt positively stated expectations and/or demonstrate other contextually appropriate behaviors.				
Actively Engage Students in Relevant Instruction				
1. I provide all students with appropriately high rates of opportunities to respond and participate during instruction.				
2. I effectively and actively engage all students in various observable ways (e.g., writing, verbalizing, gesturing) in relevant instruction.				
Implement a Continuum of Strategies to Increase Contextually Appropriate Behavior				
1. I use specific praise effectively (i.e., contingent, genuine, culturally relevant, and at a sufficient rate) and use other strategies as needed to acknowledge contextually appropriate behavior.				
Implement a Continuum of Strategies to Decrease Contextually Inappropriate Behavior				
1. I provide quick, calm, supportive, and instructional error corrections/ redirections and use other strategies (e.g., reteach, restorative conversation, differential reinforcement) as needed to respond to social, emotional, and behavioral mistakes and support skill growth.				
2. I provide more frequent acknowledgment for contextually appropriate behaviors than for contextually inappropriate behaviors, exceeding 5 positives for every correction (≥5:1 ratio).				

FIGURE 11.1. Classwide PBIS self-assessment. Based on Simonsen et al. (2008).

References

Alberto, P. A., Troutman, A. C., & Axe, J. (2021). *Applied behavior analysis for teachers* (10th ed.). Pearson Education.

Algozzine, B., Barrett, S., Eber, L., George, H., Horner, R., Lewis, T., et al. (2019). *Schoolwide PBIS tiered fidelity inventory*. Center on PBIS. *www.pbis.org*.

Allday, R. A., & Pakurar, K. (2007). Effects of teacher greetings on student on-task behavior. *Journal of Applied Behavior Analysis, 40*, 317–320.

Allen, C. T., & Forman, S. G. (1984). Efficacy of methods of training teachers in behavior modification. *School Psychology Review, 13*, 26–32.

Amato-Zech, N. A., Hoff, K. E., & Doepke, K. J. (2006). Increasing on-task behavior in the classroom: Extension of self-monitoring strategies. *Psychology in the Schools, 43*, 211–221.

American Psychological Association. (2008). Are zero tolerance policies effective in the schools?: An evidentiary review and recommendations. *American Psychologist, 63*, 852–862.

Anderson, A. R., Christenson, S. L., Sinclair, M. F., & Lehr, C. A. (2004). Check & connect: The importance of relationships for promoting engagement with school. *Journal of School Psychology, 42*, 95–113.

Anderson, C. M., & Borgmeier, C. (2010). Tier II interventions within the framework of school wide positive behavior support: Essential features for design, implementation, and maintenance. *Behavior Analysis in Practice, 3*, 33–45.

Artesani, A. J., & Mallar, L. (1998). Positive behavior supports in general education settings: Combining person-centered planning and functional analysis. *Intervention in School and Clinic, 34*, 33–38.

Baer, D. M., Wolf, M. M., & Risley, T. R. (1968). Some current dimensions of applied behavior analysis. *Journal of Applied Behavior Analysis, 1*, 91–97.

Barrett, S. B., Bradshaw, C. P., & Lewis-Palmer, T. (2008). Maryland statewide PBIS initiative: Systems, evaluation, and next steps. *Journal of Positive Behavior Interventions, 10*, 105–114.

Beaver, B. N., Ré, T. C., Griffith, A. K., Zhang, D., & Schoener, M. A. (2023). A systematic literature review of group contingencies within general education classrooms. *Contemporary School Psychology*.

Becker, W. C., & Gersten, R. (1982). A follow-up of Follow Through: The later effects of the direct instruction model on children in fifth and sixth grades. *American Educational Research Journal, 19*, 75–92.

Begeny, J. C., & Martens, B. K. (2006). Assessing pre-service teachers' training in empirically-validated behavioral instruction practices. *School Psychology Quarterly, 21*, 262–285.

Benazzi, L., Horner, R. H., & Good, R. H. (2006). Effects of behavior support team composition on the technical adequacy and contextual fit of behavior support plans. *Journal of Special Education, 40*(3), 160–170.

Bennett, K., Reichow, B., & Wolery, M. (2011). Effects of structured teaching on the behavior of young children with disabilities. *Focus on Autism and Other Developmental Disabilities, 26*(3), 143–152.

Boyd, R. J., & Anderson, C. M. (2013). Breaks are Better: A Tier II social behavior intervention. *Journal of Behavioral Education, 22*(4), 348–365.

Bradshaw, C. P., Koth, C. W., Bevans, K. B., Ialongo, N., & Leaf, P. J. (2008). The impact of school-wide positive behavioral interventions and supports (PBIS) on the organizational health of elementary schools. *School Psychology Quarterly, 23*, 462–473.

Bradshaw, C. P., Koth, C. W., Thornton, L. A., & Leaf, P. J. (2009). Altering school climate through school-wide positive behavioral interventions and supports: Findings from a group-randomized effectiveness trial. *Prevention Science, 10*, 100–115.

Bradshaw, C. P., Mitchell, M. M., & Leaf, P. J. (2010). Examining the effects of school-wide positive behavioral interventions and supports on student outcomes: Results from a randomized controlled effectiveness trial in elementary schools. *Journal of Positive Behavior Interventions, 12*, 133–148.

Bradshaw, C. P., Waasdorp, T. E., & Leaf, P. J. (2012). Effects of school-wide positive behavioral interventions and supports on child behavior problems. *Pediatrics, 130*, 1136–1145.

Bradshaw, C. P., Waasdorp, T. E., & Leaf, P. J. (2015). Examining variation in the impact of school-wide positive behavioral interventions and supports: Findings from a randomized controlled effectiveness trial. *Journal of Educational Psychology, 107*(2), 546–557.

Briere, D. E., & Simonsen, B. (2011). Self-monitoring interventions for at-risk middle school students: The importance of considering function. *Behavior Disorders, 36*, 129–140.

Briere, D. E., Simonsen, B., Sugai, G., & Myers, D. (2015). Increasing new teachers' specific praise rates using a within-school consultation intervention. *Journal of Positive Behavior Interventions, 17*(1), 50–60.

Briesch, A. M., & Chafouleas, S. M. (2009). Review and analysis of literature on self-management interventions to promote appropriate classroom behaviors (1988–2008). *School Psychology Quarterly, 24*, 106–118.

Burns, E. C. (2020). Factors that support high school completion: A longitudinal examination of quality teacher–student relationships and intentions to graduate. *Journal of Adolescence, 84*, 180–189.

Bushaw, W. J., & Lopez, S. J. (2010). A time for change: The 42nd annual Phi Delta Kappa/Gallup Poll of the public's attitudes toward the public schools. *Phi Delta Kappan, 92*(1), 8–26.

Caldarella, P., Larsen, R. A. A., Williams, L., & Wills, H. P. (2023). Effects of middle school teachers' praise-to-reprimand ratios on students' classroom behavior. *Journal of Positive Behavior Interventions, 25*(1), 28–40.

Caplan, G. (1964). *Principles of preventive psychiatry.* Basic Books.

Carr, E. G., Dunlap, G., Horner, R. H., Koegel, R. L., Turnbull, A. P., Sailor, W., et al. (2002). Positive behavior support: Evolution of an applied science. *Journal of Positive Behavior Interventions, 4*, 4–16.

Carr, J. E., Severtson, J. M., & Lepper, T. L. (2008). Noncontingent reinforcement is an empirically supported treatment for problem behavior exhibited by individuals with developmental disabilities. *Research in Developmental Disabilities, 30*, 44–57.

Carter, M., & Kemp, C. R. (1996). Strategies for task analysis in special education. *Educational Psychology, 16,* 155–170.

Cengher, M., Budd, A., Farrell, N., & Fienup, D. M. (2018). A review of prompt-fading procedures: Implications for effective and efficient skill acquisition. *Journal of Developmental and Physical Disabilities, 30,* 155–173.

Center on Positive Behavioral Interventions and Supports. (2020, July). *Creating effective classroom environments plan template.* Center on PBIS, University of Oregon. *www.pbis.org/resource/creating-effective-classroom-environments-plan-template.*

Center on Positive Behavioral Interventions and Supports. (2022a, January). *Supporting and responding to student's social, emotional, and behavioral needs: Evidence-based practices for educators* (Version 2.0). Center on PBIS, University of Oregon. *www.pbis.org/resource/supporting-and-responding-to-behavior-evidence-based-classroom-strategies-for-teachers.*

Center on Positive Behavioral Interventions and Supports. (2022b, January). *Tier 3 student-level systems guide.* Center on PBIS, Center on PBIS, University of Oregon. *www.pbis.org.*

Center on Positive Behavioral Interventions and Supports. (2022c, April). *Feedback and input surveys (FIS) manual.* Center on PBIS, University of Oregon. *www.pbis.org.*

Center on Positive Behavioral Interventions and Supports. (2022d, October). *What does research say about the effects of Tier 1 PBIS for students with disabilities?* Center on PBIS, University of Oregon. *www.pbis.org.*

Center on Positive Behavioral Interventions and Supports. (2023a, January). *Supporting and responding to educators' classroom PBIS implementation needs: Guide to classroom systems and data.* Center on PBIS, University of Oregon. *www.pbis.org.*

Center on Positive Behavioral Interventions and Supports. (2023b, July). *Positive behavioral interventions and supports (PBIS) implementation blueprint.* Center on PBIS, University of Oregon. *www.pbis.org.*

Center on Positive Behavioral Interventions and Supports. (2023c, October). *Discipline disproportionality problem solving: A data guide for school teams.* Center on PBIS, University of Oregon. *www.pbis.org.*

Center on Positive Behavioral Interventions and Supports, National Center on Deaf-Blindness, & National Deaf Center on Postsecondary Outcomes. (2023, November). *Supporting deaf students in the classroom within a PBIS framework.* Center on PBIS, University of Oregon. *www.pbis.org.*

Center on Positive Behavioral Interventions and Supports, State Implementation and Scaling up of Evidence-Based Practices Center, National Integrated Multi-Tiered Systems of Support Research Network, National Center on Improving Literacy, & Lead for Literacy Center. (2022, October). *Supporting schools during and after crisis: A guide to supporting states, districts, schools, educators, and students through a multi-tiered systems of support framework.* Center on PBIS, University of Oregon. *www.pbis.org.*

Chafouleas, S. M., Sanetti, L. M. H., Kilgus, S. P., & Maggin, D. M. (2012). Evaluating sensitivity to behavioral change across consultation cases using Direct Behavior Rating Single-Item Scales (DBR-SIS). *Exceptional Children, 78,* 491–505.

Chalk, K., & Bizo, L. A. (2004). Specific praise improves on-task behavior and numeracy enjoyment: A study of year four pupils engaged in numeracy hour. *Educational Psychology in Practice, 20,* 335–351.

Chaparro, E. A., Nese, R. N. T., & McIntosh, K. (2015). *Examples of engaging instruction to increase equity in education.* Center on PBIS, University of Oregon. *www.pbis.org.*

Cheney, D. A., Stage, S. A., Hawken, L. S., Lynass, L., Mielenz, C., & Waugh, M. (2009). A 2-year outcome study of the check, connect, and expect intervention for students at risk for severe behavior problems. *Journal of Emotional and Behavioral Disorders, 17,* 226–243.

Cho Blair, K., Park, E., & Kim, W. (2020). A meta?analysis of Tier 2 interventions implemented within school?wide positive behavioral interventions and supports. *Psychology in the Schools, 58,* 141–161.

Claes, C., Van Hove, G., Vandevelde, S., van Loon, J., & Schalock, R. L. (2010). Person-centered planning: Analysis of research and effectiveness. *Intellectual and Developmental Disabilities, 48*(6), 432–453.

Colvin, G., Sugai, G., Good, R. H., & Lee, Y. (1997). Using active supervision and pre-correction to improve transition behaviors in an elementary school. *School Psychology Quarterly, 12,* 344–363.

Condliffe, B., Zhu, P., Doolittle, F., van Dok, M., Power, H., Denison, D., & Kurki, A. (2022). *Study of training in multi-tiered systems of support for behavior: Impacts on elementary school students' outcomes* (NCEE 2022-008). U.S. Department of Education, Institute of Education Sciences, National Center for Education Evaluation and Regional Assistance. *http://ies.ed.gov/ncee.*

Cook, C. R., Fiat, A., Larson, M., Daikos, C., Slemrod, T., Holland, E. A., et al. (2018). Positive greetings at the door: Evaluation of a low-cost, high-yield proactive classroom management strategy. *Journal of Positive Behavior Interventions, 20,* 149–159.

Cook, S. C., Cook, B. G., & Cook, L. (2017). Classifying the evidence base of classwide peer tutoring for students with high-incidence disabilities. *Exceptionality, 25*(1), 9–25.

Cooper, J. O., Heron, T. E., & Heward, W. L. (2021). *Applied behavior analysis* (3rd ed.). Pearson.

Council for Exceptional Children. (1987). *Academy for effective instruction: Working with mildly handicapped students.* Author.

Crone, D. A., Hawken, L. S., & Horner, R. H. (2015). *Building positive behavior support systems in schools* (2nd ed.). Guilford Press.

Darch, C. B., & Kame'enui, E. B. (2004). *Instructional classroom management: A proactive approach to behavior management* (2nd ed.). Pearson Education.

Darling-Hammond, L., Hyler, M. E., & Gardner, M. (2017). *Effective teacher professional development.* Learning Policy Institute.

de Mooij, B., Fekkes, M., Scholte, R. H. J., & Overbeek, G. (2020). Effective components of social skills training programs for children and adolescents in nonclinical samples: A multilevel meta-analysis. *Clinical Child and Family Psychology Review, 23*(2), 250–264.

Downs, K. R., Caldarella, P., Larsen, R. A. A., Charlton, C. T., Wills, H. P., Kamps, D. M., & Wehby, J. (2019). Teacher praise and reprimands: The differential response of students at risk for emotional and behavioral disorders. *Journal of Positive Behavioral Interventions, 21,* 135–147.

Doyle, P. M., Wolery, M., Ault, M. J., & Gast, D. L. (1988). System of least prompts: A literature review of procedural parameters. *Journal of the Association for Persons with Severe Handicaps, 13,* 28–40.

Dunlap, G., dePerczel, M., Clarke, S., Wilson, D., Wright, S., White, R., et al. (1994). Choice making to promote adaptive behavior for students with emotional and behavioral challenges. *Journal of Applied Behavior Analysis, 27,* 505–518.

Dunlap, G., Iovannone, R., Wilson, K. J., Kincaid, D. K., & Strain, P. (2010). Prevent-teach-reinforce: A standardized model of school-based behavioral intervention. *Journal of Positive Behavior Interventions, 12*(1), 9–22.

Eber, L., Osuch, R., & Redditt, C. A. (1996). School-based applications of wraparound process: Early results on service provision and student outcomes. *Journal of Child and Family Studies, 5,* 83–99.

Educational & Community Supports, PBISApps. (2023). *School-wide information system (SWIS) suite* [Online App]. University of Oregon. *www.pbisapps.org.*

Embry, D. D. (2002). The Good Behavior Game: A best practice candidate as a universal behavioral vaccine. *Clinical Child and Family Psychology Review, 5,* 273–297.

Engleman, Z., & Carnine, D. (1982). *Theory of instruction: Principles and applications.* Irvington.

Fabelo, T., Thompson, M. D., Plotkin, M., Carmichael, D., Marchbanks, M. P., & Booth, E. A. (2011). *Breaking schools' rules: A statewide study of how school discipline relates to students' success and juvenile justice involvement.* Council of State Governments Justice Center. *https://csgjusticecenter. org/publications/breaking-schools-rules.*

Fairbanks, S., Sugai, G., Guardino, D., & Lathrop, M. (2007). Response to intervention: Examining classroom behavior support in second grade. *Exceptional Children, 73,* 288–310.

Faul, A., Stepensky, K., & Simonsen, B. (2012). The effects of prompting appropriate behavior on the off-task behavior of two middle school students. *Journal of Positive Behavior Interventions, 14,* 47–55.

Fefer, S., DeMagistris, J., & Shuttleton, C. (2016). Assessing adolescent praise and reward preferences for academic behavior. *Translational Issues in Psychological Science, 2*(2), 153–162.

Ferguson, E., & Houghton, S. (1992). The effects of contingent teacher praise, as specified by Canter's assertive discipline programme, on children's on-task behaviour. *Educational Studies, 18,* 83–93.

Fixsen, D. L., Naoom, S. F., Blase, K. A., Friedman, R. M., & Wallace, F. (2005). *Implementation research: A synthesis of the literature* (FMHI Publication No. 231). University of South Florida, Louis de la Parte Florida Mental Health Institute, National Implementation Research Network.

Forman, S. G. (1980). A comparison of cognitive training and response cost procedures in modifying aggressive behavior of elementary school children. *Behavior Therapy, 11,* 594–600.

Frampton, S. E., Munk, G. T., Shillingsburg, L. A., & Shillingsburg, M. A. (2021). A systematic review and quality appraisal of applications of direct instruction with children with autism spectrum disorder. *Perspectives on Behavior Science, 44*(2–3), 245–266.

Freeman, J., Simonsen, B., Briere, D. E., & MacSuga-Gage, A. S. (2014). Pre-service teacher training in classroom management: A review of state accreditation policy and teacher preparation programs. *Teacher Educational and Special Education, 37,* 106–120.

Frey, K. S., Nolen, S. B., Van Schoiack-Edstrom, L., & Hirschstein, M. K. (2005). Effects of a school-based social-emotional competence program: Linking children's goals, attributions, and behavior. *Applied Developmental Psychology, 26,* 171–200.

Gable, R. A., Tonelson, S. W., Sheth, M., Wilson, C., & Park, K. L. (2012). Importance, usage, and preparedness to implement evidence-based practices for students with emotional disabilities: A comparison of knowledge and skills of special education and general education teachers. *Education & Treatment of Children, 35*(4), 499–519.

Gage, N. A., Katsiyannis, A., Carrero, K. M., Miller, R., & Pico, D. (2021). Exploring disproportionate discipline for Latinx students with and without disabilities: A national analysis. *Behavioral Disorders, 47*(1), 3–13.

Gage, N. A., Lewis, T. J., & Stichter, J. P. (2012). Functional behavioral assessment-based intervention for students with or at risk for emotional and/or behavioral disorders in school: A hierarchical linear modeling meta-analysis. *Behavioral Disorders, 37,* 55–77.

Gion, C., McIntosh, K., & Falcon, S. (2022). Effects of a multifaceted classroom intervention on racial disproportionality. *School Psychology Review, 51*(1), 67–83.

Goh, A. E., & Bambara, L. M. (2012). Individualized positive behavior support in school settings: A meta-analysis. *Remedial and Special Education, 33,* 271–286.

Greenwood, C. R., Delquadri, J. C., & Hall, R. V. (1989). Longitudinal effects of classwide peer tutoring. *Journal of Educational Psychology, 81,* 371–383.

Gresham, F. M., Sugai, G., & Horner, R. H. (2001). Interpreting outcomes of social skills training for students with high incidence disabilities. *Exceptional Children, 67,* 331–344.

Grossman, D. C., Neckerman, H. J., Koepsell, T. D., Liu, P. V., Asher, K. N., Beland, K., et al. (1997). Effectiveness of a violence prevention curriculum among children in elementary school: A randomized controlled trial. *Journal of the American Medical Association, 277,* 1605–1611.

Harrison, J. R., Vannest, K., Davis, J., & Reynolds, C. (2012). Common problem behaviors of children and adolescents in general education classrooms in the United States. *Journal of Emotional and Behavioral Disorders, 20,* 55–64.

Hawken, L. S., Crone, D. A., Bundock, K., & Horner, R. H. (2021). *Responding to problem behavior in schools: The Check-In, Check-Out intervention* (3rd ed). Guilford Press.

Hawken, L. S., & Horner, R. H. (2003). Evaluation of a targeted intervention within a schoolwide system of behavior support. *Journal of Behavioral Education, 12,* 225–240.

Hawken, L. S., MacLeod, K. S., & Rawlings, L. (2007). Effects of the behavior education program on office discipline referrals of elementary school students. *Journal of Positive Behavior Interventions, 9,* 94–101.

Haydon, T., Conroy, M. A., Scott, T. M., Sindelar, P. T., Barber, B. R., & Orlando, A. M. (2009). A comparison of three types of opportunities to respond on student academic and social behaviors. *Journal of Emotional and Behavioral Disorders, 18,* 27–40.

Hirsch, S. E., Randall, K., Bradshaw, C., & Lloyd, J. W. (2021). Professional learning and development in classroom management for novice teachers: A systematic review. *Education & Treatment of Children, 44*(4), 291–307.

Holifield, C., Goodman, J., Hazelkorn, M., & Heflin, L. (2010). Using self-monitoring to increase attending to task and academic accuracy in children with autism. *Focus on Autism and Other Developmental Disabilities, 25,* 230–238.

Hollins-Sims, N. Y., Kauradur, E. J., & Runge, T. J. (2022). *Creating equitable practices in PBIS: Growing a positive school climate for sustainable outcomes.* Routledge.

Horner, R., Sugai, G., Smolkowski, K., Eber, L., Nakasato, J., Todd, A., et al. (2009). A randomized, wait-list controlled effectiveness trial assessing school-wide positive behavior support in elementary schools. *Journal of Positive Behavior Interventions, 11,* 133–145.

Horner, R. H., & Albin, R. (1988). Research on general-case procedures for learners with severe disabilities. *Education and Treatment of Children, 11,* 375–388.

Horner, R. H., Vaughn, B. J., Day, H. M., & Ard, W. R. (1996). The relationship between setting events and problem behavior: Expanding our understanding of behavioral support. In L. K. Koegel, R. L. Koegel, & G. Dunlap (Eds.), *Positive behavioral support: Including people with difficult behavior in the community* (pp. 381–402). Brookes.

Hunter, W., Williamson, R. L., Jasper, A. D., Baylot Casey, L., & Smith, C. (2017). Examining self-monitoring interventions for academic support of students with emotional and behavioral disorders. *Journal of International Special Needs Education, 20,* 67–68.

Infantino, J., & Little, E. (2005). Students' perceptions of classroom behaviour problems and the effectiveness of different disciplinary methods. *Educational Psychology, 25,* 495–508.

Ingram, K., Lewis-Palmer, T., & Sugai, G. (2005). Function-based intervention planning: Comparing the effectiveness of FBA indicated and contra-indicated intervention plans. *Journal of Positive Behavior Interventions, 7,* 224–236.

I-MTSS Research Network. (2023). *I-MTSS: What's in a name?* Integrated Multi-Tiered Systems of Support Research Network, University of Connecticut. *www.mtss.org.*

Johnson, C. C., Walton, J. B., Strickler, L., & Elliott, J. B. (2023). Online teaching in K–12 education in the United States: A systematic review. *Review of Educational Research, 93*(3), 353–411.

Kartub, D. T., Taylor-Green, S., March, R. E., & Horner, R. H. (2007). Reducing hallway noise: A systems approach. *Journal of Positive Behavior Interventions, 2,* 179–182.

Keane, K., & Evans, R. R. (2022). The potential for teacher–student relationships and the whole school, whole community, whole child model to mitigate adverse childhood experiences. *Journal of School Health, 92,* 504–513.

Kennedy, C. H., Long, T., Jolivette, K., Cox, J., Tang, J. C., & Thompson, T. (2001). Facilitating general education participation for students with behavior problems by linking positive behavior supports and person-centered planning. *Journal of Emotional and Behavioral Disorders, 9,* 161–171.

Kern, L., Gaier, K., Kelly, S., Nielsen, C. M., Commisso, C. E., & Wehby, J. H. (2020). An evaluation of adaptations made to Tier 2 social skill training programs. *Journal of Applied School Psychology, 36,* 155–172.

Kerr, M. M., & Nelson, C. M. (2006). *Strategies for addressing behavior problems in the classroom* (5th ed.). Pearson Education.

Kim, J. Y., Fienup, D. M., Oh, A. E., & Wang, Y. (2022). Systematic review and meta-analysis of token economy practices in K–5 educational settings, 2000 to 2019. *Behavior Modification, 46*(6), 1460–1487.

Kittelman, A., Mercer, S. H., McIntosh, K., Morris, K. R., & Hatton, H. L. (2023). Validation of a measure of district systems implementation of positive behavioral interventions and supports. *Remedial and Special Education, 44*(4), 259–271.

Kleinman, K. E., & Saigh, P. A. (2011). The effects of the Good Behavior Game on the conduct of regular education New York City high school students. *Behavior Modification, 35*, 95–105.

Konrad, M., Joseph, L. M., & Eveleigh, E. (2009). Meta-analytic review of guided notes. *Education & Treatment of Children, 32*(3), 421–444.

Lane, K. L., Wehby, J., Menzies, H. M., Doukas, G. L., Munton, S. M., & Gregg, R. M. (2003). Social skills instruction for students at risk for antisocial behavior: The effects of small-group instruction. *Behavioral Disorders, 28*, 229–248.

Lassen, S. R., Steele, M. M., & Sailor, W. (2006). The relationship of school-wide positive behavior support to academic achievement in an urban middle school. *Psychology in the Schools, 43*, 701–712.

La Salle, T. (2023, November). *Differences in perceptions of school climate based on students' identities: School climate evaluation series, first of two.* Center on PBIS, University of Oregon. *www.pbis.org.*

Layden, S. J., Crowson, T. G., & Hayden, K. E. (2023). A 30-year systematic review of self-monitoring as a strategy to improve teacher performance. *Journal of Special Education, 57*(1), 47–58.

Lazarus, B. D. (1993). Guided notes: Effects with secondary and postsecondary students with mild disabilities. *Education and Treatment of Children, 16*, 272–289.

Legge, D., DeBar, R., & Alber-Morgan, S. (2010). The effects of self-monitoring with a MotivAider® on the on-task behavior of fifth and sixth graders with autism and other disabilities. *Journal of Behavior Assessment and Intervention in Children, 1*, 43–52.

Leverson, M., Smith, K., McIntosh, K., Rose, J., & Pinkelman, S. (2021, March). PBIS Cultural responsiveness field guide: Resources for trainers and coaches. Center on PBIS, University of Oregon. *www.pbis.org.*

Lewis, T. J., Jones, S. E. L., Horner, R. H., & Sugai, G. (2010). School-wide positive behavior support and students with emotional/behavioral disorders: Implications for prevention, identification and intervention. *Exceptionality: A Special Education Journal, 18*, 82–93.

Libby, M. E., Weiss, J. S., Bancroft, S., & Ahearn, W. H. (2008). A comparison of most-to-least and least-to-most prompting on the acquisition of solitary play skills. *Behavior Analysis in Practice, 1*, 37–43.

Losen, D. J., & Martinez, P. (2020). *Lost opportunities: How disparate school discipline continues to drive differences in the opportunity to learn.* Learning Policy Institute, Center for Civil Rights Remedies at the Civil Rights Project, UCLA.

MacDuff, G. S., Krantz, P. J., & McClannahan, L. E. (2001). Prompts and prompt fading strategies for people with autism. In C. Maurice, G. Green, & R. M. Foxx (Eds.), *Making a difference: Behavioral intervention for autism* (pp. 37–50). PRO-ED.

MacSuga, A. S., & Simonsen, B. (2011). Increasing teachers' use of evidence-based classroom management strategies through consultation: Overview and case studies. *Beyond Behavior, 20*, 4–12.

MacSuga-Gage, A. S., & Simonsen, B. (2015). Examining the effects of teacher-directed opportunities to respond and student outcomes: A systematic review of the literature. *Education and Treatment of Children, 38*, 211–240.

Majeika, C. E., Wehby, J. H., & Hancock, E. M. (2022). Are breaks better? A comparison of Breaks are Better to Check-In Check-Out. *Behavioral Disorders, 47*(2), 118–133.

March, R. E., & Horner, R. H. (2002). Feasibility and contributions of functional behavioral assessments in schools. *Journal of Emotional and Behavioral Disorders, 13*, 158–170.

Mason, L., & Otero, M. (2021). Just how effective is direct instruction? *Perspectives on Behavior Science, 44*(2–3), 225–244.

McIntosh, K., Bennett, J. L., & Price, K. (2011). Evaluation of social and academic efforts of school-wide positive behaviour support in a Canadian school district. *Exceptionality Education International, 21*, 46–60.

McIntosh, K., Campbell, A. L., Carter, D. R., & Dickey, C. R. (2009). Differential effects of a tier two behavior intervention based on function of problem behavior. *Journal of Positive Behavior Interventions, 11*, 68–81.

McIntosh, K., Filter, K. J., Bennett, J. L., Ryan, C., & Sugai, G. (2010). Principles of sustainable prevention: Designing scale-up of school-wide positive behavior support to promote durable systems. *Psychology in the Schools, 47*, 5–21.

McIntosh, K., & Goodman, S. (2016). *Integrated multi-tiered systems of support: Blending RTI and PBIS.* Guilford Press.

McIntosh, K., Mercer, S. H., Nese, R. N. T., Strickland-Cohen, M. K., Kittelman, A., Hoselton, R., & Horner, R. H. (2018). Factors predicting sustained implementation of a universal behavior support framework. *Educational Researcher, 47*(5), 307–316.

McIntosh, K., Peterson, N., Robbie., K., & Simonsen, B. (2023, June). *Lesson plan: Co-creating classroom expectations with students (elementary schools).* Center on PBIS, University of Oregon. *www.pbis. org.*

McIntosh, K., Sugai, G., & Simonsen, B. (2020, February). *Ditch the clip! Why clip charts are not a PBIS practice and what to do instead.* Center on PBIS, University of Oregon. *www.pbis.org.*

Meyer, K., Sears, S., Putnam, R., Phelan, C., Burnett, A., Warden, S., & Simonsen, B. (2021). Supporting students with disabilities with universal positive behavioral interventions and supports (PBIS): Lessons learned from research and practice. *Beyond Behavior, 30*(3), 169–178.

Muldrew, A. C., & Miller, F. G. (2021). Examining the effects of the personal matrix activity with diverse students. *Psychology in the Schools, 58*(3), 515–533.

Muscott, H. S., Mann, E. L., & LeBrun, M. R. (2008). Effects of large-scale implementation of school-wide positive behavior support on student discipline and academic achievement. *Journal of Positive Behavior Interventions, 10,* 190–205.

Myers, D., Simonsen, B., & Sugai, G. (2011). Increasing teachers' use of praise with a response to intervention approach. *Education and Treatment of Children, 34*, 35–59.

Myers, D., Simonsen, B., & Freeman, J. (2020). *Implementing classwide PBIS: A guide to supporting teachers.* Guilford Press.

National Center on Intensive Intervention & Center on Positive Behavioral Interventions and Supports. (2021). *Intensive intervention: Myths and facts.* Office of Special Education Programs, U.S. Department of Education. *https://intensiveintervention.org/sites/default/files/Intensive_Intervention_Myths_and_Facts.pdf.*

Nese, R. N. T., Santiago-Rosario, M. R., Nese, J. F. T., Triplett, D., Malose, S., Hamilton, J., et al. (2023). *Instructional and restorative alternatives to exclusionary discipline: A guide to implementing the five components of the inclusive skill-building learning approach (ISLA).* Center on PBIS, University of Oregon.

Noell, G. H., Witt, J. C., Gilbertson, D. N., Rainer, S. D., & Freeland, J. T. (1997). Increasing teacher intervention implementation in general education settings through consultation and performance feedback. *School Psychology Quarterly, 12*, 77–88.

Nolan, J. D., Houlihan, D., Wanzek, M., & Jenson, W. R. (2014). The Good Behavior Game: A classroom-behavior intervention effective across cultures. *School Psychology International, 35*, 191–205.

Olson, J. R., Benjamin, P. H., Azman, A. A., Kellogg, M. A., Pullmann, M. D., Suter, J. C., & Bruns, E.

J. (2021). Systematic review and meta-analysis: Effectiveness of wraparound care coordination for children and adolescents. *Journal of the American Academy of Child & Adolescent Psychiatry, 60*(11), 1353–1366.

Ota, K., & DuPaul, G. J. (2002). Task engagement and mathematics performance in children with attention-deficit hyperactivity disorder: Effects of supplemental computer instruction. *School Psychology Quarterly, 17,* 242–257.

Pavlov, I. P. (1960). *Conditioned reflex: An investigation of the physiological activity of the cerebral cortex.* Dover. (Original work published 1927)

Ran, H., Kim, N. J., & Secada, W. G. (2022). A meta-analysis on the effects of technology's functions and roles on students' mathematics achievement in K–12 classrooms. *Journal of Computer Assisted Learning, 38*(1), 258–284.

Reinke, W. M., Herman, K. C., & Sprick, R. (2011). *Motivational interviewing for effective classroom management: The classroom check-up.* Guilford Press.

Reinke, W. M., Lewis-Palmer, T., & Merrell, K. (2008). The classroom check-up: A classwide teacher consultation model for increasing praise and decreasing disruptive behavior. *School Psychology Review, 37,* 315–332.

Reinke, W. M., Stormont, M., Herman, K. C., Puri, R., & Goel, N. (2011). Supporting children's mental health in schools: Teacher perceptions of needs, roles, and barriers. *School Psychology Quarterly, 26*(1), 1–13.

Riley, G. A. (1995). Guidelines for devising a hierarchy when fading response prompts. *Education and Training in Mental Retardation and Developmental Disabilities, 30,* 231–242.

Riley-Tillman, T. C., Kalberer, S. M., & Chafouleas, S. M. (2005). Selecting the right tool for the job: A review of behavior monitoring tools used to assess student response to intervention. *California School Psychologist, 10,* 81–91.

Rispoli, M., Zainy, S., Mason, R., Brodhead, M., Burke, M. D., & Gregori, E. (2017). A systematic review of teacher self-monitoring on implementation of behavioral practices. *Teaching and Teacher Education, 63,* 58–72.

Robbie, K., Santiago-Rosario, M., Yanek, K., Kern, L., Meyer, B., Morris, K., & Simonsen, B. (2022, August). *Creating a classroom teaching matrix.* Center on PBIS, University of Oregon. *www.pbis.org.*

Royer, D. J., Lane, K. L., Cantwell, E. D., & Messenger, M. L. (2017). A systematic review of the evidence base for instructional choice in K–12 settings. *Behavioral Disorders, 42*(3), 89–107.

Royer, D. J., Lane, K. L., Dunlap, K. D., & Ennis, R. P. (2019). A systematic review of teacher-delivered behavior-specific praise on K–12 student performance. *Remedial and Special Education, 40*(2), 112–128.

Santiago-Rosario, M. R., McIntosh, K., Izzard, S., Cohen-Lissman, D., & Calhoun, T. E. (2023). *Is positive behavioral interventions and supports (PBIS) an evidence-based practice?* Center on PBIS, University of Oregon. *www.pbis.org.*

Santiago-Rosario, M. R., McIntosh, K., & Payno-Simmons, R. (July, 2022). *Centering equity within the PBIS framework: Overview and evidence of effectiveness.* Center on PBIS, University of Oregon. *www.pbis.org.*

Schnell, L. K., Vladescu, J. C., Kisamore, A. N., DeBar, R. M., Kahng, S., & Marano, K. (2020). Assessment to identify learner-specific prompt and prompt-fading procedures for children with autism spectrum disorder. *Journal of Applied Behavior Analysis, 53*(2), 1111–1129.

Scott, T. M., & Eber, L. (2003). Functional assessment and wraparound as systemic school processes: Primary, secondary, and tertiary systems examples. *Journal of Positive Behavior Interventions, 5,* 131–143.

Shapiro, E. S. (2013). *Behavior Observation of Students in Schools (BOSS).* Pearson.

Simonsen, B., Eber, L., Black, A., Sugai, G., Lewandowski, H., Sims, B., et al. (2012). Illinois state-wide positive behavior interventions and supports: Evolution and impact on student outcomes across years. *Journal of Positive Behavior Interventions, 14,* 5–16.

Simonsen, B., Fairbanks, S., Briesch, A., Myers, D., & Sugai, G. (2008). A review of evidence based practices in classroom management: Considerations for research to practice. *Education and Treatment of Children, 31,* 351–380.

Simonsen, B., Freeman, J., Dooley, K., Maddock, E., Kern, L., & Myers, D. (2017). Effects of targeted professional development on teachers' specific praise rates. *Journal of Positive Behavior Interventions, 19,* 37–47.

Simonsen, B., Freeman, J., Myers, D., Dooley, K., Maddock, E., Kern, L., & Byun, S. (2020). Effects of targeted professional development on teachers' implementation of key classroom management skills. *Journal of Positive Behavior Interventions, 22,* 3–14.

Simonsen, B., Freeman, J., Swain-Bradway, J., George, H., Putnam, B., Lane, K., et al. (2019). Using data to support teachers' implementation of empirically-supported classroom practices. *Education and Treatment of Children, 42,* 265–290.

Simonsen, B., Goodman, S., Robbie, K., Power, M., Rodriguez, C., & Burns, D. (2021, January). *Effective instruction as a protective factor.* Center on PBIS, University of Oregon. *www.pbis.org.*

Simonsen, B., MacSuga, A. S., Fallon, L. M., & Sugai, G. (2013). The effects of self-monitoring on teachers' use of specific praise. *Journal of Positive Behavior Interventions, 15*(1), 5–15.

Simonsen, B., MacSuga-Gage, A. S., Briere, D. E., Freeman, J., Myers, D., Scott, T., et al. (2014). Multitiered support framework for teachers' classroom-management practices: Overview and case study of building the triangle for teachers. *Journal of Positive Behavior Interventions, 16,* 179–190.

Simonsen, B., Myers, D., & Briere, D. E. (2011). Comparing a behavioral Check-In/Check-Out (CICO) intervention with standard practice in an urban middle school using an experimental group design. *Journal of Positive Behavior Interventions, 13,* 31–48.

Simonsen, B., Myers, D., Everett, S., Sugai, G., Spencer, R., & LaBreck, C. (2012). Explicitly teaching social skills school-wide: Using a matrix to guide instruction. *Intervention in School and Clinic, 47,* 259–266.

Simonsen, B., Putnam, R., Yaneck, K., Evanovich, L., Shaw, S. Shuttleton, C., et al. (2020, February). *Supporting students with disabilities in the classroom within a PBIS framework.* Center on PBIS, University of Oregon. *www.pbis.org.*

Simonsen, B., Robbie, K., Meyer, K., Freeman, J., Everett, S., & Feinberg A. (2021, November). *Multi-tiered system of supports (MTSS) in the classroom.* Center on PBIS, University of Oregon. *www.pbis.org.*

Simonsen, B., & Sugai, G. (2007). Using school-wide data systems to make decisions efficiently and effectively. *School Psychology Forum, 1*(2), 46–58.

Simonsen, B., Sugai, G., Freeman, J., Kern, L., & Hampton, J. (2014). Ethical and professional guidelines for crisis procedures. *Education and Treatment of Children, 37,* 307–322.

Sinclair, M. F., Christenson, S. L., Evelo, D. L., & Hurley, C. M. (1998). Dropout prevention for youth with disabilities: Efficacy of a sustained school engagement procedure. *Exceptional Children, 65,* 7–21.

Sinclair, M. F., Christenson, S. L., & Thurlow, M. L. (2005). Promoting school completion of urban secondary youth with emotional or behavioral disabilities. *Exceptional Children, 71,* 465–482.

Skinner, B. F. (1953). *Science and human behavior.* Macmillan.

Skinner, B. F. (1963). Operant behavior. *American Psychologist, 18,* 503–515.

Skinner, B. F. (1969). Contingency management in the classroom. *Education, 90,* 93–100.

Skinner, B. F. (1974). *About behaviorism.* Random House.

Skinner, B. F. (1983). *A matter of consequences.* Knopf.

Smith, S., Barajas, K., Ellis, B., Moore, C., McCauley, S., & Reichow, B. (2021). A meta-analytic review of randomized controlled trials of the Good Behavior Game. *Behavior Modification, 45*(4), 641–666.

Snell, M. E., Voorhees, M. D., & Chen, L. Y. (2005). Team involvement in assessment-based interventions with problem behavior: 1997–2002. *Journal of Positive Behavior Interventions, 7,* 140–152.

Soares, D. A., Harrison, J. R., Vannest, K. J., & McClelland, S. S. (2016). Effect size for token economy use in contemporary classroom settings: A meta-analysis of single-case research. *School Psychology Review, 45*(4), 379–399.

Spaulding, S. A., Irvin, L. K., Horner, R. H., May, S. L., Emeldi, M., Tobin, T. J., et al. (2010). Schoolwide social-behavioral climate, student problem behavior, and related administrative decisions: Empirical patterns from 1510 schools nationwide. *Journal of Positive Behavior Interventions, 12,* 69–85.

Stokes, T. F., & Baer, D. M. (1977). An implicit technology of generalization. *Journal of Applied Behavior Analysis, 10,* 349–367.

Strickland-Cohen, M. K., Newson, A., Meyer, K., Putnam, R., Kern, L., Meyer, B. C., & Flammini, A. (September, 2022). *Strategies for de-escalating student behavior in the classroom.* Center on PBIS, University of Oregon. *www.pbis.org.*

Sugai, G., & Horner, R. H. (2006). A promising approach for expanding and sustaining school-wide positive behavior support. *School Psychology Review, 35,* 245–259.

Sugai, G., & Horner, R. H. (2009). Responsiveness-to-intervention and school-wide positive behavior supports: Integration of multi-tiered system approaches. *Exceptionality: A Special Education Journal, 17,* 223–237.

Sugai, G., & Lewis, T. J. (1996). Preferred and promising practices for social skills instruction. *Focus on Exceptional Children, 29,* 1–16.

Sugai, G., O'Keefe, B. V., & Fallon, L. M. (2012). A contextual consideration of culture and school-wide positive behavior support. *Journal of Positive Behavior Interventions, 14,* 197–208.

Sullivan, A. L., Van Norman, E. R., & Klingbeil, D. A. (2014). Exclusionary discipline of students with disabilities: Student and school characteristics predicting suspension. *Remedial and Special Education, 35,* 199–210.

Sumi, W. C., Woodbridge, M. W., Javitz, H. S., Thornton, S. P., Wagner, M., Rouspil, K., et al. (2013). Assessing the effectiveness of First Step to Success: Are short-term results the first step to long-term behavioral improvements? *Journal of Emotional and Behavioral Disorders, 21,* 66–78.

Suter, J. C., & Bruns, E. J. (2009). Effectiveness of the wraparound process for children with emotional and behavioral disorders. *Clinical Child and Family Psychological Review, 12,* 336–351.

Sutherland, K. S., & Singh, N. N. (2004). Learned helplessness and students with emotional or behavioral disorders: Deprivation in the classroom. *Behavioral Disorders, 29,* 169–181.

Sutherland, K. S., & Wehby, J. H. (2001). The effect of self-evaluation on teaching behavior in classrooms for students with emotional and behavioral disorders. *Journal of Special Education, 35,* 2–8.

Sutherland, K. S., Wehby, J. H., & Copeland, S. R. (2000). Effects of varying rates of behavior-specific praise on the on-task behavior of students with EBD. *Journal of Emotional and Behavioral Disorders, 8,* 2–8.

Tanol, G., Johnson, L., McComas, J., & Cote, E. (2010). Responding to rule violations or rule following: A comparison of two versions of the Good Behavior Game with kindergarten students. *Journal of School Psychology, 48,* 337–355.

Tingstrom, D. H., Sterling-Turner, H. E., & Wilczynski, S. M. (2006). The Good Behavior Game: 1969–2002. *Behavior Modification, 30,* 225–253.

Trice, A. D., & Parker, F. C. (1983). Decreasing adolescent swearing in an instructional setting. *Education and Treatment of Children, 6,* 29–35.

U.S. Department of Education. (2012). *Restraint and seclusion: Resource document.* Author. *www2.ed.gov/policy/seclusion/restraints-and-seclusion-resources.pdf.*

U.S. Department of Education Office for Civil Rights. (2018). *School climate and safety: Data highlights on school climate and safety in our nation's public schools.* Author. *www2.ed.gov/about/offices/list/ocr/docs/school-climate-and-safety.pdf.*

U.S. Department of Education Office for Civil Rights. (2022). *Suspensions and expulsions of students with disabilities in public schools.* Author. *www2.ed.gov/about/offices/list/ocr/docs/discipline-of-students-with-disabilities-part-3.pdf.*

Van Camp, A. M., Wehby, J. H., Martin, B. L. N., Wright, J. R., & Sutherland, K. S. (2020). Increasing opportunities to respond to intensify academic and behavioral interventions: A meta-analysis. *School Psychology Review, 49*(1), 31–46.

Van Mechelen, M., Smith, R. C., Schaper, M.-M., Tamashiro, M., Bilstrup, K.-E., Lunding, M., et al. (2023). Emerging technologies in K–12 education: A future HCI research agenda. *ACM Transactions on Computer-Human Interaction, 30*(3), 1–40.

Vargas, J. S. (2020). *Behavior analysis for effective teaching.* (3rd ed.). Routledge/Taylor & Francis.

Vincent, C. G., Randall, C., Cartledge, G., Tobin, T. J., & Swain-Bradway, J. (2011). Toward a conceptual integration of cultural responsiveness and schoolwide positive behavior support. *Journal of Positive Behavior Interventions, 13,* 219–229.

Waasdorp, T. E., Bradshaw, C. P., & Leaf, P. J. (2012). The impact of school-wide positive behavioral interventions and supports (SWPBIS) on bullying and peer rejection: A randomized controlled effectiveness trial. *Archives of Pediatrics and Adolescent Medicine, 116,* 149–156.

Walker, H. M., Horner, R. H., Sugai, G., Bullis, M., Sprague, J. R., Bricker, D., et al. (1996). Integrated approaches to preventing antisocial behavior patterns among school-age children and youth. *Journal of Emotional and Behavioral Disorders, 4,* 194–209.

Walker, H. M., Kavanagh, K., Stiller, B., Golly, A., Severson, H. H., & Feil, E. G. (1997). *First Step to Success: An early intervention program for antisocial kindergartners.* Sopris West.

Walker, H. M., Seeley, J. R., Small, J., Severson, H. H., Graham, B. A., Feil, E. G., et al. (2009). A randomized controlled trial of the First Step to Success early intervention: Demonstration of program efficacy outcomes in a diverse, urban school district. *Journal of Emotional and Behavioral Disorders, 17,* 197–212.

Walker, V. L., Chung, Y.-C., & Bonnet, L. K. (2018). Function-based intervention in inclusive school settings: A meta-analysis. *Journal of Positive Behavior Interventions, 20*(4), 203–216.

Wei, R. C., Darling-Hammond, L., & Adamson, F. (2010). *Professional development in the United States: Trends and challenges.* National Staff Development Council.

White, W. A. (1988). A meta-analysis of the effects of direct instruction in special education. *Education and Treatment of Children, 11*(4), 364–374.

Whitney, T., & Ackerman, K. B. (2020). Acknowledging student behavior: A review of methods promoting positive and constructive feedback. *Beyond Behavior, 29*(2), 86–94.

Wilkinson, S., Freeman, J., Simonsen, B., Sears, S., Byun, S. G., Xu, X., & Luh, H.-J. (2020). Professional development for classroom management: A review of the literature. *Educational Research and Evaluation, 26*(3–4), 182–212.

Wills, H., & Mason, B. (2014). Implementation of a self-monitoring application to improve on-task behavior: A high-school pilot study. *Journal of Behavioral Education, 23,* 421–434.

Wilson-Ching, M., & Berger, E. (2023). Relationship building strategies within trauma informed frameworks in educational settings: A systematic literature review. *Current Psychology: A Journal for Diverse Perspectives on Diverse Psychological Issues.*

Wolf, M. M. (1978). Social validity: The case for subjective measurement *or* How applied behavior analysis is finding its heart. *Journal of Applied Behavior Analysis, 11,* 203–214.

Zoder-Martell, K. A., Floress, M. T., Bernas, R. S., Dufrene, B. A., & Foulks, S. L. (2019). Training teachers to increase behavior-specific praise: A meta-analysis. *Journal of Applied School Psychology, 35*(4), 309–338.

Index

Note. *f* or *t* following a page number indicates a figure or a table.